Politics and Development of Contemporary China

Series Editor
Kevin G. Cai, Renison University College, University of Waterloo,
Waterloo, ON, Canada

As China's power grows, the search has begun in earnest for what super-power status will mean for the People's Republic of China as a nation as well as the impact of its new-found influence on the Asia-Pacific region and the global international order at large. By providing a venue for exciting and ground-breaking titles, the aim of this series is to explore the domestic and international implications of China's rise and transformation through a number of key areas including politics, development and foreign policy. The series will also give a strong voice to non-western perspectives on China's rise in order to provide a forum that connects and compares the views of academics from both the east and west reflecting the truly international nature of the discipline.

Kevin G. Cai · Yitan Li · Sujian Guo
Editors

China and Global Economic Governance, Volume I: China's BRI & AIIB and Global Economic Governance

palgrave
macmillan

Editors
Kevin G. Cai
Renison University College
University of Waterloo
Waterloo, ON, Canada

Yitan Li
Department of Political Science
Seattle University
Seattle, WA, USA

Sujian Guo
Department of Political Science
San Francisco State University
San Francisco, CA, USA

ISSN 2946-2355 ISSN 2946-2363 (electronic)
Politics and Development of Contemporary China
ISBN 978-3-031-73211-9 ISBN 978-3-031-73212-6 (eBook)
https://doi.org/10.1007/978-3-031-73212-6

© The Editor(s) (if applicable) and The Author(s), under exclusive license to Springer
Nature Switzerland AG 2025

This work is subject to copyright. All rights are solely and exclusively licensed by the
Publisher, whether the whole or part of the material is concerned, specifically the rights
of translation, reprinting, reuse of illustrations, recitation, broadcasting, reproduction on
microfilms or in any other physical way, and transmission or information storage and
retrieval, electronic adaptation, computer software, or by similar or dissimilar methodology
now known or hereafter developed.
The use of general descriptive names, registered names, trademarks, service marks, etc.
in this publication does not imply, even in the absence of a specific statement, that such
names are exempt from the relevant protective laws and regulations and therefore free for
general use.
The publisher, the authors and the editors are safe to assume that the advice and information in this book are believed to be true and accurate at the date of publication. Neither
the publisher nor the authors or the editors give a warranty, expressed or implied, with
respect to the material contained herein or for any errors or omissions that may have been
made. The publisher remains neutral with regard to jurisdictional claims in published maps
and institutional affiliations.

This Palgrave Macmillan imprint is published by the registered company Springer Nature
Switzerland AG
The registered company address is: Gewerbestrasse 11, 6330 Cham, Switzerland

If disposing of this product, please recycle the paper.

Preface

A novel, pressing and challenging issue has emerged in international political economy in recent decades following the rapid rise of Chinese economic power, that is, how to accommodate China as a new economic superpower within the existing structure of global economic governance. This has become not only a highly contentious geopolitical and geoeconomic issue that is complicating already complex relations between major powers, particularly between China and the US, but also a heated issue of scholarly debate in the academia.

To address this important issue in international political economy, this two-volume series, edited under the title of *China and Global Economic Governance*, is compiled from a number of relevant articles published in Springer Nature journals in recent years. Volume I explores how China's two initiatives of the Belt and Road Initiative (BRI) and the Asian Infrastructure Investment Bank (AIIB) have had impact on geopolitics and geoeconomics in general and on global economic governance in particular, while Volume II examines how China's active engagement with the BRICS, the Shanghai Cooperation Organization (SCO), and the Group of Twenty (G20) has helped shape the development of these groupings with significant implications not only for geopolitics and geoeconomics at both regional and global levels, but also for global economic governance.

It is hoped that these two volumes will contribute to the ongoing debate on this very important issue in contemporary international political economy.

Kevin G. Cai
Professor
Renison University College
University of Waterloo
Canada

CONTENTS

1	**Introduction: China Seeking Influence in Global Economic Governance Through BRI and AIIB** Kevin G. Cai	1
2	**China's Initiatives: A Bypassing Strategy for the Reform of Global Economic Governance** Kevin G. Cai	9
3	**All Roads Lead to Beijing: *Systemism*, Power Transition Theory, and the Belt and Road Initiative** Enyu Zhang and Patrick James	33
4	**Putting the BRI in Perspective: History, Hegemony, and Geoeconomics** Mark Beeson and Corey Crawford	69
5	**The Maritime Silk Road Initiative and Its Implications for China's Regional Policy** Charles Chong-Han Wu	93
6	**Building Blocks or Walls? BRI, Globalization, and the Future of East Asian Regionalization** Serafettin Yilmaz and Bo Li	123

vii

viii CONTENTS

7 **Infrastructure and the Politics of African State Agency: Shaping the Belt and Road Initiative in East Africa** 155
Frangton Chiyemura, Elisa Gambino, and Tim Zajontz

8 **The AIIB and China's Normative Power in International Financial Governance Structure** 191
Zhongzhou Peng and Sow Keat Tok

9 **The Asian Infrastructure Investment Bank and Status-Seeking: China's Foray into Global Economic Governance** 215
Hai Yang

10 **Conclusion** 241
Yitan Li

Index 251

ABBREVIATIONS

ADB	Asian Development Bank
AfDB	African Development Bank
ADMM-Plus	ASEAN Defence Ministers' Meeting Plus
AIIB	Asian Infrastructure Investment Bank
AMF	Asian Monetary Fund
AOA	Articles of Agreement (AIIB)
APT	ASEAN Plus Three
ARF	ASEAN Regional Forum
BCIMEC	Bangladesh–China–India–Myanmar Economic Corridor
BFA	Boao Forum for Asia
BOT	Build-Operate-Transfer
BRFIC	Belt and Road Forum for International Cooperation
BRI	Belt and Road Initiative
BRICS	Brazil, Russia, India, China and South Africa
B3W	Build Back Better World
BWIs	Bretton Woods Institutions
CAF	Andean Development Corporation
CCM	*Chama Cha Mapinduzi*
CCP	Chinese Communist Party
CCWAEC	China–Central Asia–Western Asia Economic Corridor
CGCOC	China Geo-Engineering Corporation Overseas Construction Group
CICPEC	China–Indochina Peninsula Economic Corridor
CMIM	Chiang Mai Initiative Multilateralization
CMREC	China–Mongolia–Russia Economic Corridor
CMS	China Maritime Surveillance

CNM	The Chief Negotiators Meeting
CNOOC	China National Offshore Oil Corporation
COC	Code of Conduct (in South China Sea)
CMPort	China Merchants Port Holdings
CPEC	China–Pakistan Economic Corridor
CRA	Contingent Reserve Arrangement
CRBC	China Road Bridge Corporation
CSIS	Center for Strategic and International Studies
DAC	Development Assistance Committee
DOC	Declaration on the Conduct of Parties in the South China Sea
EAS	East Asia Summit
EBRD	European Bank for Reconstruction and Development
EDCA	Enhanced Defense Cooperation Agreement
EEU	Ethiopia Electric Utility
EEZ	Exclusive Economic Zone
EIB	European Investment Bank
EPC	Engineering-Procurement-Construction
EPRDF	Ethiopian People's Revolutionary Democratic Front
EU	European Union
FLEC	Fisheries Law Enforcement Command
GATT	General Agreement on Tariffs and Trade
GDP	Gross Domestic Product
GEF	Global Environment Facility
GFC	Global Financial Crisis
GIZ	German Society for International Cooperation
G-7/G7	Group of Seven
GTP	Growth and Transformation Plan (Ethiopia)
G-20/G20	Group of Twenty
HydroChina	HydroChina Corporation
ICA	Infrastructure Consortium for Africa
ICOW	Issue Correlates of War
IDB	Inter-American Development Bank
IMF	International Monetary Fund
IOs	International Organizations
IR	International Relations
JCF	China-Philippines Joint Committee on Fisheries
JMSU	Joint Marine Seismic Undertaking
LAPSSET	Lamu Port–South Sudan–Ethiopia Transport (Corridor)
LMC	Lancang-Mekong Cooperation
MDB	Multilateral Development Bank
MIDs	Militarized Interstate Disputes
MOFA	Ministry of Foreign Affairs (China)
MOFCOM	Ministry of Commerce (China)

MOFEC	Ministry of Finance and Economic Cooperation (Ethiopia)
MOU	Memorandum of Understanding
MOWIE	Ministry of Water, Irrigation and Electricity (Ethiopia)
MSR	Maritime Silk Road
MSRI	Maritime Silk Road Initiative
NDB	New Development Bank
NDRC	National Development and Reform Commission (China)
NEA	Northeast Asia
NELBEC	New Eurasian Land Bridge Economic Corridor
OECD	Organization for Economic Cooperation and Development
PFMs	Prospective Founding Members (AIIB)
PLA	Chinese People's Liberation Army
PLAN	PLA Navy
PNOC	Philippine National Oil Corporation
PRC	People's Republic of China
RCEP	Regional Comprehensive Economic Partnership
S&P	Standard & Poor's
SCO	Shanghai Cooperation Organization
SCS	South China Sea
SDR	Special Drawing Rights
SEZ	Special Economic Zone
SIR	*Systemist* International Relations
SIT	Social Identity Theory
SLOCs	Sea Lines of Communication
SOEs	State-Owned Enterprises
SREB	Silk Road Economic Belt
SRF	Silk Road Fund
SWERA	Solar and Wind Energy Resource Assessment (Ethiopia)
TAZARA	Tanzania-Zambia Railway Authority
TCS	Trilateral Cooperation Secretariat
TERNA	Technical Expertise for Renewable
TFP	Total Factor Productivity
TPA	Tanzania Ports Authority
TPP	Trans-Pacific Partnership
UK	United Kingdom
UNEP	United Nations Environment Programme
USIDFC	International Development Finance Corporation
WB	World Bank
WTO	World Trade Organization

LIST OF FIGURES

Fig. 3.1 Map of the Belt and Road Initiative, 2020 (*Source* Mercator Institute for China Studies, https://merics.org/sites/default/files/2020-06/Silkroad-Projekt_EN_2020_) 36

Fig. 3.2 Functional relations in a social system (*Source* Adapted from Bunge, 1996, p. 149) 41

Fig. 3.3 Regions of war and peace (Lemke 2002). Diagrammed by: Douglas William Lemke, Sarah Gansen, and Patrick James 45

Fig. 3.4 Systemism, power transition, and BRI (Zhang and James 2022). a–d Elaboration based on further evidence. Diagrammed by: Enyu Zhang, Sarah Gansen, and Patrick James 48

Fig. 7.1 Energy projects implementation framework (*Source* Authors' compilation from field data) 171

xiii

LIST OF TABLES

Table 3.1	Systemist notation	43
Table 5.1	Territorial and maritime claims, 1900–2001	103
Table 6.1	China's trade with major partner regions and their share in China's total trade (2008–2017)	140
Table 6.2	Official discourse on globalization and regionalization	142
Table 6.3	Academic discourse on globalization and regionalization	142
Table 7.1	Adama wind farms project terms and conditions. From: Infrastructure and the Politics of African state agency: Shaping the belt and road initiative in East Africa	175
Table 9.1	Three identity management strategies (Tajfel and Turner 1979; Larson and Shevchenko 2003, 2010)	222
Table 9.2	A brief comparison of WB, ADB, and AIIB (Kawai 2015, p. 9; official websites of the three banks)	230

CHAPTER 1

Introduction: China Seeking Influence in Global Economic Governance Through BRI and AIIB

Kevin G. Cai

Following the rise of Chinese economic power in recent decades, how to accommodate China as a new economic superpower within the existing structure of global economic governance has become a novel challenging issue in international political economy.

From the Chinese perspective, the existing structure of global economic governance no longer corresponds to the new reality of the changed balance of economic power in the world economy following the rise of Chinese economic power. Hence, in recent years Beijing has become increasingly dissatisfied with United States (US) and Western dominance of the existing international economic system. It was against this backdrop that China launched two significant initiatives of the Belt

---

K. G. Cai (✉)
Renison University College, University of Waterloo, Waterloo, Canada
e-mail: kcai@uwaterloo.ca

© The Author(s), under exclusive license to Springer Nature Switzerland AG 2025
K. G.Cai et al. (eds.), *China and Global Economic Governance, Volume I: China's BRI & AIIB and Global Economic Governance*, Politics and Development of Contemporary China,
https://doi.org/10.1007/978-3-031-73212-6_1

and Road Initiative (BRI) and the Asian Infrastructure Investment Bank (AIIB) in 2013 after Xi Jinping took office as the country's new leader.[1] Unprecedented in the diplomatic history of the People's Republic of China (PRC), the two initiatives, which clearly reflected Xi's new perception of China's position in global politics and economics in the context of rising Chinese power, ushered in a new period of Chinese foreign policy, moving away from the previous period of *tao guang yang hui* (low profile) foreign policy initiated by Deng Xiaoping.[2] As foreign policy initiatives, the BRI and AIIB were intended to help Beijing pursue its multiple important foreign policy objectives in geopolitics, security, and geoeconomics. One of these important foreign policy objectives was to increase China's influence in the world economy and help the nation play a more important role in global economic governance.[3]

After Deng Xiaoping initiated economic reforms and opening to the outside world in 1978, China took a crucial step to join the liberal international economic system by resuming its membership in the International Monetary Fund (IMF) and the World Bank in 1980 and the Asian Development Bank (ADB) in 1986. With its accession to the World Trade Organization (WTO) in 2001, China completed the process of its integration with the capitalist world economy, turning the nation into a full member of the global economic system. Despite this, however, it is important to note that given its weak economic capacity at the time, China entered the IMF and the World Bank on terms that had been set by the Western powers. Hence, China had very limited voice and weight within these institutions under the existing governance structure that had been formed at the end of World War II. Over time, however, with its economic power gradually rising following the nation's rapid economic growth, China inevitably started to quest for the reform of the global economic system that had long been dominated by the Western powers, the US in particular so that its voice and influence in global economic governance (which was particularly reflected in voting power in both

---

[1] Kevin G. Cai, "One Belt One Road and the Asian Infrastructure Investment Bank: Beijing's New Strategy of Geoeconomics and Geopolitics." *The Journal of Contemporary China*, Vol.27, No.114, 2018. pp.838–39.

[2] Ibid., *China's Foreign Policy since 1949: Continuity and Change* (Routledge, 2022).

[3] Ibid, "One Belt One Road and the Asian Infrastructure Investment Bank," pp.831, 838–39.

the IMF and the World Bank) could be increased in conformity with its increased economic power.

On the other hand, however, the US and other Western countries were hardly enthusiastic about any substantial reform of the existing international economic system that would weaken their own position in global economic governance. Especially, despite its relative declining economic power vis-à-vis other major economies and increasingly retreating from liberal economic policies in its external economic relations, the US continued to maintain its dominant position as the status-quo power in the global economic system. It was within this context that China's launching of the BRI and the AIIB can be understood as a bypassing strategy adopted by Beijing to exert pressure on the US and other developed countries for the reform of the structure of global economic governance from outside the existing global economic system.[4]

Beijing's initiatives of the BRI and the AIIB have apparently been posing a great challenge to the leadership position of the US in the existing international economic order and bringing significant implications on global politics and economics. Despite this, however, it is also important to note that by launching these two high-profile initiatives, Beijing has primarily intended to increase its voice and influence in global economic governance rather than replace the US as a new leader in the international economic system. This is not only because China lacks the overall economic capability that is required of a global leader but also because Beijing's existing economic system and policy are far from liberal to allow it to play such a leadership role in the existing global economic order. With such limitation in both of its economic capability and the openness of its economic policy, it is highly unlikely that the Chinese leadership should have such an ambition of replacing the US as a new leader in the global economic order. Whatever Beijing's motivations, however, the initiatives of the BRI and the AIIB have apparently been bringing significant implications on multiple areas of contemporary international political economy, particularly the global economic governance.

This volume comprises a collection of papers that have been published in *Chinese Political Science Review* on this topic in recent years. The volume is intended to explore some most important aspects of China's twin initiatives of the BRI and the AIIB. While representing the views

---

[4] See Chapter 2.

of the authors, these articles provide analyses of the BRI and the AIIB from various perspectives. Chapter 2 presents an overall analysis of how China's initiatives of the BRI and the AIIB (as well as the BRICS) have been bringing implications on global economic governance. Focusing on the BRI, Chapters 3 to 7 examine various aspects of this global investment initiative of China, ranging from a theoretical explanation of China's BRI and historical comparison of China's BRI with America's Marshall Plan to the assessment of various implications of China's initiative on multiple areas in geopolitics and geoeconomics. Chapters 8 and 9 investigate how China has attempted to enhance its power and status in global financial/economic governance through its AIIB initiative. The volume ends with a conclusion.

Chapter 2 by Kevin G. Cai, "China's Initiatives: A Bypassing Strategy for the Reform of Global Economic Governance" seeks to explain why Beijing has initiated the BRI and the AIIB. According to Cai, one of Beijing's important motivations behind the BRI and the AIIB (as well as the BRICS) is to push for the reform of global economic governance from outside the existing global economic system dominated by the Western status-quo powers. Because of the resistance of Western powers, the US in particular, to any reforms that would weaken their position in the existing multilateral system, Beijing has adopted a two-track approach to push for the reform of the existing structure of global economic governance. On the one hand, Beijing has been explicitly and vigorously calling for the reform of the multilateral institutions (the IMF and the World Bank in particular) within the existing international economic system; on the other hand, Beijing has also adopted a bypassing strategy by launching new initiatives outside the existing multilateral system that was dominated by the US as a vehicle to increase Beijing's voice and influence within the existing multilateral institutions. Cai further argues that while the BRI and the AIIB can hardly be transformed directly into the nation's enhanced status within the existing global economic order, they have been posing normative and structural challenges to the existing global economic order dominated by the Western powers and bringing significant implications on the existing global economic architecture in multiple important areas, including patterns of regional and global trade, investment, and infrastructure development, which will, in turn, have strategic impact on global economic governance.

In Chapter 3, "All Roads Lead to Beijing: *Systemism*, Power Transition Theory and the Belt and Road Initiative," Enyu Zhang and Patrick James apply power transition theory to the explanation of China's BRI. Through the prism of *systemism*, this chapter seeks to address two major questions of (1) how the BRI looks in the context of power transition theory, and (2) whether it is a time-honored theory that is able to explain the characteristics of the BRI, notably its impact upon policies and outcomes at the regional and international levels. According to Zhang and James, this *systemist* approach emphasizes the graphic portrayal of cause and effect, which is well suited to the task of comparing and evaluating theoretical arguments about developments such as the BRI. The chapter uses a visualization of power transition theory to obtain insights about the likely direction of China's BRI in terms of the US and China as leading states and rivals faced with the challenge of managing conflict short of war in East Asia.

Chapter 4 by Mark Beeson and Corey Crawford, "Putting the BRI in Perspective: History, Hegemony and Geo-economics" compares America's Marshall Plan and China's BRI from the perspectives of 'hegemonic transitions' and 'comparative hegemony' in order to highlight some striking similarities and noteworthy differences, and to assess the prospects for the BRI and its possible scenarios. According to Beeson and Crawford, the two initiatives are equally unprecedented and ambitious, designed to simultaneously facilitate the (re)development of some of the world's key economies and reinforce their respective positions as a global leader. Both the Marshall Plan and the BRI are important expressions of geoeconomic influence and power. By comparison, however, the authors argue that the BRI does not have the same sort of compelling geopolitical imperatives and narrative that the emerging Cold War provided for American hegemonic leadership. The two authors further point out that Beijing's BRI also lacks the comprehensive global institutional architecture developed in the aftermath of World War II that facilitated American influence. Consequently, the authors anticipate, it may prove more difficult for China to utilize the BRI to translate potential geoeconomic leverage into the sort of hegemonic influence that the US enjoyed during the Cold War.

In Chapter 5, "The Maritime Silk Road Initiative and Its Implications for China's Regional Policy," Charles Chong-Han Wu compares previous maritime issues between China and neighboring countries in Southeast Asia. Wu argues that the promotion of the Maritime Silk Road Initiative (MSRI) can mitigate relevant maritime militarized interstate disputes in the region and help prevent conflict. According to the author, the empirical findings of this study help identify the crucial elements that determine how China can improve its maritime policies under the MSRI with a special focus on the case of the Philippines, a country that has experienced most continuously a friction over maritime boundaries with China.

In Chapter 6, "Building Blocks or Walls? BRI, Globalization and the Future of East Asian Regionalization," Serafettin Yilmaz and Bo Li provide an analysis of the dynamic interaction between the processes of globalization and regionalization in East Asia within the context of the BRI. The authors aim (1) to examine the BRI as a comprehensive blueprint for an alternative type of globalization based on a new set of economic, cultural, and political ideas that are qualitatively and quantitatively different from what has been promoted under the existing US-led global system; and (2) to explore the potential impact of new globalization on the prospects of region building in East Asia in terms of China's role in it. Yilmaz and Li argue that the BRI-driven globalization may have certain dampening and diluting effects on China's participation in and contribution to the East Asian regionalization. The authors hope that their study will shed further light on the nature of relationship between globalization and regionalization and extrapolate on the future course of regionalism in East Asia.

In Chapter 7, "Infrastructure and the Politics of African State Agency: Shaping the Belt and Road Initiative in East Africa," Frangton Chiyemura, Elisa Gambino, and Tim Zajontz examine the BRI with respect to China-Africa cooperation. According to the authors, infrastructure development has experienced a political renaissance in Africa and is again at the center of national, regional, and continental development agendas, and China has been identified by African policymakers as a particularly suitable strategic partner. The authors note that as infrastructure has become a main pillar of Sino-African cooperation, there has been growing literature in China-Africa studies on the role of African state and non-state actors in shaping the terms and conditions and, by extension, the implementation of infrastructure projects with Chinese participation. The authors identify their work as part of this growing body of literature on the subject.

Chapters 8 and 9 move to explore China's AIIB initiative. In Chapter 8, "The AIIB and China's Normative Power in International Financial Governance Structure," Zhongzhou Peng and Sow Keat Tok investigate the role of the AIIB in China's emerging normative power in international financial governance. The chapter scrutinizes the AIIB's role in China's normative power from three angles, namely, normative principles, norm diffusion, and external perception. According to Peng and Tok, the AIIB's policy framework has inherited Chinese norms of unconditionality and infrastructure construction. In the meantime, the management structure of the AIIB manifests China's preference of a lean internal arrangement. Furthermore, the authors contend, the AIIB's voting structure, under which Asian developing countries hold the majority of voting power, falls in line with China's appeal of a fair governance structure in international financial institutions. Peng and Tok are optimistic that the AIIB will significantly enhance China's normative power in international society and that the cooperation between the AIIB and the other financial institutions will provide an opportunity to improve the Western countries' perception of China's normative power.

Chapter 9 by Hai Yang, "The Asian Infrastructure Investment Bank and Status-Seeking: China's Foray into Global Economic Governance" uses the AIIB as a case study to examine how China is seeking to enhance its international status. To do so, the author employs a symbiotic approach of social identity theory (SIT) in international relations (IR) and institutional innovation. According to Yang, in the IR context, SIT assumes that an aspiring state resorts predominantly to one of the three status-seeking strategies, namely, social mobility, social competition, and social creativity. On the other hand, institutional innovation is introduced as a construct to understand the crystallization of social creativity in the AIIB. Yang notes that the research findings show that in the case of the AIIB, China largely adopted, albeit not exclusively, the social creativity strategy to mitigate the doubt of the West and boost the legitimacy of the bank. This is because Beijing presented its status-seeking initiative of the AIIB as a legitimate addition to the existing global financial system by following the relevant rules of the game in the institution-building process. The author further argues that the case study of China's AIIB initiative can help understand Beijing's other similar initiatives and the strategic thinking of the Chinese leadership in seeking the nation's greater international status.

In a concluding chapter, Yitan Li notes that China today enjoys a much higher level of leadership in global economic governance than before. This said, however, there are still limits on China's playing a true leadership role. On balance, the contributors in this volume point to a mixed view about the efficacy of China's endeavors to reform global economic governance.

It is hoped that by pursuing the topic from multiple perspectives, this volume will make valuable contributions to the literature on China's BRI and AIIB and their implications on geopolitics and geoeconomics in general and on global economic governance in particular.

CHAPTER 2

China's Initiatives: A Bypassing Strategy for the Reform of Global Economic Governance

Kevin G. Cai

Since the mid-2000s, China has vigorously launched three significant diplomatic initiatives in the economic area either jointly with other countries or of its own, namely, the BRICS (a grouping that involves Brazil, Russia, India, China, and South Africa), the One Belt One Road (now

---

This chapter is a reproduction of the journal article: Cai, K.G. "China's Initiatives: A Bypassing Strategy for the Reform of Global Economic Governance." *Chin. Polit. Sci. Rev.* **8**, 1–17 (2023). https://doi.org/10.1007/s41111-022-00215-7

K. G. Cai (✉)
Renison University College, University of Waterloo, Waterloo, Canada
e-mail: kcai@uwaterloo.ca

© The Author(s), under exclusive license to Springer Nature Switzerland AG 2025
K. G.Cai et al. (eds.), *China and Global Economic Governance, Volume I: China's BRI & AIIB and Global Economic Governance*, Politics and Development of Contemporary China,
https://doi.org/10.1007/978-3-031-73212-6_2

known as the Belt and Road Initiative (BRI) in English) and the Asian Infrastructure Investment Bank (AIIB). While China played a key role in the formation of the BRICS, it solely launched the significant twin initiatives of the BRI and the AIIB. A most notable feature of all these initiatives is the exclusion of the US, a superpower that has dominant influence in the existing global economic order. Apparently, China has launched these initiatives as a new diplomatic strategy to pursue its multiple foreign policy objectives (Cai 2018), one of which is to push for the reform of the existing global governance in the economic area, a topic that this paper aims to investigate. These initiatives are pursued by Beijing outside the existing global economic system to bypass the Western status-quo powers' resistance to such a reform. Hence, it can be seen as a "bypassing strategy" adopted by the Chinese leadership. In Beijing's view, the current global economic governance is far from reflecting the reality of China's increased economic capacity and power, thus needing a reform.

This paper is intended to explore why and how Beijing has launched the three initiatives in question to pursue the reform of the existing global economic governance so that China's voice and weight in the existing international economic order can be more reflective of its economic power. The paper is divided into three sections. Section 1 examines the geoeconomic background in which China has launched the initiatives under investigation. Section 2 analyzes the progress and limit of China's initiatives in helping achieve Beijing's objective of increasing its influence in the regional and global economy and reforming the existing global economic governance. The concluding section assesses the implications of these initiatives on the existing global economic governance.

2.1 Geoeconomic Background for China's Launch of the BRICS, the BRI, and the AIIB

The post-Mao Chinese leadership initiated economic reforms in late 1978, dramatically moving away from the command economy of the Mao era with an objective of achieving the nation's rapid economic development and modernization. A very important component of this new policy orientation was to open the nation to the outside world and integrate the country into the capitalist world economy so that China would be able to obtain foreign capital, technology, market, and all the other resources that were needed for China to achieve the nation's modernization. As an integral part of integrating into the capitalist world economy, China resumed its membership of the International Monetary Fund (IMF) and the World Bank in 1980, joined the Asian Development Bank (ADB) in 1986, and entered the World Trade Organization (WTO) in 2001. China's membership in these mainstream international economic institutions proved substantially beneficial to the nation, greatly contributing to the nation's achievement of the economic miracle and the rise of Chinese power.

When China joined these postwar mainstream multilateral organizations of the capitalist world economy, the structure and rules of these institutions had already been solidly established by the Western powers, the US in particular. So China had to enter these institutions on terms that had been set by the Western countries. Given its weak economic position at the time, China had very limited voice and weight within these multilateral institutions under the existing governance structure that had been formed in the wake of World War II. Over time, China gained increasing economic and political power as a result of its rapid economic growth following the nation's dramatic economic reforms, which gradually tilted the balance of power in the world economy in favor of China. However, the existing structure and rules of major international institutions (the IMF and the World Bank in particular) remained basically unchanged to the advantage of the developed countries, while China continued to be disadvantageous. Particularly, China's voting power within these mainstream multilateral institutions was increasingly deviating from the nation's true economic power vis-à-vis the US and other developed countries. For example, by the early 2000s, China had only 63,942 votes (2.95% of total) within the IMF as compared with Belgium's 46,302 votes (2.14%) and Netherlands's 51,874 votes (2.40%), while China's 2005 GDP ($2286 billion) was 5.9 times Belgium's ($386 billion) and 3.3 times the Netherlands's ($685 billion).[1] Beijing wanted to increase its voting power commensurate with its economic capacity in

---

[1] The data on voting rights in the IMF come from Leo Van Houtven, *Governance of the IMF Decision Making, Institutional Oversight, Transparency, and Accountability*, Pamphlet Series, No. 53, International Monetary Fund, 2002, Appendix II. IMF Executive Directors and Voting Power, pp.75–80, https://www.imf.org/external/pubs/ft/pam/pam53/pam53.pdf (accessed December 12, 2021); the data on GDP are from the World Bank, "GDP (current US$)—China, Belgium, Netherlands," https://data.worldbank.org/indicator/NY.GDP.MKTP.CD?locations=CN-BE-NL (accessed December 12, 2021).

the IMF and the World Bank so that it could have more voice and influence in the mainstream multilateral institutions in defense of its interests. Hence, by the first half of the 2000s, Beijing was increasingly disappointed with US and Western dominance of the existing multilateral institutions. In Beijing's view, the existing global economic governance could no longer reflect the new reality of the changed global balance of economic power, thus, a reform was needed (Momani 2013). However, Beijing's call for the reform of the existing international economic system could hardly be echoed by the US and other Western status-quo powers, as such a reform would help increase China's voice and influence and weaken the power and influence of the Western countries in these institutions. As such, the major Western powers resisted the reform that China and other less privileged countries had called for.

It was within this context that around 2005, Beijing started to adopt a two-track approach to push for the reform of the existing global economic governance dominated by the Western status-quo powers. On one hand, Beijing started to more vigorously call for the reform of the multilateral institutions (the IMF and the World Bank in particular) within the existing international economic system; on the other hand, Beijing began to adopt a bypassing strategy by launching new initiatives outside the existing multilateral system that was dominated by the US as a vehicle to increase Beijing's influence in the regional and global economy.

As the first track of the new policy approach, China started to explicitly call for the reform of the IMF and the World Bank within the existing mainstream multilateral system (Cai 2018, p. 838). In a statement to the IMF in 2005, the Governor of the Bank for China stated,

> the two institutions (the IMF and the World Bank) should reform their own governance structure, increasing participation of developing countries in decision making. In doing so, the increasing strength of developing countries as a whole should be reflected, and the views of all member countries expressed in a balanced way, to ensure that the policies of the two institutions will be in the interest of the vast developing countries as well as the world at large. At the same time, the two institutions should also stick to their development mission and professionalism. (IMF 2005)

By 2009, China had become even more critical of the existing global economic system dominated by the Western countries. On March 23, 2009, Zhou Xiaochuan, the Governor of China's Central Bank, even openly proposed the creation of an international reserve currency to replace the US dollar with a new global system that would be controlled by the IMF (Anderlini 2009). In a speech to commemorate the 95th anniversary of the Chinese Communist Party on July 1, 2016, Xi Jinping further made it clear that the world order should be decided not by one country or a few but by the people of all countries through consultations and that China would actively participate in the building of global governance system and contribute to the improvement of global governance (China Daily 2016). Apparently, it was Beijing's belief that the existing global economic governance should be reformed in a way that would let China have more voice commensurate with its economic power.

While calling for the reform of the mainstream multilateral system, Beijing also started to initiate a second track of pushing for the reform of the existing global governance from outside. The initiatives of the BRICS, the BRI, and the AIIB were precisely launched within this geoeconomic background with an aim of creating what Zhimin Chen calls a "parallel order" outside the existing Western-dominated order (Chen 2016, p. 781) as a new bypassing strategy to exert pressure on the Western powers for the reform of the existing multilateral economic system.

Beijing's first move of its bypassing strategy was to join like-minded Brazil, Russia, and India in 2006 to start a process of forming a grouping of emerging economies, which was later joined by South Africa in 2010. Although the bloc, which became to be known as the BRICS, was created to deal with multiple global issues (like security issues, drug smuggling, and others) that concerned its member states, its utmost attention was given to the reform of global economic governance. The BRICS states shared the same disappointment with the existing global economic governance dominated by the Western powers. Particularly, the BRICS was strongly discontented with the existing voting system and president appointment system of both the IMF and the World Bank, which acutely favored the Western countries, the US in particular. Hence, it was the belief of the BRICS states that the current president appointment system of the IMF and the World Bank must be changed and the voting system of both institutions must be reformed so that the share of voting power for emerging economies could be increased, given their status in terms of their combined population (41.5% of the global total) and GDP (24.4% of world GDP).[2]

In 2009, the BRICS held its first summit meeting, which thereafter became routine. By 2021, 13 BRICS summits had been held. Over more than a decade of development, the BRICS has developed a set of procedures and practices of consultation and cooperation on issues regarding global economic governance with increased and intensified exchanges of views among BRICS members. Today, BRICS members usually have their preparatory meetings to discuss their positions before Group of Twenty (G20) summits and IMF and World Bank meetings and frequently speak with one voice on the issues of global economic governance (Miller 2021). Particularly, the most remarkable achievement of the BRICS was the creation of the New Development Bank (NDB) (formerly called BRICS Development Bank) and the Contingent Reserve Arrangement (CRA) in 2014. The establishment of the NDB (headquartered in Shanghai) and the CRA represents a big move toward the institutionalization of cooperation among BRICS members. As two global institutionalized financial arrangements that are independent of major developed countries, the NDB and the CRA explicitly pose a challenge to the mainstream multilateral financial system dominated by the Western powers as embodied in the IMF and the World Bank.

Overwhelming all the other BRICS partners combined economically, China was a crucial member of the BRICS.[3] The rising influence of the BRICS as a grouping in the global political economy was largely due to China's economic clout. By sharing similar concerns with other BRICS states regarding global economic governance, China hoped to use the combined weight and voice of the BRICS as a diplomatic weapon to push for the reform of the global economic governance from outside the existing multilateral economic system. But on the other hand, however, the five BRICS members were highly diversified in almost all major aspects, including economic system, economic structure, trade pattern,

---

[2] Both data are for 2020, which are respectively calculated from Worldometer, "Countries in the world by population" (2021), https://www.worldometers.info/world-population/population-by-country/ and World Bank Data, "GDP," https://data.worldbank.org/indicator/NY.GDP.MKTP.CD (both accessed December 25, 2021).

[3] For example, China's 2020 GDP was $14.723 trillion, which was about 2.5 times the combined GDP of Brazil ($1445 billion), India ($2660 billion), Russia ($1483 billion) and South Africa ($335 billion), calculated from World Bank Data, "GDP," https://data.worldbank.org/indicator/NY.GDP.MKTP.CD (accessed December 25, 2021).

financial system, level of income, level of education, social inequality, and the like, let alone political system and power status within the UN system (i.e., China and Russia were permanent members of the UN Security Council, while the others were not). Hence, the five BRICS countries had their own respective concerns and major policy objectives. Furthermore, because of the concerns of the other BRICS members about Beijing's dominance within the grouping, China's overwhelming economic power was not translated into Beijing's more influence and voice within the current BRICS structure, which was so designed and constructed as a political compromise among the BRICS states. This was most illustratively reflected in the NDB's system of equal voting, which was designed for purely political considerations rather than for economic rationale. Such an organizational structure of the BRICS could hardly make Beijing enthusiastic. As such, China could hardly rely on the BRICS for pursuing its favored policy agenda to promote its influence in the regional and global economy. As a matter of fact, the BRICS could at most be used by Beijing as a symbolic diplomatic gesture rather than an effective and substantial economic weapon in its pursuit of advancing the nation's global influence.

It was under such circumstances that not long after the formation of the BRICS, Beijing started to develop two more vigorous initiatives of its own. China first tossed an idea of creating a development bank for Asia by calling for closer financial cooperation among Asian countries at the Boao Forum for Asia on April 17–19, 2009. Thereafter, China also started to promote the establishment of closer economic ties between China and its neighboring countries. In his speech to the Chinese Communist Party (CCP)'s 18th National Congress on November 8, 2012, the Chinese leader Hu Jintao called for the construction of infrastructure in neighboring counties (including highways, railways, communications, energy channels, etc.) to establish a network of interconnected and interoperable infrastructure so that neighboring countries could be connected to China (Xinhua 2012). These two ideas eventually led to Beijing's launch of two high-profile and significant initiatives in 2013 under Xi's leadership, that is, the BRI and the AIIB. Never before in its diplomatic history had the People's Republic of China (PRC) ever actively launched any diplomatic initiative comparable to the BRI and the AIIB (Cai 2018, p. 832).

The BRI is fully known as the Silk Road Economic Belt and the 21st Century Maritime Silk Road. It was first officially proposed by Chinese leader Xi Jinping when he visited Kazakhstan and Indonesia respectively in September and October 2013. The BRI was initiated as a plan for the construction of a network of infrastructure projects for the vast areas of the developing world through Chinese investments, including roads, railways, oil and natural gas pipelines, telecommunications, electricity projects, ports, and other coastal infrastructure projects. While the Belt includes the countries that are located on the historical Silk Road through Central Asia, West Asia, the Middle East, and Europe, the Road makes the initiative extended to cover South Asia, Southeast Asia, Oceania, and Africa. While over 60 countries are said to be located along the route of the BRI initiative, many other countries outside the BRI route are also either involved or are considering getting involved in BRI projects. By December 2021, 142 countries from all the continents had joined the BRI by signing a Memorandum of Understanding (MOU) with China (Green Finance & Development Center). According to one estimate, if the whole plan were fully implemented, it could cost as high as $8 trillion (Hillman 2018). As such, the ambitious BRI initiative has been dubbed "China's Marshall Plan" (The Wall Street Journal 2014).[4]

On March 28, 2015, the Chinese government released an official document, entitled "Vision and Actions on Jointly Building Silk Road Economic Belt and 21st-century Maritime Silk Road," which provided a more detailed plan for the initiative and moved the initiative well beyond infrastructure construction to comprehensive economic cooperation between China and the rest of Eurasia, Oceania, and Africa (Xinhua 2015). According to the document, in addition to infrastructure development, the initiative would promote policy coordination, financial integration, the use of *renminbi* (RMB) by other countries, liberalization of trade and investment, creation of information and communication networks, and people to people connectivity in the vast areas of East and Southeast Asia, Oceania, South Asia, Central Asia, Europe, and Africa.

---

[4] However, there is a major difference between the US's Marshall Plan in the immediate postwar years and China's BRI of today in that the US's funds for Western European countries did not need to be repaid, while China's BRI funds for developing countries are primarily in the form of loans, which are, in theory, required to be paid back. See Ammar A. Malik, et al., *Banking on the Belt and Road: Insights from a new global dataset of 13,427 Chinese development projects*, AIDDATA, September 29, 2021, https://docs.aiddata.org/ad4/pdfs/Banking_on_the_Belt_and_Road__Insights_from_a_new_global_dataset_of_13427_Chinese_development_projects.pdf (accessed January 30, 2022). Thanks are given to an anonymous reviewer for bringing my attention to this point and useful source.

As a result, the BRI turned to be a grand scheme of expanding China's economic sphere of influence in the region and the world.

The AIIB was also first officially proposed by the Chinese leader Xi Jinping in October 2013 as a development bank dedicated to lending for infrastructure projects in Asia. Thereafter, there were bilateral and multilateral discussions and consultations on core principles and key elements of the proposed bank, which led to the official launch of the bank on October 24, 2014, with a Memorandum of Understanding (MOU) being signed by 22 of 57 original founding members, known as Prospective Founding Members (PFMs). The Chief Negotiators Meeting (CNM) was then established by the PFMs as the forum to negotiate on the AIIB's Articles of Agreement and other related issues. Through five CNMs of negotiation and discussion, the text of the AIIB's Articles of Agreement (Articles), which provided a legal framework, was finalized and adopted on May 22, 2015. By June 29, 2015, the Articles were signed by 50 of the 57 PFMs in Beijing, and by December 31, 2015, all 57 PFMs signed the Articles. Following the ratification of the AIIB's Articles of Agreement by 17 member states, representing 50.1 percent of the bank's capital stock, the AIIB entered into force on December 25, 2015. By August 4, 2016, the Articles had been ratified by all the 57 PFMs with their instruments deposited (Cai 2018, 834). By the end of 2020, the AIIB had a total of 103 approved members, which represented about 79% of the global population and 65% of global GDP (AIIB, a).

The AIIB has a registered capital of $100 billion,[5] 30.8% of which comes from China. As the single largest stakeholder, China therefore holds 26.6% of voting power, which marks a major milestone in China's bid to play a more active role in global governance and development (AIIB, b). Dubbed as a China's "World Bank" for the Asia–Pacific region, the AIIB is widely seen as Beijing's efforts to provide an alternative to the postwar US-dominated financial institutions like the IMF and the World Bank. It is also viewed as a challenge to the ADB, which is dominated by the US and Japan.

Unlike the BRICS where China's efforts to pursue its policy objectives are frequently hindered by political constraints derived from different policy priorities and/or policy orientations of member states and even from conflicting national interests between member states, the BRI and

---

[5] The AIIB's registered capital is only about 50% of the World Bank and 2/3 of the ADB.

the AIIB have been launched solely by China using its growing economic wealth and economic power as a leverage, which, therefore, allows Beijing to more conveniently steer these two initiatives in the direction it prefers.

In a speech at a high-level party meeting in June 2018, Xi Jinping called for China to "… proactively participate in and show the way in reform of the global governance system, creating an even better web of global partnership relationships" (Reuters 2018). The launch of the BRICS, the BRI, and the AIIB has represented Beijing efforts to shape new rules of the multilateral system and to transform the global economic governance in a way that reflects China's values and priorities (Council on Foreign Relations). The three initiatives have been, therefore, used by Beijing as a bypassing strategy to push for such a reform of global economic governance from outside the existing multilateral system to overcome the resistance to such a reform by the Western status-quo powers.

2.2 Progress and Limit of China's Initiatives

The launch and operation of the three initiatives have been changing the geoeconomic map of the world to some extent and enabling China to enjoy increasing influence in the regional and global economy.

When the BRICS was first formed in the 2000s, its member states were largely marginalized from the global economic governance of the mainstream global economic order. Over a decade and half of development, the BRICS has now become growingly visible as a grouping in the global economy, claiming to serve as a bridge between the developing and developed countries. In the meantime, accounting for about 41.5% of the world's population, 24.4% of the global GDP, and 18.1% of the world trade of today,[6] the BRICS makes itself a critical economic engine for the global economy.

Internally, the BRICS provides a mechanism for member countries to share information, build trust and consensus, understand each other's intentions, mitigate conflicts, manage disagreements and develop common positions. Particularly impressive was the establishment of the CRA and the NDB. While the CRA is tasked with providing mutual financial support among BRICS states, the NDB helps finance development

---

[6] The data on trade is for 2020, which is calculated from WTO STATS, "International Trade Statistics," https://stats.wto.org/ (accessed December 25, 2021).

projects of member countries as an alternative to the World Bank and other development banks that are dominated by the developed countries. Notably, since its founding in 2014, the NDB had approved 73 loans with a total of $29.1 billion by September 23, 2021 in support of infrastructure projects of BRICS member countries, covering multiple sectors (NDB, a). It is particularly important to note that the NDB has received high credit ratings from two major credit rating agencies, Standard & Poor's (S&P) and Fitch Ratings, both of which have given AA+ ratings for NDB (NDB, a). The high credit ratings can, therefore, allow the NDB to raise more capital easily and quickly.

It is also important to note that partly because of the efforts of BRICS states, both the IMF and World Bank have adjusted their voting arrangements so that developing economies and emerging economies have more voice than before. The new arrangement in the IMF has particularly benefited China, India, and Brazil, although the BRICS has failed to support South Africa's call for a third African seat on the board of the IMF, which has left Africa as the most underrepresented region on the board (Bradlow 2017).

Despite the progress of the BRICS as a bloc over the past decade, the grouping apparently has its own significant internal weaknesses. Particularly, the BRICS is highly uninstitutionalized as a grouping, which is characterized by such organizational principles as decision-making by consensus, absence of treaty obligations, voluntary commitment and respect for national sovereignty (Hooijmaaijers 2021, p. 33). As such, it is difficult for the BRICS to develop and adopt a common position, let alone play a constructive role in establishing a new foundation for global economic governance.

Moreover, the solidarity of the BRICS is further weakened by the lack of common ideology and mutual political trust among its members. Particularly, inherent conflicting national interests between some member states, most notably between China and India, prevent any possibility of having the BRICS develop into a true unified body in pursuit of the common objective of reforming global economic governance, although the BRICS claims to set conflicts between member countries aside. Indeed, it can hardly be imagined that China and India would wholeheartedly cooperate with each other on global issues when the two countries are involved in territorial disputes and rivalry in multiple areas and see each other as a threat to their respective national interests and even national security.

In a further analysis, the huge disparity between China and the other BRICS states in terms of economic capacity provides another source of worry within the BRICS. For example, China's GDP is 2.5 times the combined GDP of the other four BRICS countries and China's total trade volume is 2.6 times the combined trade volume of the other four states of the grouping with China's exports being 2.9 times and imports 2.4 times the total of the other four (2020).[7] With such a huge economic gap between China and the other members of the BRICS, there is fear of the grouping to be dominated by Beijing, which explains the widespread uneasiness and nationalist sentiment in other BRICS states. The equal voting system of the NDB precisely reflects such an uneasiness and nationalist sentiment as well as the lack of political trust among BRICS members.

With such huge insurmountable weaknesses of the grouping, it is almost impossible for the BRICS states to engage in sincere and true cooperation and develop a common strategy in pursuing the reform of the existing global economic governance that they are all dissatisfied with. At most, the BRICS can impose a big challenge rather than provide a constructive and effective alternative to the existing multilateral economic system. This largely explains why after 15 years of its founding, the BRICS has failed to become an effective force in transforming the existing global economic governance and making it more responsive to the concerns of developing countries, a mission that the BRICS set for itself at the onset. By the 2020s, the BRICS states seem to have more conflicting interests than common interests (Hooijmaaijers 2021, p. 32).

By comparison, the BRI and AIIB have been solely launched by Beijing and are, therefore, either fully steered (BRI) or substantially influenced (AIIB) by China. Consequently, these two initiatives have been more effectively helping achieve Beijing's objective of enhancing China's influence in the regional and global economy and promoting the transformation of the existing global economic order.

Despite the name, the BRI has a truly global coverage in geography with 142 countries from all the continents joining this giant scheme. The BRI is a massive ambitious program that provides funds to support infrastructure projects in developing countries, particularly those big infrastructure projects in transportation and power, which otherwise can

---

[7] Calculated from WTO STATS, "International Trade Statistics," https://stats.wto.org/ (accessed December 25, 2021).

hardly be funded by any other sources. The funds under the BRI have been on the order of $50–100 billion a year. BRI funds are commercial loans, but the terms are more generous than those from private investors for developing countries, although less favorable than funds from Western donors or multilateral development banks (Dollar 2020). By the first quarter of 2020, the total value of BRI projects had exceeded $4 trillion, involving over 3000 projects (Dezan Shira & Associates). Consequently, China has now become a major source of infrastructure investments for many developing countries. Moreover, as a result of such a magnitude of the Chinese state-sponsored and ever-expanding global infrastructure investments, the BRI has also helped gradually form a comprehensive relationship of connectivity between China and the vast areas of East and Southeast Asia, Oceania, South Asia, Central Asia, Europe, and Africa through policy coordination, financial integration, the use of RMB, liberalization of trade and investment, creation of information and communication networks, and people-to-people contacts. Hence, the BRI has become a grand scheme of advancing China's economic influence in the region and the world. In this process, the world economic order that is currently dominated by the Western powers has been bypassed and BRI countries, and the world at large, have been growingly drawn into a China-defined orbit of global order.

China's another initiative AIIB is also designed to provide funds to support infrastructure projects in developing countries, mostly in Asia. However, unlike the BRI that is solely administered by Beijing, the AIIB is a multilateral development bank, which is organized along the line of Western standard of development banks. Nevertheless, having the overwhelmingly largest share of subscribed capital and voting power of the AIIB, China has a crucial say in the AIIB's operation.[8] Ever since the start of its operation in 2016, the AIIB has vigorously financed infrastructure investment projects across Asia and beyond. By December 22, 2021, the AIIB had approved a total of $31.97 billion of loans, involving 159 infrastructure projects in 31 member economies. Among the countries that have got most investment projects financed by the AIIB so far are India

---

[8] China has 30.77% of the AIIB's subscribed capital and 26.57% of voting power, much ahead of India, the member country that has the second largest subscribed capital (8.65%) and voting power (7.60%). AIIB, "Members and Prospective Members of the Bank," https://www.aiib.org/en/about-aiib/governance/members-of-bank/index.html (accessed December 22, 2021).

(29 projects), Bangladesh (14), Turkey (14), Indonesia (10), China (9), Pakistan (8), and Uzbekistan (7). The other 24 countries each have 1–4 investment projects approved. Besides, there are also 15 approved projects that involve multiple countries (AIIB, c). Notably, the majority of these infrastructure investment projects have been approved for financing by the AIIB in conjunction with the World Bank, the ADB, and other international financial institutions to reduce the risk. Apparently, joint financing by the AIIB and other international financial institutions allow the AIIB to finance more infrastructure investment projects in developing countries. As a multilateral development bank for Asia, the AIIB has performed well since its start of operation in 2016 and received high credit ratings from major credit rating agencies, AAA/A-1+ from S&P, Aaa/Prime-1 from Moody's and AAA/F1+ from Fitch (AIIB, d).

It is important to note that the AIIB has greatly enhanced Beijing's voice and influence in the international monetary area not only because China holds the largest share of the AIIB's capital subscriptions and voting power, but also because the bank involves the US's many allies in Western Europe and the Asia–Pacific as its members (including Britain, France, Germany, Italy, Australia, South Korea, Canada, etc.), which have ignored Washington's opposition and joined this China-initiated multilateral development bank. By today, the AIIB has a total of 88 approved members, well surpassing the ADB's 68 members. More significantly, with 30.77% of subscribed capital and 26.57% of voting power, China enjoys more weight and influence within the AIIB as compared with Japan and the US within the ADB, each of which has 15.57% of subscribed capital and 12.75% of voting power. This is also the case with the US within the World Bank, where the US has 15.73% of voting power as the largest capital subscriber (AIIB, b; ADB, b; World Bank).

By offering huge amounts of investment funds to support infrastructure projects, the BRI and the AIIB provide developing countries with attractive opportunities for economic development. As such, compared with the BRICS, both the BRI and the AIIB have more effectively and directly helped greatly expand and enhance China's political and economic influence in the region and the world at large and significantly reshape global political economy.

It is important to note that by launching the BRI and the AIIB (as well as the BRICS), China does not necessarily intend to replace the existing multilateral system, which Beijing is unable to do. However, the BRI and the AIIB have indeed enabled China to play a more active and prominent role in global economic governance and development and to form and develop a parallel regional and global economic order that is based on China-defined norms and rules alongside the Western-dominated global economic order. It is interesting to note that this seemingly emerging China-centered global economic order is apparently endorsed by the UN, the World Bank, the IMF, the ADB, etc., as all these mainstream multilateral institutions have been cooperating well with China on the BRI and the AIIB. Such endorsements from the mainstream international institutions have further confirmed the significant role of China in global economic governance and development. Indeed, with its rising power and influence, China is now clearly capable of operating outside the existing global economic order that is still largely led by the US. Today, China has already surpassed the World Bank as the most important aid provider at least on the African continent with its aid budget for Africa larger than that of the latter. With such a significant role in financing the economic development of the vast developing world, it is inevitable that China's increasing influence has been ramifying from the China-centered global order over into the mainstream global economic order. China's rising status within the mainstream global economic order is most illustratively reflected in China's increased voting power in both the IMF and the World Bank in recent years as well as in the inclusion of the RMB in the IMF's Special Drawing Rights (SDRs) basket of currencies in October 2016, although it is not, technically speaking, the direct result of China's rising influence derived from its BRI and AIIB.

Despite their impressive achievements so far, however, China's BRI and AIIB have their own limit in helping Beijing achieve the objective that has been set for these two initiatives.

In the first place, the BRI and the AIIB are largely contradictory to the BRICS. This is because if successfully implemented, China's twin initiatives (the BRI in particular) will inevitably entrench China's regional hegemony at the expense of the other BRICS states like Russia and India (Beeson and Zeng 2018, p. 9). This dilemma can be well explained by India's ambivalent attitude toward Beijing's twin initiatives of the BRI and the AIIB. On the one hand, New Delhi is acceptive of Beijing's AIIB initiative and has timely joined the AIIB, seeing the AIIB as a useful additional source for India's much needed funds in support of its infrastructure investment. On the other hand, however, India is very critical of Beijing's BRI, fearing that rising BRI infrastructure investment in South Asia would not only weaken its own dominance in what New Delhi sees as its backyard, but also undermine the country's national security. Particularly, the $46 billion China–Pakistan Economic Corridor (CPEC) project, which runs through the part of Kashmir that is under Pakistan's control, is even seen as a direct challenge to India's sovereignty claim over the disputed region. It is within such a context that at least, the BRI functions to weaken rather than strengthen the solidarity of the BRICS. With respect to the AIIB, although all the BRICS states are either the approved members or a prospective member (South Africa) of this development bank, China's dominance of the bank can hardly make the other BRICS states comfortable. The adoption of the equal voting system within the NDB precisely explains the true attitude of the other BRICS members toward China's economic dominance.

Second, while it is believed that BRI investment projects would help narrow the huge infrastructure gap and boost economic development in many developing countries, their success is largely subject to how efficiently these investment projects are introduced and run by both Chinese-invested companies and host governments of developing countries. However, some BRI investment projects, instead of bringing hope of economic development for host developing countries, have led to a "trail of trouble" (e.g., wasteful spending, environmental destruction, skyrocketing costs, untenable debt, etc.) as a result of irregularities like corruption, lack of transparency, ill planning and mismanagement. In some cases, there is even outbreak of violence and negative sentiment against BRI projects in local areas. A most publicized case of such irregularities is BRI mega infrastructure projects in Hambantota of Sri Lanka. Scandals are also reported to be found in huge multiple BRI infrastructure investment projects in Malaysia and Bangladesh (Shepard 2020). If such problems continue and even proliferate, the reputation of the BRI would be impaired, which might eventually ruin China's whole ambitious BRI program.

Third, as a development bank, the AIIB is still incomparable to the World Bank and the ADB in terms of the amount of registered capital. The registered capital of the AIIB is only about 50% of the World Bank and 2/3 of the ADB. In terms of the amount of loans lent, the AIIB is even farther behind the ADB. In 2020, for example, the ADB approved $22.47 billion of loans, while the amount of the approved loans provided by the AIIB was only $9.88 billion. Particularly, it is interesting to note that China still borrows much more from the ADB than from the AIIB. To use the 2020 data again, China borrowed a total of $2,012.5 million of loans from the ADB, but only \$385 million from the AIIB (ADB, b; AIIB, e). Apparently, there is still a long way to go for the AIIB to become on par with the ADB in terms of the amount of investment loans that are provided, which is a crucial indicator of how important and significant a development bank is for developing countries.

Finally, and most importantly, although the BRI and the AIIB have helped increase China's influence in regional and global economy and promote the emergence of a China-centered global economic order (if it can be seen as an "order"), this order is still very primitive. Compared with the well-established existing mainstream international economic order, this so-called China-centered order is more of ad hoc nature and its most important feature is the lack of institutionalization. Hence, this China-led order is far from being able to really shake, let alone replace, the existing US-led mainstream global economic order that is institutionalized in the UN, the IMF, the World Bank, and the WTO. This China-centered order can at most play a supplementary role in helping contribute to economic development in the developing world, through which China is able to increase its influence in the regional and global economy. This probably explains why all the main multilateral institutions like the UN, the IMF, the World Bank, the ADB, etc., have endorsed the BRI and the AIIB and cooperated with China on investment projects in developing countries under these initiatives, because they all view China's twin initiatives from the perspective of the economic development of developing countries as well as global economic growth. By contrast, the US and some other powers (like Japan, India, etc.) are critical of one or both of China's initiatives, because they perceive one or both of China's initiatives from the perspective of geopolitics and geoeconomics. It is under such circumstances that China's BRI and AIIB can help increase its influence in the regional and global economy, but such increased influence of China can hardly be directly transformed into its enhanced status within the existing mainstream global economic order, which is still fundamentally based on the rules and procedures that have been established by the Western powers. For example, China's increased voting power in both the IMF and the World Bank in recent years is, technically speaking, based on the rules and procedures of these institutions regarding the voting weights of member states. In a similar fashion, the inclusion of the Chinese RMB in the IMF's SDRs basket currencies in 2016 is precisely based on the relevant rules and procedures of the IMF rather than any other criteria.

2.3 Conclusion: The Implications of China's Initiatives on Global Economic Governance

It is Beijing's belief that the existing global economic governance, which was established in the immediate postwar years, becomes increasingly unfair, as China's voice as reflected in its voting weights in the IMF and the World Bank is far from reflecting the nation's true economic capacity. Due to the difficulty in pushing for the reform of the existing global economic governance from within at a pace and magnitude that China desires, Beijing has, therefore, resorted to a bypassing strategy to push for such a reform from outside. It is in this context that China's launch of the three initiatives reflects Beijing's intention and efforts to reconfigure the global governance of the existing international economic order dominated by the Western powers in a way that would allow China to have more say in the mainstream global economic system and to play a more important role in the regional and global economy. In this regard, the BRI and the AIIB that China has solely launched reflect the nation's growing capacity and economic clout that Beijing intends to use in pursuit of its multiple diplomatic objectives, one of which is the reform of the global economic governance. Obviously, China's initiatives (the BRI and the AIIB in particular) have been bringing significant implications on the existing global economic architecture in multiple important areas, including patterns of regional trade, investment and infrastructure development, which will in turn have strategic impact on global economic governance.

Apparently, China's initiatives have been posing normative and structural challenges to the existing global economic order dominated by the Western powers. Most notably, China has bypassed the World Bank and other mainstream development banks by lending unilaterally under the BRI and multilaterally through the AIIB to developing countries in support of their infrastructure investment projects. This, together with the NDB that is designed to finance development in emerging economies, will weaken the prominence of the World Bank, the ADB, and other mainstream development banks. As the demand for infrastructure investment in developing countries is very high and Western funds provided to developing countries are primarily related to social services, administration, and democracy-promotion while shy away from hard infrastructure (Dollar 2020), China's BRI and AIIB play an irreplaceable significant role in infrastructure development and economic growth in the developing world. It is in this sense that the BRI and the AIIB are bound to help increase China's role in the economic development of developing countries, which in turn helps enhance China's influence in the developing world. Furthermore, the BRI and the AIIB have also helped promote the global use of the RMB, which is unavoidably bringing an effect of weakening the US dollar and other Western currencies. Consequently, these high-profile initiatives (the BRI and the AIIB in particular) have enabled China to play a more active and prominent role in global economic governance and development. This has been leading to increasing pressure for the reform and change of the existing US-led mainstream global economic order in terms of not only its structure but also its rules, posing a huge challenge to the Western powers in general and the US in particular.

This said, however, of the three initiatives, the BRI is the most significant in terms of the level and scope that the existing global economic order is being challenged. This is because the BRI is unilaterally controlled and run by the Chinese state and BRI investment projects can, therefore, be used by China directly and effectively to pursue its geoeconomic as well as geopolitical objectives and to promote its national interests. To make Beijing's BRI program even more formidable is its huge scale of worldwide infrastructure investment by a single individual country, which has been unparallel in the world history. As such, it is the BRI that has been bringing most significant and complex implications for the existing global economic order as well as for Western powers, the US in particular.

Most significantly, in the medium to long term, successful implementation of the BRI will strengthen China-centered economic links among BRI countries. Within the vast BRI area, the markets of BRI countries are more closely connected with not only products made in China moving more freely into these markets but also products made by Chineseinvested companies in BRI countries moving into the Western markets at even lower costs. In the meantime, BRI countries will also be linked through digital infrastructure that is constructed by Chinese high-tech companies like Huawei, Tencent, ZTE, etc. Consequently, BRI countries will be truly incorporated into a China-defined economic order of trade, financial flows, investment, and infrastructure on the basis of Chinese norms, rules, and standards. Such development will be enhancing China's not only geoeconomic but also geopolitical influence in the region and the world at large.

Such a formidable and mounting challenge from China's BRI has already aroused the concerns of the Western powers (the US in particular), which view China's BRI and other initiatives increasingly from a geopolitical as well as geoeconomic perspective. Particularly, in Washington's view, the BRI is presenting "significant risks for US economic, political, climate change, security, and health interests" (Lew et al. 2021, p. 20). It is within this context that during the G7 summit on June 12, 2021, the seven leaders of developed countries agreed to set up an infrastructure plan for developing countries, known as the Build Back Better World (B3W) initiative, to jointly compete with China's massive BRI. While the Chinese state-sponsored BRI investment primarily focuses on infrastructure projects in transportation and power, the G7's B3W initiative is intended to "mobilize private-sector capital in areas such as climate, health and health security, digital technology, and gender equity and equality" for investment in developing countries (Holland and Guy 2021). Given the nature of the G7's initiative, it is apparent that China's BRI program can hardly be challenged and stopped by the Western powers.

Finally, despite China's rising influence through its initiatives (the BRI in particular) and the bumping-up efforts of the Western powers to compete with China's BRI, the existing global economic order will continue to function as usual and the reform of the existing global governance will still proceed at its own pace according to its established rules and procedure. Likewise, China will continue to stay within the mainstream global economic order, as it has well been benefitting from this order. But on the other hand, Beijing will also continue to make efforts to push for the reform of the global economic governance within the existing international economic order to make the nation's status therein more reflective of its economic power.

REFERENCES

ADB (a). Members, Capital Stock, and Voting Power. In *ADB Annual Report 2020*, file:///C:/Users/Kevin20Cai/Downloads/oi-appendix1.pdf. Accessed 22 Dec 2021.

ADB (b). *ADB Annual Report 2020*, https://www.adb.org/sites/default/files/institutional-document/691766/adb-annual-report-2020.pdf and AIIB, "Our Projects, 2020", https://www.aiib.org/en/projects/list/year/2020/member/All/sector/All/financing_type/All/status/All. Accessed 24 Dec 2021.

AIIB (a). https://www.aiib.org/en/about-aiib/index.html. Accessed 14 Dec 2021.

AIIB (b). https://www.aiib.org/en/about-aiib/governance/members-of-bank/index.html. Accessed 14 Dec 2021.

AIIB (c). Approved Projects. https://www.aiib.org/en/projects/list/index.html?status=Approved. Accessed 22 Dec 2021.

AIIB (d). https://www.aiib.org/en/treasury/_other_content/rating-reports/index.html. Accessed 25 Dec 2021.

AIIB (e). Our Projects, 2020, https://www.aiib.org/en/projects/list/year/2020/member/All/sector/All/financing_type/All/status/All. Accessed 24 Dec 2021.

Anderlini, Jamil. 2009. China Calls for New Reserve Currency. *Financial Times*, March 23, https://www.ft.com/content/7851925a-17a2-11de-8c9d-0000779fd2ac. Accessed 18 Jan 2021.

Beeson, Mark, and Jinghan Zeng. 2018. The BRICS and Global Governance: China's Contradictory Role. *Third World Quarterly* 39 (10): 1962–1978.

Bradlow, Danny. 2017. Why Has the BRICS Failed to be an Effective Force? *Wire*, September 27, https://thewire.in/economy/brics-reform-socio-economic-justice. Accessed 7 Dec 2021.

Cai, Kevin G. 2018. One Belt One Road and the Asian Infrastructure Investment Bank: Beijing's New Strategy of Geoeconomics and Geopolitics. *Journal of Contemporary China* 27 (114): 831–847.

Chen, Zhimin. 2016. China, the European Union and the Fragile World Order. *Journal of Common Market Studies* 54: 775–792. https://doi.org/10.1111/jcms.12383, Accessed 12 Dec 2021.

China Daily. 2016. Xi: China to Contribute Wisdom to Global Governance. July 1, http://www.chinadaily.com.cn/china/2016-07/01/content_25933506.htm. Accessed 23 Nov 2017.

Council on Foreign Relations. China's Approach to Global Government. https://www.cfr.org/china-global-governance/. Accessed 28 Jan 2021.

Dezan Shira & Associates, China Belt and Road Projects Value Now Exceeds US$4 Trillion, *Silk Road Briefing*, https://www.silkroadbriefing.com/news/2020/11/25/china-belt-and-road-projects-value-now-exceeds-us4-trillion/. Accessed 17 Dec 2021.

Dollar, David. 2020. Seven Years into China's Belt and Road, *Brookings*, October 1, https://www.brookings.edu/blog/order-from-chaos/2020/10/01/seven-years-into-chinas-belt-and-road/. Accessed 16 Dec 2021.

Green Finance & Development Center, Countries of the Belt and Road Initiative (BRI), https://greenfdc.org/countries-of-the-belt-and-road-initiative-bri/. Accessed 16 Dec 2021.

Hillman, Jonathan E. 2018. How Big is China's Belt and Road? April 3, Center for Strategic & International Studies, https://www.csis.org/analysis/how-big-chinas-belt-and-road. Accessed 26 Dec 2021.

Holland, Steve, and Guy, Faulconbridge. 2021. G7 rivals China with Grand Infrastructure Plan, *Reuters*, June 13, https://www.reuters.com/world/g7-counter-chinas-belt-road-with-infrastructure-project-senior-us-official-2021-06-12/. Accessed 27 Dec 2021.

Hooijmaaijers, Bas. 2021. China, the BRICS, and the Limitations of Reshaping Global Economic Governance. *The Pacific Review* 34 (1): 29–55.

IMF. 2005. Press Release No. 13, 24–25 September, http://www.imf.org/external/am/2005/speeches/pr13e.pdf. Accessed 7 May 2017.

Lew, Jacob J., Gary Roughead, Jennifer, Hillman, and David Sacks. 2021. *China's Belt and Road: Implications for the United State*, Independent Task Force Report No. 79, Council on Foreign Relations, https://www.cfr.org/report/chinas-belt-and-road-implications-for-the-united-states/. Accessed 27 Dec 2021.

Malik, Ammar A., et al. 2021. *Banking on the Belt and Road: Insights from a New Global Dataset of 13,427 Chinese Development Projects*, AIDDATA, September 29, https://docs.aiddata.org/ad4/pdfs/Banking_on_the_Belt_and_Road__Insights_from_a_new_global_dataset_of_13427_Chinese_development_projects.pdf. Accessed 30 Jan 2022.

Miller, Manjari Chatterjee. 2021. Why BRICS Still Matters—BRICS May be a Young Institution, But It Shouldn't be Underestimated, *Foreign Policy*, September 27, https://foreignpolicy.com/2021/09/27/brics-members-summit-brazil-russia-india-china-south-africa/. Accessed 26 Nov 2021.

Momani, Bessma. 2013. China at the International Monetary Fund: Continued Engagement in Its Drive for Membership and Added Voice at the IMF Executive Board. *Journal of Chinese Economics* 1 (1): 125–150.

NDB (a). Approved Projects. https://www.ndb.int/projects/list-of-all-projects/approved-projects/. Accessed 7 Dec 2021.

NDB (b). Credit Ratings. https://www.ndb.int/investor-relations/credit-ratings/. Accessed 7 Dec 2021.

Reuters. 2018. Xi says China Must Lead Way in Reform of Global Governance, June 23, https://www.reuters.com/article/us-china-diplomacy/xi-says-china-must-lead-way-in-reform-of-global-governance-idUSKBN1JJ0GT. Accessed 28 Jan 2021.

Shepard, Wade. 2020. How China's Belt and Road Became a 'Global Trail of Trouble,' *Forbes*, January 29, 2020, https://www.forbes.com/sites/wadeshepard/2020/01/29/how-chinas-belt-and-road-became-a-global-trail-of-trouble/?sh=31ed3a8f443d. Accessed 25 Dec 2021.

The Wall Street Journal. 2014. China's 'Marshall Plan:' Xi Jinping Bids to Take Leadership Away from the U.S, November 11, http://online.wsj.com/articles/chinas-marshall-plan-1415750828. Accessed 26 Dec 2021.

The World Bank, https://thedocs.worldbank.org/en/doc/1da86cb968275b9 4ab30b3d454882208-0330032021/original/IBRDEDsVotingTable.pdf. Accessed 22 Dec 2021.

Xinhua. 2012. Full Text of Hu Jintao's Report at the 18th Party Congress, November 19, http://en.people.cn/90785/8024777.html. Accessed 5 Dec 2021.

Xinhua. 2015. Full Text: Vision and Actions on Jointly Building Belt and Road, March 28, http://www.china.org.cn/china/Off_the_Wire/2015-03/28/con tent_35182638.htm. Accessed 27 Dec 2021.

CHAPTER 3

All Roads Lead to Beijing: *Systemism*, Power Transition Theory, and the Belt and Road Initiative

Enyu Zhang and Patrick James

3.1 Introduction

Like the Ancient Silk Road, the Belt and Road Initiative (BRI) will change the world. The People's Republic of China (PRC), under Xi Jinping's leadership, has committed to building international and inter-regional connectivity through the BRI—a series of Beijing-backed infrastructure, trade, and investment projects, along with bilateral and multilateral diplomatic and cultural cooperation activities across Eurasia, Africa, and Latin

---

This chapter is a reproduction of the journal article: Zhang, E., James, P. "All Roads Lead to Beijing: Systemism, Power Transition Theory and the Belt and Road Initiative." *Chin. Polit. Sci. Rev.* **8**, 18–44 (2023). https://doi.org/10.1007/s41111-022-00211-x

---

E. Zhang (✉)
Seattle University, Seattle, USA
e-mail: zhange@seattleu.edu

© The Author(s), under exclusive license to Springer Nature
Switzerland AG 2025
K. G.Cai et al. (eds.), *China and Global Economic Governance, Volume I: China's BRI & AIIB and Global Economic Governance*, Politics and Development of Contemporary China,
https://doi.org/10.1007/978-3-031-73212-6_3

America. Since its inception in 2013, the BRI has gone from a loosely coordinated infrastructure development program to the cornerstone of foreign policy for the PRC under Xi Jinping's leadership. The BRI is an ambitious step forward for the PRC as it openly questions the long-standing Anglo-American world order in significant ways.

Much has been said already about the scope, intentions, goals, and significance, and connection to domestic politics, among other aspects of the BRI. However, little research so far has examined the complex causal mechanisms of the BRI in a rigorously visualized way. How, for example, does the BRI look in the context of power transition between the US and China? Is the time-honored power transition theory, which focuses on the dynamics of capabilities, able to explain the characteristics of BRI, most notably its impact upon outcomes at the international level? These are questions with great academic and policy-related significance for today and the years beyond.

Through the prism of *systemism*, this paper seeks to answer such questions with an examination of ideas about the dynamics of capabilities, such as power transition theory in international relations. This is intended to obtain greater insight about the characteristics and development of China's Belt and Road Initiative. *Systemist* International Relations (SIR) (James 2019, 2022), which emphasizes graphic portrayal of cause and effect, is well suited to the task of comparing and evaluating theoretical arguments about developments such as the BRI. The goal is to produce a better theoretical model to explain the China-led multilateral initiative and identify the most significant policy-related aspects of its ongoing implementation.

This study proceeds in five further sections. The second section provides an overview of the BRI and associated academic literature. Section 3 introduces SIR, a graphic approach toward communication of theories. In Sect. 4, power transition theory is conveyed through visualizations based on SIR as a potential explanation for development and characteristics of the BRI. The fifth section employs SIR to convey and assess the story about the cause and effect of BRI in the power transition dynamics between the US and China. A sixth and final section

---

P. James
University of Southern California, Los Angeles, USA
e-mail: patrickj@usc.edu

reviews what has been accomplished and offers a few suggestions for future research about the BRI, in particular, and the evolving role of the PRC as a rising world power in general.

3.2 The BRI: A Comprehensive Diplomatic and Development Strategy

Initially articulated in President Xi Jinping's 2013 speech in Kazakhstan to build the "Silk Road Economic Belt" (丝绸之路经济带)[1] and his address to the Indonesian parliament on building the "21st Century Maritime Silk Road" (21世纪海上丝绸之路), the BRI serves as the framework of contemporary Chinese foreign policy. This vision of a new world order is referred to as either the "One Belt, One Road" Initiative (一带一路倡议) or the BRI. Its vision is to establish economic, diplomatic, and cultural connections between and among China and Eurasia, Africa, and Oceana through six economic corridors.[2] Entitled "Vision and Actions on Jointly Building Silk Road Economic Belt and 21st Century Maritime Silk Road," the official narrative jointly released by the National Development and Reform Commission (NDRC), the Ministry of Foreign Affairs (MOFA), and the Ministry of Commerce (MOFCOM) in March 2015 defines the scope of the BRI as follows:

The Belt and Road run through the continents of Asia, Europe, and Africa, connecting the vibrant East Asia economic circle at one end and developed European economic circle at the other, and encompassing countries with huge potential for economic development. The Silk Road Economic Belt focuses on bringing together China, Central Asia, Russia, and Europe (the Baltic); linking China with the Persian Gulf and the Mediterranean Sea through Central Asia and West Asia; and connecting China with Southeast Asia, South Asia, and the Indian Ocean. The twenty-first Century Maritime Silk Road is designed to go from China's coast to Europe through the South China Sea and the Indian Ocean in

---

[1] Key terms will be provided in Mandarin as well as English for the benefit of area specialists who will be able to assess the translation in each instance.

[2] The six economic corridors include the New Eurasian Land Bridge, the China–Central Asia–West Asia Corridor, the China–Pakistan Corridor, the Bangladesh–China–India–Myanmar Corridor, the China–Mongolia–Russia Corridor, and the China–Indochina Peninsula Corridor.

one route, and from China's coast through the South China Sea to the South Pacific in the other.

Figure 3.1 displays a map of the BRI. As a modern, state-sponsored version of the Silk Road, the BRI stands out as a grand strategy that should enhance the position of China over time. This is to be anticipated precisely because of its comprehensive approach toward implementation of foreign policy, international trade and investment, and security.

Economically, through a series of hard and soft infrastructures, the BRI seeks to build intra-regional and inter-regional connectivity by linking China's economic centers and underdeveloped regions with key cities across land corridors in the "Silk Road Economic Belt" and connecting a string of ports across the South China Sea, the Indian Ocean, and the Mediterranean in the "21st Century Maritime Silk Road." The BRI not only focuses on infrastructure building in partner countries and regions, it also is a vehicle to strengthen trade and cultivate cooperative relations.

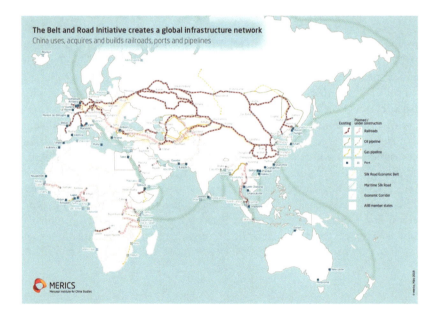

Fig. 3.1 Map of the Belt and Road Initiative, 2020 (*Source* Mercator Institute for China Studies, https://merics.org/sites/default/files/2020-06/Silkroad-Projekt_EN_2020_)

From 2013 to 2018, China's direct investment in BRI partners reached US$90 billion. In October 2020, *China Daily* reports that trade between China and BRI partners totaled US$7.8 trillion in over 2,000 projects.[3]

The BRI goes beyond construction that consists of 'bricks and mortar.' Since 2015, BRI has included a "Digital Silk Road," also called a "community of common destiny in cyberspace." The hardware in the digital infrastructure abroad includes most notably the 5G telecommunication networks, next-generation fiber-optic cables, and data centers built by Huawei and other Chinese high-tech champions. These elements are essential to integrate modern international trade and financial markets.[4] The software of the Digital Silk Road consists of various initiatives for international cooperation in implementing standards of cyber security and cyber sovereignty through intergovernmental institutions. China also offers Internet training programs that take place in some BRI partners (e.g., Egypt, Zimbabwe, etc.), highlighting the internet as a legitimate domain for state governance and intervention. It has great potential to enhance China's digital connectivity and cyber free trade zones with BRI partners with China-centered digital infrastructure—a Chinese model of digital sovereignty and internet governance (Yang 2020).

Another highlight of the BRI, "people-to-people exchanges," involves study abroad and exchange programs between China and its BRI partners. China now ranks third globally in attracting international students to universities and vocational schools, behind the US and the UK. The Ministry of Education in Beijing reported 489,200 international students studying in China in 2017, up from 290,000 in 2011 ("Is China both a source and hub for international students?" 2017). Over half of the inbound international students came from China's Asian neighbors, many of which are BRI partners. International students from BRI partner countries have risen steadily from just around 207,847 in 2012 to 284,141 in 2018. Among these, students from Pakistan studying in China doubled from 2012 to 2016 to 19,000. In 2016, China became the

---

[3] https://www.chinadaily.com.cn/a/202010/29/WS5f9a0e99a31024ad0ba81ba1. html. Given the geographical scope and variety of projects under the BRI, the nature of the BRI defies an accurate overall characterization. Some projects make better economic sense, but other projects make more strategic sense, from the PRC's standpoint.

[4] The domestic component of the digital infrastructure aims to develop the crown jewels of advanced technologies for the twenty-first century, such as artificial intelligence, *Beidou* Satellite Navigation System, quantum computing, and blockchain.

second most popular international destination—after France—for African students, attracting 61,594 students from African countries majoring in economics and sciences.[5] As of 2017, according to the Ministry of Education, 350,000 Chinese students have studied in BRI partner countries and 45 educational agreements had been signed with BRI partner countries since 2012. By March 2017, to promote the Chinese language and culture, 137 Confucius Institutes had been established in 53 BRI partner countries.[6] These numbers, moreover, have risen rapidly from the outset of the BRI onward until the COVID-19 pandemic.

In addition, other "new strategic territories" have been incorporated to expand BRI's footprint, including China's involvement in the Polar regions through the "Silk Road on Ice" in the Arctic, the deep sea through the three ocean-based "blue economic passages," and outer space through the Space Information Corridor.

Since its inception, the Chinese Communist Party (CCP) and Chinese government have expended enormous financial, economic, diplomatic, political, and human resources to promote the BRI. The Initiative was officially endorsed at the Third Plenum of the 18th CCP Congress in November 2013. Since 2015, the BRI has been featured in the State Council's annual reports on the work of the government. It is a prominent feature of China's 13th Five-Year Plan that has guided the national investment plan from 2016 to 2020. The BRI also has been elevated to represent Xi Jinping's strategic vision of China's place in world order and thus enshrined in the PRC Constitution in 2017 and the CCP Constitution in 2018.

Over and beyond Xi Jinping's personal leadership from the beginning, policy coordination for the BRI since 2015 has been under the guidance of the CCP Central Leading Small Group on "Advancing the Development of the OBOR." This ongoing process of coordination involves four top-ranking Politburo members. Involvement of the highest leadership with the BRI, through the Leading Small Group, is able to "project an image of global Chinese economic accomplishment and prestige domestically, that in turn delivers satisfaction to the populace, and insures against

---

[5] The top five home origins of these students are Ghana, Nigeria, Tanzania, Zambia, and Zimbabwe.

[6] Xinhua, "350,000 Chinese students study in Belt and Road Countries," *China Daily*, 13 May 2017. http://www.xinhuanet.com//english/2017-05/13/c_136279200.htm.

regime stability" (He 2019, p. 185). Thus, the BRI can be identified as the PRC's 'signature' foreign policy.

Beyond active promotion within China, the Chinese government has put forward the BRI as the cornerstone of Xi Jinping's signature "major country diplomacy" (大国外交), notably through the two One Belt and One Road Forums for International Cooperation. In May 2017, 29 heads of state and 60 representatives of international organizations, among over 1600 delegates, attended the first BRI forum and achieved 279 practical outcomes. In April 2019, among over 6000 foreign guests, 38 heads of state attended the second BRI forum and achieved 283 practical outcomes. Chinese Foreign Minister Wang Yi reported that, by March 8, 2019, 123 countries and 29 international organizations already had signed on to the BRI (Wang 2019).[7] By July 2019, China had signed 195 intergovernmental cooperation agreements with 136 countries and 30 international organizations across Eurasia, Africa, Latin America, and the South Pacific (Belt and Road Portal 2019).

As of March 2020, BRI partners include 38 in sub-Saharan Africa, 34 in Europe and Central Asia (including 18 EU member states), 25 in East Asia and the Pacific (including China), 17 in the Middle East and North Africa, 18 in Latin America and the Caribbean, and in Southeast Asia (Belt and Road Portal 2019). These 138 BRI partners not only consist of China's various circles of allies and friends in the developing countries, emerging markets, and advanced economies, but also include some of the allies (notably, Australia, Greece, Italy, South Korea, Poland, Saudi Arabia, United Arab Emirates) and enemies (notably, Iran) of the US.[8]

Existing studies of the BRI have been developed within the broader contexts of China's historical connections with the West through the Ancient Silk Road and contemporary IR inter- and intra-paradigmatic debates on the rise of China, along with its impact on world order (examples include Ikenberry 2011a, 2011b; Kirshner 2010; Mearsheimer 2010; Han and Paul 2020). Much of the existing scholarship outside

---

[7] According to a World Bank study (*Belt and Road Economics*, 2019), some of the countries that have signed BRI collaboration agreements with China are not geographically located within the BRI corridors. Not all countries located within the BRI corridors have signed collaboration agreements with China.

[8] Given the wide variety of BRI partners, a more nuanced categorization and analysis of these partnerships are beyond the scope of this paper. This could be taken up in a follow-up study in the future.

China about the BRI has focused on Beijing's official discourses and strategic narratives (Callahan 2016; Rolland 2017; Lams 2018; Yang 2020), grand strategy (Rolland 2017; Cai 2018; Rudd 2020), domestic politics (He 2019; Ye 2019, 2020), roots within China's strategic culture (Farwa 2018), challenges and implications (e.g., Djankov et al. 2016), and perceptions, effects, and implications in specific recipient countries and regions (e.g., Ba 2019).

Some scholars view BRI as a cohesive strategy. For instance, Callahan (2016, p. 226) asserts that China intends to "weave neighboring countries into a Sino-centric network of economic, political, cultural, and security relations. Beijing's grand strategy thus is to reconstitute the regional order—and eventually global order—with new governance ideas, norms, and rules." Furthermore, Rudd (2019, p. 22) observes that "the strategic imperative is clear: to consolidate China's relationships with its neighboring states. And by and large, this means enhancing its strategic position across the Eurasian continent, thereby consolidating China's continental periphery." Other scholars, on the other hand, point out that BRI's rapid advancement is accompanied by ongoing fragmentation and fragility in its domestic politics and economy (Shirk 2007; Tatom 2007; Ye 2020). In addition, some studies emphasize the BRI as a poorly-coordinated program to address China's domestic fragmentation and economic crises (He 2019; Ye 2019).

IR theories have been modified to advance understanding of BRI as a comprehensive foreign policy and development strategy. For instance, "contested multilateralism" (e.g., Knoerich and Urdinez 2019; Liang 2019) and "institutional balancing" (e.g., He 2015, 2018; Stephen 2017; Yuan 2018) have been developed to study the BRI and other Chinese-initiated multilateral institutions. The underlying logic of such a framework is essentially balance of power.

However, little research has examined the complex causal mechanisms of the BRI in a rigorously visualized way. This paper intends to fill that gap through implementation of SIR, which emphasizes a graphic approach that is intended to facilitate communication about theories in application to substantive issues of policy. A visual format can help to illustrate the ongoing debate about the BRI as a tangible contingency whether China remains satisfied or grows dissatisfied with the status quo.

3.3 Systemist International Relations

Systemism is an *approach* rather than a substantive theory (Bunge 1996, p. 265). It focuses on building comprehensive explanations; *systemism* transcends individualism and holism as the other available "coherent views" with respect to operation of a social system (Bunge 1996, p. 241). *Systemism* as a method emphasizes diagrammatic exposition of cause and effect that promotes comprehension and rigor. Thus, the overall value of *systemism* is that its visual representations clarify relationships expressed in a theory.

Systemism goes beyond holism and reductionism through a focus on *all* types of connections needed to fully specify a theory.[9] Figure 3.2 depicts functional relations in a social system from a *systemist* point of view. The varying shapes and colors that appear will be explained momentarily.

Figure 3.2 depicts the system and its environment. Variables that operate at macro (VARIABLE X, VARIABLE Y) and micro (variable

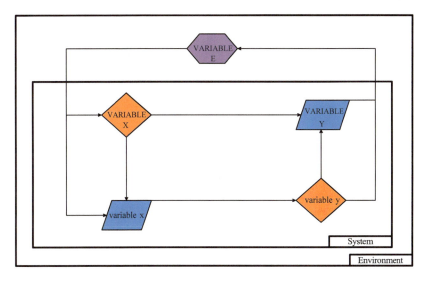

Fig. 3.2 Functional relations in a social system (*Source* Adapted from Bunge, 1996, p. 149)

---

[9] The diagrammatic exposition that follows is based primarily upon James (2019).

x, variable y) levels of the system appear at the upper and lower levels of the system. In this diagram and others based on *systemism, UPPER- and lowercase characters correspond to MACRO- and microlevel variables*, respectively. Four basic types of linkages are possible: macro–macro (VARIABLE X → VARIABLE Y), macro–micro (VARIABLE X → variable x), micro–macro (variable y → VARIABLE Y), and micro–micro (variable x → variable y). The figure also includes a variable to represent the environment (VARIABLE E). The environment can be expected to stimulate the system and vice versa: (i) 'VARIABLE E → VARIABLE X' and 'VARIABLE E → variable x' and (ii) 'variable y → VARIABLE E' and 'VARIABLE Y → VARIABLE E.' All potential types of connection for a theory to incorporate now are in place.[10]

Table 3.1 provides the notation for *systemist* figures. Color and shape are used to designate roles for variables. An initial variable takes the form of a green oval, while a terminal variable is depicted as a red octagon. With exactly one connection coming in and out, a generic variable appears as a plain rectangle. A blue parallelogram (orange diamond) designates a point of convergence (divergence) for pathways. A purple hexagon denotes both convergence and divergence—a nodal variable. A co-constitutive variable—one with mutually contingent variables—appears in bifurcated form. Line segments are depicted in different ways, depending on what they are supposed to represent, and will be explained as relevant within respective figures.

3.4   Power Transition Theory with a *Systemist* Graphic Turn

Power transition theory, introduced more than 60 years ago by Organski (1958), continues to provide the foundation for one of the most successful programs of research in the field (Tammen et al. 2017a, b). The theory focuses on the dynamics of power between the first- and second-place states in the system. The basic intuition of power transition is that tension rises as the challenger gains ground on the leader. Danger of war is at a maximum in a zone where the difference between the two top

---

[10] Beyond the scope of the present exposition is specification of functional form for proposed connections; this is required by *systemism* to completely articulate a theory (Bunge 1996). While incremental change is assumed as the default position, it is important to recognize that functional relationships can be non-linear as well.

Table 3.1 Systemist notation

	Systemist Notation	
Initial variable		The starting point of a series of relationships
Generic variable		A step in the process being depicted
Divergent variable		Multiple pathways are created from a single linkage
Convergent variable		A single pathway is created from multiple linkages
Nodal variable		Multiple pathways are created from multiple linkages
Co-constitutive variable		Two variables that are mutually contingent upon each other
Terminal variable		The end point of a series of relationships
Connection stated in study		A linkage explicitly made by the author
Connection crossing over		Two separate linkages that do not interact
Connection inferred from study		A linkage inferred by the reader but is not made explicit by the author
Interaction effect		Two variables that depend upon the effect of each other

states is within a 20% margin. This creates the potential for ambiguity about who is at the apex and therefore should be expected to enforce the existing order. Thus, the theory is about international hierarchy rather than anarchy.

While the original power transition theory focuses on the power and conflict dynamics between a dominant state and a rising challenger in the international system, more recent research has expanded application of power transition dynamics to regional conflicts, civil wars, deterrence and proliferation, democratic peace, national identity and socialization, and the international monetary system (Tammen et al. 2017b). For the present purposes, the power transition theorizing of Lemke (2002) is ideal for application. Rather than looking at the global system, Lemke (2002) unpacks regional hierarchies.

Figure 3.3 displays the *systemist* visualization of Lemke (2002) on regions of war and peace.[11] The network of cause and effect in the diagram contains 12 variables. One is initial, three are divergent, one is convergent, two are nodal, and two are terminal. The figure is sufficiently complex to convey the dynamics of power transition theory as a vision of war. At the same time, it is straightforward enough to avoid charges of "hyperactive optical clutter," identified by Tufte (2006) as a challenge to all forms of visual communication.

Figure 3.3 depicts a region in the international system. Interactions with the potential to escalate into war at the level of the international system are likely to begin in proximity to the challenger rather than the leader. Many pathways appear in Fig. 3.3, as a result of six variables that are either divergent, convergent, or nodal. Thus, it is beyond the scope of the present investigation to explore all of the routes that can lead from power transition theory in operation at the international level to either preservation of the status quo or war. Instead, a few basic properties are highlighted along the way.

Power transition theory produces hierarchy in the international order, with a single state recognized as the regional leader. The region, therefore, experiences preponderance of a dominant power as the result. Gradual buildup in potential capabilities in the rising power can lead to significant changes in power dynamics between the dominant state and the rising state. In this scenario, escalation is possible and this part of the story begins within the challenger. Domestic politics in the challenger can lead in multiple directions. One possibility is that the dominant power will remain preponderant in the region if the rising power remains satisfied with the status quo and chooses not to challenge the regional order.

If the rising power, with favorable demographic and economic transitions, rapidly reaches power parity with the dominant power, the other possibility is a vicious cycle in which the rising power will become increasingly dissatisfied with the status quo and thus seek to challenge and eventually replace the dominant power as the preponderant state in the regional and even the international order. In this scenario, escalation of conflict is a likely result of rising demands in the challenger's domestic

---

[11] This figure has benefited from a consultation with Doug Lemke.

3 ALL ROADS LEAD TO BEIJING: *SYSTEMISM*, POWER ... 45

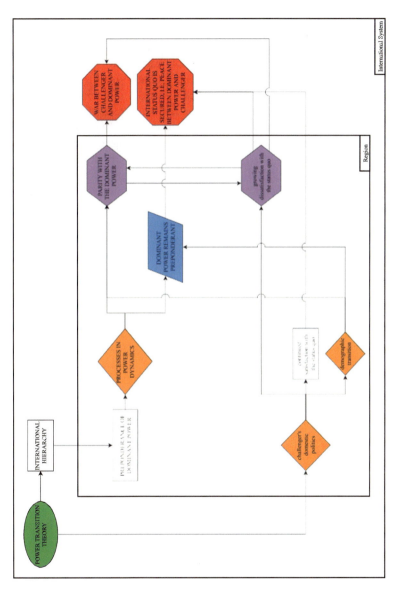

Fig. 3.3 Regions of war and peace (Lemke 2002). Diagrammed by: Douglas William Lemke, Sarah Gansen, and Patrick James

politics and growing insecurity in the dominant state with its relative decline. When the challenger's desire for change is poorly managed by the current dominant state, war can be expected.

Contingency is significant within the power transition's outlook. Tammen et al. (2017b, p. 19) observe that war "is not predetermined by structures, but structures set the necessary conditions for war." If the challenger adopts a hostile foreign policy toward the dominant power and the dominant power adopts a similar hostile foreign policy toward the challenger, severe conflict is the likely outcome. "As the defender begins to question the rise of the challenger," according to Tammen et al. (2017b, p. 19), "small increases toward a hostile policy stance produce sharp increases in dyadic conflict. Hence, the structural stage is set for prompting an early conflict initiation and war escalation." With evenly matched capabilities, it becomes relatively easy for each side to imagine that war will produce victory and hence the increased chance of conflict.

Power transition theory also acknowledges that the changes in power dynamics do not always lead to war, especially when the rising power is satisfied with the status quo (Tammen et al. 2017a, b). Power transition studies have shown that changing power dynamics and various situations of power parity can lead to contradictory outcomes ranging from war to integration, depending on the levels of satisfaction (Kugler et al. 2015) and specific indicators of power transition. When the dominant power and the rising power are in power parity, the latter does not necessarily challenge the former if both are satisfied with the status quo. In this sense, the dominant power has a key responsibility to create conditions for peace.[12]

Power transition theory is a dynamic theory of power precisely because its ability to account for the variety of outcomes of conflict and cooperation in a regional system (Tammen et al. 2017a, b). This highly successful theory therefore emerges as an ideal choice for application to the BRI in the quest to explain its characteristics and development against the backdrop of the rise of the PRC and mounting debate about an armed conflict or a new "Cold War" between the PRC and the US, most likely in East Asia (Navarro and Autry 2011; Friedberg 2012; Jacques 2012; Roy 2013; Pillsbury 2016; Allison 2017; Mahbubani 2020). While not

---

[12] Still, critics have pointed out that power transition theorists have failed to pinpoint the structural origins of these different levels of satisfaction toward behavior because of the different assumptions about domestic coalitions (Schenoni 2018, pp. 471–472).

acknowledged openly, these expositions, for the most part, tend to rely on the logic of the power transition.

3.5 The BRI Through Power Transition Theory and *Systemist* IR

3.5.1 *Overview*

This section applies power transition theory, now in the SIR-based graphic form of Fig. 3.4, to the Belt and Road Initiative. Figure 3.4 depicts a network of 26 variables. There are 17 in East Asia, with 7 macro and 10 micro, and 9 variables in the international system. The distribution by type is as follows: one initial, seven generic, six divergent, five convergent, five nodal, and two terminal variables. (One variable also is co-constitutive.) It is beyond the scope of the present article to unpack the entire series of connections in the diagram, one at a time, so instead there will be an overview of cause and effect in four sub-figures.[13] Four sub-sections therefore follow, in each instance linking features of Fig. 3.4 with aspects of the BRI to illustrate how the initiative may change the power dynamics between the US and China. It is worth noting that the *systemist* approach demonstrates BRI as a critical nodal variable linking the micro and macro variables within the system and the environment.

3.5.2 *The Logic of BRI and Power Dynamics between the US and China*

Figure 3.4a shows that the US, although outside of East Asia, has established and maintained its economic and military preponderance in that region since the end of World War II. The US military dominance is manifested in the hub-and-spokes security alliance system with Japan, South Korea, the Philippines, and the Republic of China on Taiwan (terminated in 1979). Its economic dominance is solidified with the US dollar as the dominant international currency in the open trading system. This status quo in the economic realm has been challenged by Japan temporarily in the 1980s and the PRC in a sustained way since the 2000s.

Since its reform and opening to the world in the late 1970s, as illustrated in Fig. 3.4b, China has achieved unprecedented economic growth

---

[13] Appendix A contains the sub-figures for future reference.

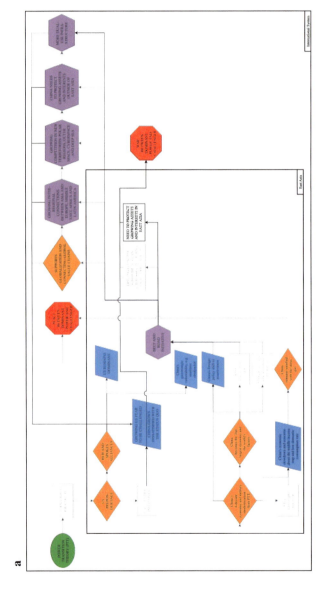

Fig. 3.4 Systemism, power transition, and BRI (Zhang and James 2022). a–d Elaboration based on further evidence. Diagrammed by: Enyu Zhang, Sarah Gansen, and Patrick James

3 ALL ROADS LEAD TO BEIJING: *SYSTEMISM*, POWER … 49

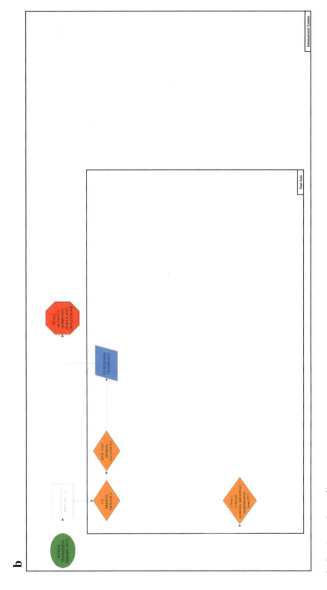

Fig. 3.4 (continued)

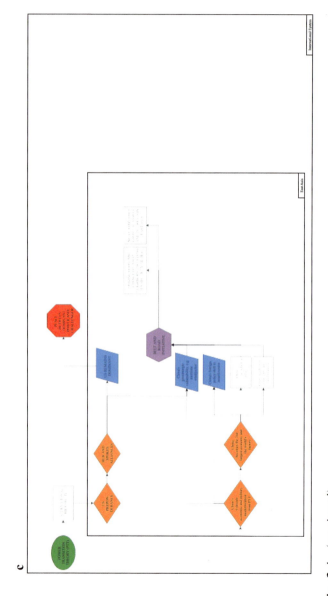

Fig. 3.4 (continued)

3 ALL ROADS LEAD TO BEIJING: *SYSTEMISM*, POWER ... 51

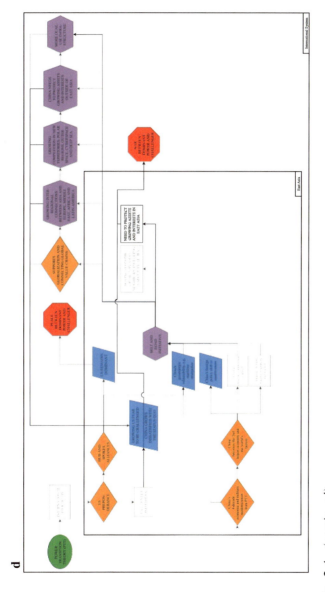

Fig. 3.4 (continued)

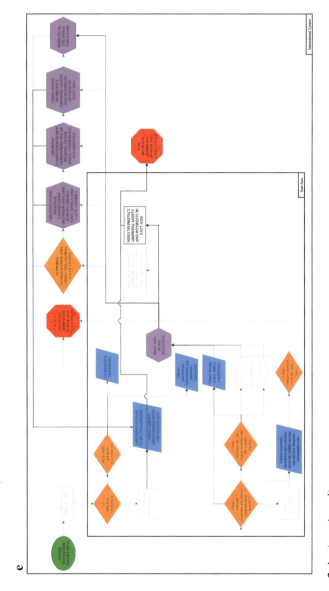

Fig. 3.4 (continued)

for and lifted over 500 million people out of abject poverty, a root cause for social unrest and extremism (Rolland 2017).[14] A combination of market-oriented reforms, and since 2006, state-driven industrial policies, well-trained, low-cost labor forces, and expanding modern infrastructure, and sustained export-driven economic growth have made China the world's factory, the hub of the global supply chain, and more recently, the second largest technological powerhouse. With such a foundation, China has become the world's largest exporter. In 2018, China exported US$2.5 trillion worth of goods worldwide, US$800 billion more than the US, the second largest exporter of goods. In this process, China has amassed the world's largest foreign exchange reserves, at US$3.15 trillion in 2020. Chinese companies also have accumulated unrivaled industrial capacity and experience in infrastructure building. These engineering skills, financial, and capacity surpluses put China in a favorable position to help fill the infrastructure gap across Asia and beyond through the BRI partnerships and projects. The Asian Development Bank (2017) estimated that Asia would need US$26 trillion of infrastructure between 2016 and 2030, including climate-related infrastructure.

As a globally oriented infrastructure development strategy, BRI aims to "promote the economic prosperity of the countries along the Belt and Road, promote regional economic cooperation, strengthen exchanges and mutual learning between civilizations, and promote world peace and development" ("Visions and Actions on Jointly Building Silk Road Economic Belt and 21st Century Maritime Silk Road," 2015) by matching up the developing world's pent-up demand for physical infrastructure and China's knowhow, surplus capacity and financial resources.[15]

In this sense, given the strong political mobilization and economic backing from the Chinese government and business circles, the BRI accelerated the power dynamics between the US and China, propelling the latter to reach economic power parity with the former. According to the World Bank International Comparison Program database, in 1950, the US had 27.3% of the world's GDP in purchasing power parity terms while

---

[14] China has lifted as many as 800 million of its citizens out of poverty, according to the World Bank estimate (Sanchez 2017).

[15] McKinsey Global Institute estimated that the world will have a total spending gap on infrastructure of US$5.5 trillion between 2017 and 2035, with 63% of the infrastructure needs from the emerging economies. https://www.mckinsey.com/business-functions/ope rations/our-insights/bridging-infrastructure-gaps-has-the-world-made-progress.

China had only 4.5%. When the Cold War ended in 1990, the US had 20.6% of the world's GDP and China's share stood at a mere 3.86%. In 2018, by contrast, the US's share dropped to 15% of the world's GDP, while China's share increased to 18.6% (Mahbubani 2020, p. 10). In 2019, China's nominal GDP was 66% of that of the US, up from 6.4% in 1978 when China began its economic reform and modernization.[16] In addition, China has become a top trading partner to over 120 countries and regions, including the European Union. It is the only major economy that managed to grow its economy during the COVID pandemic. In a best-case scenario, China has been projected to surpass the US in GDP size as early as 2031 (e.g., Tatom 2007).[17]

In 2016, the International Monetary Fund (IMF) granted the *renminbi* Special Drawing Rights (SDR) status and thus elevated it to the status of an international reserve currency. In 2017, the World Bank estimated that China made the world's largest share of investment at 26% while the US total investment share was only 14%.[18] The bulk of these monetary transactions and investment involved BRI projects.

In the meantime, China's meteoric rise remains uneven. China's western inland regions, especially rural areas, continue to lag economically while infrastructure building and industrial capacity in the eastern coastal regions have increasingly become saturated. In recognition of these challenges, the Chinese government started actively diverting resources and investment to boost economic development in the western inland regions as early as 1998 in the Great Western Development Program. To address these ongoing economic and strategic challenges, the BRI has served as a coherent development strategy to shift policy focus and resources to infrastructure building in inland regions by connecting the less-developed regions with their Eurasian neighbors overland and Southeast Asian neighbors via maritime routes.

---

[16] Measured in purchasing power parity (PPP) terms, according to the World Bank's International Comparison Program, China's GDP in 2017 (US$19.617 trillion) surpassed that of the US (US$19.519 trillion). However, when measured at actual exchange rates, China's nominal GDP is about 62.22% of the US's.

[17] However, China's standard of living measured by GDP per capita will continue to play 'catchup' with that of the US even after their GDPs reach parity. This is mainly due to China's four times larger population size and lower productivity (Tatom 2007).

[18] https://blogs.worldbank.org/opendata/new-results-international-comparison-pro gram-shed-light-size-global-economy.

Within the US–China power dynamics, the BRI serves as an assertive strategic response to the US's "Pivot" or rebalance to Asia proposed by the Obama administration, especially through the Trans-Pacific Partnership (TPP) and subsequent confrontation politics from the Trump administration. In 2011 and 2012, Wang Jisi (王缉思), one of China's most influential international relations scholars, articulated the "March West" strategy in his articles published in *Foreign Affairs* and *Global Times*. Wang Jisi called for China to pursue a grand strategy of moving westward from Central Asia to the Middle East, from which the US has started to retreat. This also is a strategic choice to avoid direct confrontation with the US (Liang 2019).

Beijing perceives the US's military dominance along the Western Pacific as a "maritime straitjacket" (Yoshihara 2014, p. 47) and considers the US-led security alliances in East Asia as strategic encirclement and a menace to China's national rejuvenation. In this sense, energy-related infrastructure and cooperation with Russia, along with China's Central, Southeastern, and Western Asian neighbors, are seen as strategic diversification of energy sources and circumvention of transportation routes away from the so-called Malacca Dilemma, the security concerns about any potential hostile naval blockade of the Malacca, Sunda, and Lombok Straits that would choke off the flow of maritime trade and energy supply upon which China relies.

In Chinese official discourse, the BRI effectively merges the main themes of peace and development in its foreign policy into a coherent strategic vision. Chinese leaders since Deng Xiaoping all strongly believe that cultivating friendly and cooperative relations with its neighbors and surrounding regions is crucial to create a peaceful environment for China's modernization and prosperity. Many of the initial projects that have been incorporated in the BRI had been conceptualized or even implemented in the Great Western Development Program and the Going Out Strategy from 1999 to 2012 under Jiang Zemin's and Hu Jintao's leaderships and some had been implemented years before BRI's official launch (Yuliantoro and Dinarto 2019; Ye 2020). Overall, although it is widely considered as Xi Jinping's signature proactive foreign policy, the strategic goals and many of the specific projects within the BRI umbrella had been consistent with Chinese strategic thinking about war avoidance and its neighborly foreign policy approach in the last four decades. On both conceptual and policy levels, the BRI is a continuation of Chinese foreign policy that prioritizes periphery diplomacy (周边外交) to tap into

China's comparative advantages to meet the vast infrastructure demand in East, Southeast, and Central Asia.

Approaching the centenaries of the founding of the CCP in 2021 and the PRC in 2049, Chinese leaders envision the BRI to play a key role in embodying the "Chinese Dream" of national rejuvenation and building a more equitable global order toward the ideal of the "Community for Common Destiny" (Lams 2018). These are all essential parts of Xi Jinping's political legitimacy and eventual legacy. Symbolically, the active promotion of BRI directly followed Xi's call for "striving for achievement" (奋发有为) to achieve China's "great rejuvenation" (伟大复兴), the "Chinese Dream" (中国梦) and a "Community of a Shared Future for Mankind" (人类命运共同体). This was a major shift in Chinese foreign policy from Deng Xiaoping's axiom of "keeping a low profile and biding our time" (韬光养晦) (Zhu 2019).

While acknowledging the risks and obstacles ahead, China-based scholars highlight the connections between the Ancient Silk Road and the BRI, as the modern Silk Road, which represents China's extraordinary civilizational revival. They see this embodiment of Chinese civilizational values to be an alternative to Western Imperialism via globalization (e.g., Wang Yiwei 2015; Zheng 2015). For instance, Wang Yiwei (2015, p. 29) argues,

> The [ancient] Silk Road was a road of friendship and prosperity, a road of exchange and mutual respect' that offers a superior model of globalization. BRI thus will help to spread around the globe the benefits of traditional Chinese civilization and the China model of development. China's 'superior' culture, therefore, is seen as a resource that will reshape the rules and norms of international institutions: the success of BRI will show how China no longer 'submits' to globalization but is proactive in 'creating new standards of globalization.'

From the PRC's point of view, greatness can be achieved without hegemonic war, but instead through the awe-inspiring effects from an impressive role model for politico-economic progress.

However, as China's economic and strategic interests and influence expand rapidly overseas under the BRI, it is increasingly imperative for the Chinese People's Liberation Army (PLA) to develop capabilities and expand its own footprint to protect Chinese nationals, assets, and other financial interests.[19] Most notably, the PLA launched its very first overseas naval base in Djibouti in 2017, alongside the American and Japanese bases. In addition, the China-initiated Shanghai Cooperation Organization (SCO) is poised to play a more prominent role in fighting against terrorism, separatism, and extremism in Central Asia, a crucial region in the BRI.

Meanwhile, such power dynamics in the security realm are at a preliminary stage. While since 2010 China has flexed its military muscles in the Taiwan Strait, East and South China Seas, the US remains the preponderant power in East Asia. The US military budget is about three times larger than the PRC's. The US still has about 600 military bases overseas, maintaining its air and naval dominance around the world since World War II.

3.5.3 The BRI and China's Complex Engagement with the Status Quo

Power transition theory asserts that the "level of cooperation among nations does vary in direct proportion to the proximity to the status quo among competing parties" (Tammen et al. 2017b, p. 6). One possibility, as portrayed in Fig. 4b, is that the US will remain preponderant both economically and militarily, leading to an accommodation with China and preservation of the status quo. On the global level, Beijing has boosted its active participation and sought to expand its influence through the existing international institutions created by the US post-World War II, including the United Nations, World Bank, International Monetary Fund (IMF), World Trade Organization (WTO), etc.[20] China is now the largest contributor of UN peacekeepers among the five permanent members of the Security Council and the second largest financial contributor of the UN behind the US. With Beijing's proactive diplomacy, these international institutions have endorsed the BRI and started collaboration on BRI-associated projects. In April 2019, for instance, UN Secretary-General António Guterres remarked at the opening ceremony of the

---

[19] For instance, over one million Chinese citizens were working overseas in 2014, and that number more than doubled in just 2 years.

[20] As a case in point, the China-IMF Capacity Development Center was established in 2018 to provide training and assistance to make BRI projects more transparent, more sustainable, and with better risk assessment.

second BRI global forum, "the UN is poised to support the alignment of the Belt and Road Initiative with the Sustainable Development Goals, to share knowledge, and to make the most of the opportunities of this large-scale initiative for maximum sustainable development dividends."[21]

On the other hand, as the BRI continues to expand its footprint, China may be increasingly dissatisfied with the status quo and thus seek to challenge, or even replace, the US as the preponderant state in East Asia and even the international order. To accomplish the economic and strategic goals of BRI, Beijing founded the Asian Infrastructure Investment Bank (AIIB)[22] and the Silk Road Fund as the financial arms to fund various BRI projects, along with the Shanghai-based New Development Bank (formerly known as the BRICS Bank) and other major Chinese policy banks (e.g., the Export–Import Bank of China and the Agricultural Development Bank of China).[23]

In addition, to further internationalize the *renminbi*, China has signed 36 bilateral currency-swap agreements between 2008 and 2016, including 20 BRI partners such as Pakistan, Iran, Egypt, and more. China also signed seven bilateral *renminbi* clearing agreements with its BRI partners. These agreements have boosted *renminbi*-denominated trade and investment deals, lowering exchange rate risks for the parties involved. According to the global payments platform SWIFT, the *renminbi* accounted for 2.79% of the world's total in value of payments in 2015, thus surpassing the *yen* as the fourth most-used global currency in cross-border financial transactions.[24]

---

[21] "United Nations Poised to Support Alignment of China's Belt and Road Initiative with Sustainable Development Goals, Secretary-General Says at Opening Ceremony." 26 April 2019. https://www.un.org/press/en/2019/sgsm19556.doc.htm.

[22] China initiated the AIIB in 2013—the idea had been floated in the Bo'ao Forum (博鳌论坛) in 2009—and officially became established on 25 December 2015 with 52 founding members and starting capital of $100 billion. As of May 2020, the AIIB includes 103 members, although prominent notable non-members include Japan, Mexico, and the US.

[23] It is important to note that China has sought to enhance its status and influence in the international economic institutions founded and backed by the US, such as the International Monetary Fund (IMF) and the World Bank through vigorous push for institutional reforms.

[24] By contrast, the US dollar remains the dominant global currency in 38% of all cross-border financial transactions.

Some BRI partnerships seem to indicate Beijing's dissatisfaction with the status quo. As noted earlier, the grand strategy of BRI partially is intended to address China's geostrategic vulnerability and partially is designed to build a coalition of like-minded allies to balance against or challenge the dominant power. Consider two cases in point: Pakistan and Iran.

Beijing's "all-weather" ally Pakistan has been the center of the Chinese–Pakistani Economic Corridor (CPEC), the flagship of the BRI. The PRC has a projected investment of US$62 billion in development projects for Pakistan, focusing on energy and communication infrastructures and industrial zones. Opening the CPEC not only can alleviate China's "Malacca Dilemma" and help pacify its peripheral regions but also can speed up Pakistan's pursuit for energy independence and economic development.[25]

In July 2020, China and Iran, as part of BRI's China–Central Asia–West Asia Corridor, announced a comprehensive strategic partnership agreement that includes trade and investment worth US$400 billion in the next 25 years. By far, this is the largest deal with a single BRI partner, dwarfing the previous 'poster-child,' the China–Pakistan Economic Corridor (CPEC). About US$280 billion is marked for developing Iranian petrochemical, gas, and oil sections and US$120 billion is targeted for upgrading Iran's roads and railways connecting Tehran with Urumqi through Kazakhstan, Kyrgyzstan, Uzbekistan, and Turkmenistan. The plan is to connect China with the Tehran-Urumqi road to Europe through Turkey. Bilateral military cooperation also will be enhanced with regular military exercises, intelligence sharing, training, weapons development, and, potentially, China's access to Iranian dual-use air bases.

All in all, as illustrated in Fig. 3.4c, the BRI seeks to increase cross-regional connectivity in a globalized world with "win–win" solutions with its partners and cooperates with the US-backed international institutions by aligning with some of the key priorities of the UN, World Bank, IMF, etc. It hints at a desire to challenge US economic dominance, but not all-out competition or confrontation, as yet, with the US-led coalition that has been in control of the international system since the end of World War II. In 2017, Chinese defense officials have publicly denied any connection

---

[25] This, however, led to India's opposition, mainly due to the CPEC's passing through the disputed Kashmir region.

between the BRI and China's military-security intentions. Some analysts point out that the BRI infrastructure facilities built by Chinese companies around the world have the potential for dual use for commercial and military purposes.

3.5.4 US Perceptions and Responses to BRI

The US generally views China's BRI with caution, ambivalence, skepticism, and increasingly open criticism and hostility. Most notably, the US refused to join China-initiated AIIB, the key financial arm of BRI. The US also pressured its allies not to join the AIIB on the grounds that Chinese lending practices lack transparency and thus are not in line with international standards. However, American pressure and criticism have failed to stop its allies Australia, France, Germany, Israel, Italy, New Zealand, Saudi Arabia, the UAE, South Korea, and the UK from joining AIIB as founding members in December 2015.

Such responses from the US in part originate from the growing consensus of a zero-sum competition with China among American political elites, including key officials in the White House and US Congress. For instance, in 2018, FBI Director Christopher Wray testified before Congress, "One of the things we're trying to do is view the China threat as not just a whole-of-government threat, but as a whole-of-society threat." On 23 July 2020, in his speech at the Nixon Library on the most significant turn of the US policy toward China, Secretary of State Michael Pompeo remarked, "President Reagan said that he dealt with the Soviet Union on the basis of 'trust but verify.' When it comes to the CCP, I say we must distrust and verify." Strategic documents of the US government and military frequently label the PRC as the strategic competitor.

Growing tension and hostility in US–China relations have cast a long shadow over the American perception of BRI. For instance, China's Digital Silk Road is viewed as an integral part of the ongoing contest for technological supremacy. In February 2019, in a panel discussion on China's Digital Silk Road hosted by the Center for Strategic and International Studies (CSIS), William C. Mayville, former deputy commander of US Cyber Command, said China was "unfit to own large chunks of the world's communication infrastructure, given its extensive surveillance, given its censorship, given the fact that it has for years been stealing property—intellectual property… I start with an inherent distrust of this actor. And I question the motivations behind all of its modernization…" Such rhetoric is consistent with the US global efforts to lobby and pressure other countries not to adopt China's Huawei as the supplier of the most advanced 5G telecommunication networks." Since the US trade war with China began in July 2018, the US has explicitly restricted export of sensitive technologies to China's AI and other high-tech champions with the Department of Commerce's Entity List.[26]

As China is poised to reach economic parity with the US along several key dimensions, Chinese vision of overseas development assistance has increasingly come to clash with the American one. The US official development assistance overseas and US-based nongovernmental organizations tend to shy away from physical infrastructure projects due to their relative higher costs and risks, especially in less developed and less stable regions with poor governance. Instead, the US tends to focus on official assistance with public health, civil society building, disaster relief, and democratization.[27]

The US seems threatened by China's efforts to internationalize the *renminbi* and its state-led, large-scale, fast-pace, and opaque financing through BRI. From the standpoint of Washington, DC, all of that may undermine the US-led global economic order and the dominance of the US dollar in the global economy. The US also openly criticized China's BRI as "debt-trap diplomacy" with massive infra-structure loans whose terms are "opaque at best, and the benefits invariably flow overwhelming to Beijing" (Pence 2018). According to the World Bank, between 2014 and 2018, 72 low-income countries owed Chinese creditors $104 billion out of a total outstanding debt of $514 billion (Huang and Brautigam 2020). China is the largest bilateral official creditor for 51 of the 72 low-income countries and for 32 of the 40 African countries (Huang and Brautigam 2020). Whether and how these countries are able to pay back the debts are the main concerns in the West.[28] As indicated earlier, a

---

[26] https://www.federalregister.gov/documents/2019/10/09/2019-22210/addition-of-certain-entities-to-the-entity-list.

[27] The US's negative responses to BRI are associated with its neglect of physical infrastructure in economic development, both domestically and internationally. The American Society of Civil Engineers rated a D-plus for the US infrastructure in 2017, citing lack of leadership, vision, and funding as the main causes of such failure. As the latest case in point, the ailing port infrastructure in Long Beach and Los Angeles has exacerbated the pandemic-induced bottleneck in the US supply chain.

[28] Assessing China's financing for the variety of projects across a wide range of countries is beyond the scope of this study. What seems clear so far is that the AIIB lending practice

priority for the US-backed international institutions, such as the IMF, is to offer technical assistance to enhance debt sustainability.[29]

A direct response to BRI from the US is the bipartisan Better Utilization of Investment Leading to Development (BUILD Act of 2018) to create a new US development agency International Development Finance Corporation (USIDFC) with funding of US\$60 billion. The USIDFC is charged with partnering with private sectors in providing development assistance to small and medium-sized enterprises in low-income and lower-to-middle-income countries. This is proposed as a market-based alternative to China's big-ticket, "no-string-attached," state-to-state development financing. In June 2021, the US Congress passed the Innovation and Competition Act of 2021 (\$200 million), one of the US's largest industrial bills, to invest in scientific research and technological innovation and manufacturing to compete with China. The Biden Administration also rallied the Group of Seven and other democracies to launch the Build Back Better World (B3W) Partnership as a "values-driven, high-standard, and transparent" alternative China's BRI to support infrastructure needs in low- and middle-income countries.

These responses largely reflect the dominate power's growing fear to be challenged and even replaced by the rising power. However, given the divisive politics and lack of financial resources within the US, the responses as a whole are not necessarily a unified, long-term strategy in response to China's BRI. Former Secretary Defense Robert Gates commented, "[T]he biggest concern I have is that even though we now have a bipartisan understanding that China is a challenge for us, we have no strategy. Where do we want this relationship to be in five or 10 or 15 years and, more broadly, how do we counter the Chinese in all the different areas where competition is going to take place?" (McCullough 2020) Most US allies increasingly rely on China to boost their own economies, so the extent to which they are willing to form a united front against China will be limited.

Alongside these developments, as portrayed in Fig. 3.4d, it is also important to note that China's economic and demographic challenges may lead to Beijing's continued accommodation with the status quo.

---

is widely acknowledged to have met international standards, although it has yet to become a major player in BRI financing.

[29] In June 2020, due to the COVID-19 pandemic, China joined the G-20 moratorium to provide debt relief to the developing world.

One of the greatest economic challenge is that China's growth has slowed down from the annual average rate of 11% from 2001 to 2007 to around 7% since 2008 (Dollar 2015). Given its large population size, China is still an "upper middle-income" country, according to the World Bank classification. This puts growing pressure on the country's investment-intensive, export-driven development model. To escape from the "middle-income trap" that many middle-income economies have failed to avoid, China must find alternative means to expand the global market for its excess capital and industrial capacity through BRI and it must boost household consumption and enhance its total factor productivity (TFP) by focusing on technological advancement.

On top of its projected economic slowdown (even though Chinese economy still grows faster than most major economies), China faces the long-term demographic challenge of a gender-imbalanced, rapidly aging, and shrinking working-age population. The one-child policy implemented between the late 1970s and mid-2010s has succeeded in slowing down population growth and thus contributing to China's economic takeoff. However, the unintended consequences of such policy include the sharp decline of both birth rate and fertility rate (1.6 children per woman)[30] to an unsustainable level. According to China's National Bureau of Statistics, the birth rate in China has kept falling since 2017—2 years after the repeal of the one-child policy—to 14.6 million births in 2019. With a declining workforce in the next few decades, China may grow old before it overcomes the "middle-income trap." Challenges like these do not bode well for China's long-term prospects for seeking power parity with the US.

After seeing *systemism* in action, it is reasonable to reflect in at least an initial way upon the value added from its implementation. At least five favorable observations about *systemism* are in order at this point. First, its graphic presentation facilitates assessment of completeness and logical consistency of arguments about power transition and BRI. Second, the *systemist* visualization can be used to zero in on areas of disagreement, which in turn would enable more constructive debate about the BRI. Third, the diagram connecting power transition with the BRI could have pedagogical value—to cite just two examples, the graphic could be presented alongside a lecture in a classroom or used by doctoral students

---

[30] The "replacement level" fertility rate to maintain population levels is 2.1 children per woman. According to Professor Yi Fuxian at the University of Wisconsin-Madison, China's average fertility rate between 2010 and 2018 was as low as 1.18.

studying for their qualifying examinations. Fourth, the sub-figures present the arguments in stages and thereby strengthen all of the preceding points related to comprehension and retention. Fifth, and finally, the graphic fits onto one page and uses non-technical language, which increases its accessibility to policymakers across the board.

3.6   Conclusion

This study contributes to the growing literature on the BRI, as China's signature foreign policy agenda for its national rejuvenation in the twenty-first century, by examining and visualizing the causal links of BRI in the context of power transition between the US—the dominate power—and China—the rising power. This specifically takes the form of a *systemist* graphic that conveys power transition theory in the context of East Asia.

While not a cause of power transition between the US and China, BRI has catalyzed China's efforts to expand its economic connectivity and footprint in a global contest for economic primacy. Our analysis has shown that this ambitious foreign policy and economic development initiative seems to have propelled China, as the rising power, to close the economic gaps with the US, as the dominant power, in East Asia and beyond. In the present political climate in both countries, China and the US increasingly see each other in zero-sum terms. China's (potential) gains through the Belt and Road Initiative often are perceived as losses for the US or as signs of the US's further decline from dominant status. Equally important, China seems to have a grand strategy to advance its interests through BRI, while the US seems to scramble for long-term, strategic responses. In the context of the US's reduced level of global leadership under the Trump administration, China's proactive advancement through the BRI, especially if Beijing can reasonably adapt to address the concerns of its BRI partners, may offer a rare opportunity for China to build an alliance to unseat the US's dominance.

While our analysis focuses on the structural dynamics driving the BRI, we acknowledge that the agency of political leadership on both sides may be able to change the structural dynamics between the US as the dominant power and China as the challenger. The insights of power transition theory show that a key factor in avoiding an armed conflict between the US and China is trust and satisfaction. Satisfaction leads to trust, which in turn leads to cooperation. Figure 3.4 contains a wide range of connections that could be evaluated on either an individual or collective basis through techniques such as statistical data analysis and process tracing.

The security and military implications for the expansive scope of BRI's economic vision point to the need for China to expand the PLA's responsibilities and footprint beyond its territory. It may generate power transition dynamics in the security realm and raise the risks for war. Short of such development, BRI is poised to be a super-charger in the economic power transition between China and the US.

REFERENCES

Allison, G.T. 2017. *Destined for War: Can America and China Escape Thucydides's Trap?* Boston: Houghton Mifflin Harcourt.

Asian Development Bank. 2017. Meeting Asia's Infrastructure Needs. https://www.adb.org/sites/default/files/publication/227496/special-report-infrastructure.pdf.

Ba, A. D. 2019. China's 'Belt and Road' in Southeast Asia: Constructing the Strategic Narrative in Singapore. *Asian Perspective* 43: 249–272.

Bunge, M. 1996. *Finding Philosophy in Social Science.* New Haven: Yale University Press.

Cai, K.G. 2018. The One Belt One Road and the Asian Infrastructure Investment Bank: Beijing's New Strategy of Geoeconomics and Geopolitics. *Journal of Contemporary China* 27 (114): 831–847.

Callahan, W.A. 2016. China's 'Asia Dream': The Belt Road Initiative and the New Regional Order. *Asian Journal of Comparative Politics* 1 (3): 226–243.

Djankov, S. et al. 2016. China's Belt and Road Initiative: Motives, Scope and Challenges. Peterson Institute for International Economics. https://piie.com/publications/piie-briefings/chinas-belt-and-road-initiative-motives-scope-and-challenges.

Dollar, D. 2015. The AIIB and the 'One Belt, One Road.' https://www.brookings.edu/opinions/the-aiib-and-the-one-belt-one-road/.

Farwa, U. 2018. Belt and Road Initiative and China's Strategic Culture. *Strategic Studies* 38 (3): 40–56.

Frankopan, P. 2018. *The New Silk Roads: The New Asia and the Remaking of the World Order.* New York: Vintage Books.

Friedberg, A. 2012. *A Contest for Supremacy: China, America, and the Struggle for Mastery in Asia.* New York: W. W. Norton.

Han, Z., and T.V. Paul. 2020. China's Rise and Balance of Power Politics. *The Chinese Journal of International Politics* 13 (1): 1–26.

He, K. 2015. Contested Regional Orders and Institutional Balancing in the Asia Pacific. *International Politics* 52 (2): 208–222.

He, K. 2018. Role conceptions, Order Transition and Institutional Balancing in the Asia-Pacific: A New Theoretical Framework. *Australian Journal of International Affairs* 72 (2): 92–109.

He, B.G. 2019. The Domestic Politics of the Belt and Road Initiative and its Implications. *Journal of Contemporary China* 28: 180–195.

Huang, Y., and Brautigam, D. 2020. Putting a Dollar Amount on China's Loans to the Developing World. *The Diplomat 24 June.* https://thediplomat.com/2020/06/putting-a-dollar-amount-on-chinas-loans-to-the-developing-world/.

Ikenberry, G.J. 2011a. The Future of the Liberal World Order: Internationalism after America. *Foreign Affairs* 90 (3): 56–68.

Ikenberry, G.J. 2011b. *Liberal Leviathan: The Origins, Crisis, and Transformation of the American World Order.* Princeton: Princeton University Press.

Jacques, M. 2012. *When China Rules the World: The Rise of the Middle Kingdom and the End of the Western World.* London: Penguin Books.

James, P. 2019. Systemist International Relations. *International Studies Quarterly* 63: 781–804.

James, P. 2022. *Realism and International Relations: A Graphic Turn Toward Scientific Progress.* Oxford: Oxford University Press.

Kirshner, J. 2010. The Tragedy of Offensive Realism: Classical Realism and the Rise of China. *European Journal of International Relations* 18 (1): 53–75.

Knoerich, J., and F. Urdinez. 2019. Contesting Contested Multilateralism: Why the West Joined the Rest in Founding the Asian Infrastructure Investment Bank. *The Chinese Journal of International Politics* 12 (3): 333–370.

Kugler, J., A. Fisunoglu, and B. Yesilada. 2015. Consequences of Reversing the European Union Integration. *Foreign Policy Analysis* 11 (1): 17–39.

Lams, L. 2018. Examining Strategic Narratives in Chinese Official Discourse under Xi Jinping. *Journal of Chinese Political Science* 23: 387–411.

Lemke, D.W. 2002. *Regions of War and Peace.* Cambridge: Cambridge University Press.

Liang, W. 2019. China and the "Belt and Road Initiative" (BRI): Contested multilateralism and innovative institution-building. In *Handbook of the International Political Economy of China*, ed. K. Zeng, 361–376. Cheltenham: Edward Elgar.

Mahbubani, K. 2020. *Has China Won? The Chinese Challenge to American Primacy.* New York: Public Affairs.

McCullough. 2020. Tracking China. *W&M Magazine.* https://magazine.wm.edu/issue/2020-spring/tracking-china.php?ref=aiddata.

Mearsheimer, J.J. 2010. The Gathering Storm: China's Challenge to US Power in Asia. *The Chinese Journal of International Politics* 3: 381–396.

N.A. 2019. "Six Years of 'Belt and Road'!" Belt and Road Portal. https://eng.yidaiyilu.gov.cn/qwyw/rdxw/105854.htm. Accessed 11 August 2020.

Navarro, P., and G. Autry. 2011. *Death by China: Confronting the Dragon—A Global Call to Action*. Hoboken: Pearson FT Press.

Organski, A.F.K. 1958. *World Politics*. New York: Alfred A. Knopf.

Pence, M. 2018. Remarks by Vice President Pence on the Administration's Policy Toward China. https://www.whitehouse.gov/briefings-statementsre marks-vice-president-pence-administrations-policy-toward-china/.

Pillsbury, M. 2016. *The Hundred-Year Marathon: China's Secret Strategy to Replace America as the Global Superpower*. New York: St. Martin's Griffin.

Rolland, N. 2017. China's Eurasian Century? Political and Strategic Implications of the Belt and Road Initiative. National Bureau of Asian Research. https://www.nbr.org/publication/chinas-eurasian-century-political-and-strategic-implications-of-the-belt-and-road-initiative/.

Roy, D. 2013. *Return of the Dragon: Rising China and Regional Security*. New York: Columbia University Press.

Rudd, K. 2019. The Avoidable War: Reflections on U.S.-China Relations and the End of Strategic Engagement. New York: Asia Society Policy Institute. https://asiasociety.org/sites/default/files/2019-01/The%20Avoidable%20War%20-%20Full%20Report.pdf.

Rudd, K. 2020. The Coming Post-COVID Anarchy: The Pandemic Bodes Ill for Both American and Chinese Power—And for the Global Order. *Foreign Affairs*. https://www.foreignaffairs.com/articles/united-states/2020-05-06/coming-post-covid-anarchy.

Sanchez, C. 2017. From Local to Global: China's Role in Global Poverty Reduction and the Future of Development. https://www.worldbank.org/en/news/speech/2017/12/07/from-local-to-global-china-role-global-pov erty-reduction-future-of-development.

Schenoni, L.L. 2018. The Argentina-Brazil Regional Power Transition. *Foreign Policy Analysis* 14: 469–489.

Shirk, S.L. 2007. *China: A Fragile Superpower*. Oxford: Oxford University Press.

Stephen, M.D. 2017. Emerging Powers and Emerging Trends. *Global Governance: A Review of Multilateralism and International Organizations* 23 (3): 483–502.

Tammen, R.R., J. Kugler and D. Lemke. 2017a. Power Transition Theory. *Oxford Bibliographies in International Relations*.

Tammen, R.R., J. Kugler and D. Lemke. 2017b. Foundations of Power Transition Theory. *Oxford Research Encyclopedia*.

Tatom, J.A. 2007. Will China Surpass the United States? *International Economy Spring*: 38–41.

The Economist Intelligence Unit. 10 April 2018. "Renminbi Internationalization and the BRI: Rebuilding Momentum?" https://www.business.hsbc.com/china-growth/renminbi-internationalisation-and-the-bri-rebuilding-momentum.

Tufte, E. 2006. *Beautiful Evidence.* Cheshire: Graphics Press LLC.

Visions and Actions on Jointly Building Silk Road Economic Belt and 21st Century Maritime Silk Road. 2015. National Development and Reform Commission, Ministry of Foreign Affairs, and Ministry of Commerce of the People's Republic of China, with the State Council authorization. http://2017.beltandroadforum.org/english/n100/2017/0410/c22-45.html.

Wang, Yiwei. 2015. *"Yidai Yilu": Jiyu yu tiaozhan [One Belt, One Road: Opportunities and Challenges].* Beijing: Renmin Publisher.

Wang, Yi. 2019. "Full Text of Foreign Minister Wang Yi's News Conference at 2nd Session of 13th National People's Congress.

Yang, Y.E. 2020. China's Strategic Narratives in Global Governance Reform under Xi Jinping. *Journal of Contemporary China* 30 (128): 299–313.

Ye, M. 2019. Fragmentation and Mobilization: Domestic Politics of the Belt and Road in China. *Journal of Contemporary China* 28 (119): 696–711.

Ye, M. 2020. *The Belt Road and Beyond: State-Mobilized Globalization in China: 1998–2018.* Cambridge: Cambridge University Press.

Yoshihara, T. 2014. Chinese Maritime Geography. In *Strategy in Asia: The Past, Present, and Future of Regional Security*, ed. T.G. Mahnken and D. Blumenthal, 43–60. Stanford University Press.

Yuan, J. 2018. Beijing's Institutional-balancing Strategies: Rationales, Implementation and Efficacy. *Australian Journal of International Affairs* 72 (2): 110–128.

Yuliantoro, N. R., and Dinarto, D. 2019. Between Revisionist and Status Quo: The Case of China's Leadership in the AIIB. *Jurnal Hubungan Internasional* 7 (2).

Zhu, Z. 2019. China's Global Power Ambition: Expectations, Opportunities and Challenges. In *Handbook on China and Globalization*, ed. H. Wang, M. Lu. Edward Elgar Publishing

CHAPTER 4

Putting the BRI in Perspective: History, Hegemony, and Geoeconomics

Mark Beeson and Corey Crawford

4.1 Introduction

The 'rise of China' or—more accurately—China's re-emergence as the most important actor in what we now think of as East Asia is one of the most important developments in world history. This may strike some readers as an extravagant claim, but it is not without foundation. Until recently, the economy of the People's Republic of China (PRC) was set to overtake the US's as the world's largest (Cheng and Lee 2021; Curran

---

This chapter is an updated version of the journal article: Beeson, M., Crawford, C. "Putting the BRI in Perspective: History, Hegemony and Geoeconomics." *Chin. Polit. Sci. Rev.* **8**, 45–62 (2023). https://doi.org/10.1007/s41111-022-00210-y

---

M. Beeson (✉)
University of Technology Sydney, Ultimo, Australia
e-mail: Mark.Beeson@uts.edu.au

© The Author(s), under exclusive license to Springer Nature
Switzerland AG 2025
K. G.Cai et al. (eds.), *China and Global Economic Governance, Volume I: China's BRI & AIIB and Global Economic Governance*, Politics and Development of Contemporary China,
https://doi.org/10.1007/978-3-031-73212-6_4

2023). It still may. Either way, the PRC remains the first credible candidate to become a non-Western hegemonic power in the modern era. The fact that it is from Asia is noteworthy enough; the idea that it is a 'communist' power that subscribes to a very different idea about the best ways of organizing social, political, economic, and strategic activities is even more remarkable. At the very least, the PRC's ascension provides a striking illustration of the possibility that very different routes to global power are conceivable. The key questions in this context are not just whether 'Chinese hegemony' is possible, but how it might differ from the more familiar American variety that has dominated the international system and the world views of nearly everyone alive today.

To try and answer these questions, we focus on China's Belt and Road Initiative (BRI). If successfully realized, the BRI will be the most ambitious and expansive developmental project the world has ever seen. While there has been an unsurprising flurry of interest inside and outside China about the development of the BRI (Beeson 2020a, b; Clarke 2017; Winter 2019), there have been few attempts to place the BRI in comparative perspective, or to consider it as an expression of possible hegemonic influence. Given that the BRI is not unprecedented, this is surprising. After all, in the aftermath of the Second World War, the US developed what was then an equally unprecedented and ambitious initiative designed to simultaneously facilitate the (re)development of some of the world's key economies and reinforce its own position as the leader of the non-communist world (Pollard 1985).

Both the American Marshall Plan and China's BRI are, therefore, important expressions of what has been described as 'geoeconomic' influence and power (Blackwill and Harris 2016; Luttwak 1990). In what follows, we compare the two projects to try and gauge the prospects for the BRI and some of its associated institutions. Significantly, the BRI lacks the same sort of geopolitical imperatives and narrative that the emerging Cold War provided for the US and its allies (Gaddis 1982). At this point, at least, the Chinese project also lacks the comprehensive institutional architecture that facilitated American 'hegemonic' influence. Consequently, we argue that it may prove more difficult for China to

---

C. Crawford
University of Western Australia, Perth, Australia
e-mail: 22219007@student.uwa.edu.au

impose or develop the same sort of coherent vision and geopolitical goals that the Americans did, raising doubts about its long-term significance, despite its unparalleled ambitions (Beeson 2009).

The paper is organized as follows. After first making, some theoretical observations about the nature of hegemony and the historical context within which it has developed, we briefly consider the nature of American dominance in the period following the Second World War. The distinctive Cold War geopolitical context helps to explain the importance of ideology and institution building that was so characteristic of this period. Following this, we provide a more extensive consideration of the BRI, highlighting some striking similarities, but also some noteworthy differences and even weaknesses in China's recent experience. Finally, we conclude by considering the implications of the BRI and China's growing international importance for international relations in theory and practice more generally.

4.2 Historicizing Hegemony

Hegemony can be described in several ways, and generally reflects the theoretical or even the cultural assumptions of the observer. For realists such as John Mearsheimer (2001, p. 40), a hegemon is 'so powerful that it dominates all other states in the system.' The principal source of this preponderance, Mearsheimer argues, is the fact that 'no other state has the military wherewithal to put up a serious fight against it.' To be sure, economic weight is also important, but primarily because it allows the hegemon to reinforce its military superiority. As we shall see, there is no doubt that increased economic importance combined with a willingness and capacity to invest heavily in military assets during and in the wake of the Second World War were crucial factors in America's hegemonic rise.

There were, however, other aspects of the 'hegemonic transition' that saw the US replace Great Britain as the most powerful country in the world that were distinctive and possibly unique (Silver and Arrighi 2003). Most consequentially, Britain's status as a great power, let alone, a hegemonic one, had been profoundly undermined by two world wars. The US, by contrast, had had a 'good war': not only was the Great Depression definitively ended by the mobilization of the national economy, but the US remained unaffected by the ravages of the war itself; potential rivals, such as Britain, Germany, and Japan, were devastated by the conflict. At the end of the war, the US accounted for nearly half of global GDP

(Maddison 2002). By any measure, this was a huge material advantage that helps to explain America's ascendance and the assumption of an international role it had hitherto eschewed. The fact that the US was another Western power undoubtedly made the transition less problematic for many of the world's historically influential states.

4.2.1 The Benign Hegemon?

Despite these overwhelming military and economic advantages, however, they do not explain the distinctive, highly institutionalized, nature of American dominance. As Ruggie (1992, p. 568 [emphasis in original]) pointed out, 'it was less the fact of American *hegemony* that accounts for the explosion of multilateral arrangements than it was the fact of *American* hegemony.' Two points are especially noteworthy and salient in this context. First, the experience of the interwar period and the economic and political traumas induced by the Great Depression meant that postwar policymakers were especially alert to the idea that it was necessary to create institutions that would ensure that international economic activity was not simply encouraged, but governed by particular principles, norms, and even rules. Charles Kindleberger (1973) had persuasively argued that the absence of a hegemon with the will and capacity to underpin an 'open' liberal international order was primarily responsible for the outbreak and duration of the Great Depression.

Second, no sooner had World War II ended than the Cold War began. Though there were numerous close calls, the struggle between the Soviet Union and the US did not spill over into hegemonic war. Ideological contestation was thus a key focus for both sides. It is important to remember that for all its increasingly evident shortcomings, the Soviet model had its admirers, especially when the failings of the capitalist alternative were generally seen as the primary cause of the Depression.

The Chinese economic and political system we describe is not 'communist' in the Soviet sense, and the Chinese Communist Party's role in the economy is not as significant—all the commentary about 'state capitalism' notwithstanding (Bremmer 2009). For our comparative purposes, the fact that the US was willing to use what we might now describe as 'geoeconomic' power to consolidate its influence and prop up fragile economies devastated by the war, is of particular interest, both theoretically and practically.

The specific historical circumstances in which American hegemony evolved and in which the US assumed the leadership of the so-called free world are, therefore, crucial components of any explanation of its distinctive form and objectives. The US's willingness to turn a blind eye to, or actively support, authoritarian regimes if they were non-communist, became one of the defining features of the era (Cumings 2009; Owen and Poznansky 2014). The construction of the 'Bretton Woods Institutions' (BWIs)—the World Bank, the International Monetary Fund (IMF), and the General Agreement on Tariffs and Trade (GATT)—was vital expressions of America's liberal norms, especially the economic variety (Steil 2013).

As important as the institutions were, they were only part of the US's post-1945 grand strategy of containing the Soviet Union. This included the physical containment of the Soviet Union, particularly around its southern rim. At a time when there was little difference between airfields used for military purposes and commercial aviation, the newly inaugurated President Harry S. Truman said that, along with reparations, control of the international air transport system was 'the most important post-war international problem' for his administration (Converse 2011, p. 114). As State Department official Fred Searles Jr. argued at a strategy meeting in February 1946, 'If [Soviet leader Joseph] Stalin knows we have airfields in India that fact will serve as a greater deterrent to him than the United Nations Charter' (Converse 2011, pp. 156–157).

Access to overseas bases provided the US with the ability to destroy Soviet cities with nuclear weapons. Mastery of the atom demonstrated the superiority of American science, technology, and industry, and it gave the US a dominant role in the postwar international system. As Secretary of the Navy James V. Forrestal wrote in 1947, 'As long as we can outproduce the world, can control the seas, and can strike inland with the atomic bomb, we can assume certain risks otherwise unacceptable' (Sherwin 2020, p. 46). Though the size of the US base network shrank dramatically from its Second World War peak of more than 3,000 facilities, the US Navy had 13 overseas bases and the US Air Force operated from 85 foreign installations in 1950 (Converse 2011, p. 210). These bases were intended to limit the foreign policy ambitions of the Soviet Union, but, ironically, led to the Cold War's greatest calamity. With the US having 'surrounded us with military bases and kept us at gunpoint [with nuclear weapons],' Soviet leader Nikita Khrushchev believed that sending such weapons to Cuba in 1962 would create 'a balance of fear'

(Sherwin 2020, p. 31). The ensuing Cuban Missile Crisis is generally considered the closest the world has ever come to nuclear annihilation.

4.2.2 International Institutions

Significantly, even 'critical' scholars operating in a broadly Marxist framework recognized that one of the most important features of American hegemony was that—for all the criticisms that have subsequently been made about its practice—for many countries, it was highly attractive. As Robert Cox (1987, p. 7) put it, effective hegemonic power and influence is 'dominance of a particular kind…based ideologically on a broad measure of consent…but at the same time offer[ing] some measure or prospect of satisfaction to the less powerful.' In other words, there was potentially something in it for those states desperate to rebuild their economies, or kickstart economic development where it had been lackluster or dependent. Whatever we may think of American hegemony as a whole, there is little doubt that in some parts of the world, at least—Western Europe, Japan, and South Korea being the most consequential—it succeeded brilliantly (Stubbs 2005).

In retrospect postwar development is seen as the 'golden age of capitalism,' distinguished by a remarkable growth spurt across many nations that was consciously fueled by American support and largesse (Glyn et al. 1990). The most celebrated manifestation of this possibility was the Marshall Plan, which saw the US provide more than $15 billion to the distressed economies of Western Europe (Hogan 1987). Japan was a major beneficiary of American aid, too, even if this was seen by the US primarily as a way of curbing communist expansion in East Asia, not to mention nullifying any possible future strategic threat from Japan itself (Pyle 2007). Again, whatever the motivation might have been, there is little doubt that this goal was spectacularly realized as Japan went from being a radioactive wasteland to the world's second biggest economy in little more than 2 decades. Significantly, Japan was able to take advantage of precisely the sort of open economic order that the US had helped to create, just as the PRC did several decades later (Tabb 1995; Lardy 2002).

After the Cold War ended, however, the inability of the Washington Consensus to provide for the economic needs of developing nations became increasingly clear. The 'stabilize, privatize and liberalize' agenda promoted by the World Bank and the IMF had produced disappointing results in terms of economic growth, employment, and poverty reduction in Africa and South America, and had also increased inequality and the occurrence of financial crises in some recipient states (Halper 2012, p. xix). As Western governments and financial institutions retreated into their domestic markets following the 2008 financial crisis, developing nations struggled to secure finance for infrastructure projects to an even greater extent than usual. China's capacity to influence the developing world grew accordingly: a loan of just 0.1% of China's foreign reserves to Africa would have easily surpassed the World Bank's annual contribution to the impoverished continent (Wei 2009).

4.2.3   Comparative Hegemony

It is precisely because American hegemony appeared to have such beneficial effects—in some strategically important parts of the world, at least—that so many observers, especially in the US itself, regard its dominance as essentially benign. True, critical scholars such as John Agnew (2005, p. 1/2) may be right to describe hegemony as 'the enrolment of others in the exercise of your power by convincing, cajoling, and coercing them that they should want what you want,' but for many American liberals this was—and remains—no bad thing. John Ikenberry (2011, pp. 57/8) claims that even when other powers are rising America's dominant position is not challenged.

> ...today's power transition represents not the defeat of the liberal order but its ultimate ascendance. Brazil, China, and India have all become more prosperous and capable by operating inside the existing international order -- benefiting from its rules, practices, and institutions, including the World Trade Organization (WTO) and the newly organized G20. Their economic success and growing influence are tied to the liberal internationalist organization of world politics, and they have deep interests in preserving that system.

Even though the PRC has been one of the principal beneficiaries of an international order predominantly created by the US, its leaders have been perennially nervous about, and critical of, America's hegemonic influence (Deng 2001). At one level, perhaps, China's leaders are right to be alert about the possible transformative influence of America's institutionalized influence. China's accession to the World Trade Organization (WTO) is emblematic of the continuing importance of the BWIs: not only did China's integration into the WTO accelerate its economic development, but it profoundly influenced social development within China, too. The growth of a middle-class consumer culture in China is a striking change, but not one that has led to the sort of concomitant political culture many expected. On the contrary, the CCP has become more powerful under Xi Jinping (Economy 2018), and it is far from clear that China is 'playing by our rules,' as American analysts such as Edward Steinfeld (2010) claim.

Even before Xi stamped his authority on the CCP and intellectual and ideological attitudes more generally, a number of scholars had begun to develop a distinctive national approach to International Relations (IR) scholarship, with increasingly Chinese characteristics (Qin 2011). Significantly, much of this literature has the same sorts of benign interpretations of China's rise that had characterized American interpretations of the US's hegemonic ascension. One of the most distinctive and influential expressions of this possibility is the notion of *Tianxia*, or 'all under heaven.' Dating back to at least to the Zhanguo or 'Warring States' era (circa 453–221 BCE), and in conjunction with the consolidation of China's Tributary system, *Tianxia* was predicated on the idea that— unlike much Western IR theory—international relations are inescapably hierarchical, and that Chinese hegemony was actually a stabilizing force in what we now think of as East Asia (Zhao 2009). However, self-serving some Western observers may consider this formulation, it is a claim that is not without some empirical foundation. As David Kang (2003) has pointed out, the historical record suggests that when China has been unified and powerful, the region has generally been peaceful, too. In this context, Xi's (2014a) claims about the benefits of creating a Community of Common Destiny and a distinctively Asian approach to security problems are not entirely unprecedented and draw on some common and distinctive regional approaches to strategic policy' (Beeson 2014; Mardell 2017).

Whatever the merits of arguments about a distinctive Asian approach to security, what is of most interest and importance for the purposes of this discussion is the way China is attempting to assert its influence and pursue what its leaders take to be its 'national interest.' It is not necessary to be a constructivist to recognize that the way national interests are conceived can vary across time and space (Weldes 1996), or that some conceptions may resonate more powerfully than others in a specific context (Kirshner 2006). Many Chinese believe that restoring China's pre-eminence and overcoming the legacy of the 'century of shame' are worthy and appropriate goals. This explains much of Xi's popular support.

As 'Gries et al. (2011, p. 16) point out, 'nationalist historical beliefs are integral to the structure of Chinese national identity.' In this context, China is not so different to the US; the populations and leaders of both countries generally see themselves as occupying a uniquely 'exceptional' place in world history and act accordingly (Lipset 1996; Zhang 2013). Indeed, as the eccentric presidency of Donald J. Trump reminds us, making a country 'great again' is an idea that has popular support in the US, too. Paradoxically, however, of late, it has been China rather than the US that has paid the most attention to the *external* dimensions of this challenge.

4.3 Hegemony with Chinese Characteristics?

For many observers outside China, especially in the US, there is no doubt that China is bent on replacing America as the dominant power in the world (Mosher 2000). Indeed, for some observers, China's elites are following nothing less than a 100-year plan to replace the US as the world's dominant power (Pillsbury 2015). Prominent realist scholars worry that there is a certain structurally determined inevitability about both China's rise and the chances of a conflict between the US and the PRC as the latter increasingly seeks to assert its growing power and influence (Allison 2017). While Western IR's collective failure to predict the end of the Cold War, the dramatic decline in inter-state wars, or recognize the importance of national strategic cultures and beliefs in shaping thinking about security, suggests that we should be very cautious about its collective epistemic authority, there is no doubt that China's behavior has changed.

One of the most important expressions of this possibility can be seen in the sophistication of China's political and diplomatic elites as they have come to play a more prominent part in what some IR theorists describe as 'international society' and the institutional architecture that constitutes it (Clark 2014). At one level, hopes and expectations about China's leaders being 'socialized' into the ways of Western diplomacy have been realized: China is nothing like the disruptive, revolutionary force that it was under before Richard Nixon and Henry Kissinger engineered the celebrated rapprochement with the PRC (Kissinger 1994; van Ness 1970). At another level, however, it is clear that China's foreign policy goals continue to reflect 'national interests' and values, especially under the increasingly coordinated and centralized leadership of Xi Jinping (Lampton 2015). Indeed, not only are Chinese policymakers still pursuing national goals, but they are doing so in ways that are also often strikingly similar to those employed by the US in an earlier era.

4.3.1 The BRI's Origins and Attractions

When Xi announced China's ambition to revitalize the fabled Silk Road during a visit to Kazakhstan in 2013, it was an indication of both his and the PRC's growing ambitions. Invoking the Silk Road not only harked back to an earlier period of Chinese regional dominance, but it also reflected some very contemporary concerns, too. Central Asia was a major area of geopolitical attention for China, its possible importance already institutionalized in the Shanghai Cooperation Organization (SCO), which the PRC initiated and dominated (Chung 2004). In keeping with the goals of the SCO, what was then called the One Belt, One Road (OBOR) initiative was seen as a way of 'firmly support[ing] each other and mak[ing] joint efforts to crack down on the "three evil forces" of terrorism, extremism and separatism, as well as drug trafficking, transnational organized crime' (MoF 2013). While the rebadged BRI also shares the goal of helping to develop and stabilize Central Asia, its geographical scope and ambitions have significantly expanded.

In keeping with China's deliberative and broad-based approach to foreign policy in the post-Mao era, Chinese economic analysts and policymakers spent several years developing an ambitious global infrastructure initiative. Prominent Chinese scholar Justin Yifu Lin, for example, was not only the first person from the 'developing world' to be appointed chief economist of the World Bank, but in 2009, he also argued that China should 'donate' some of its extensive forex reserves as part of a 5-year, $2 trillion 'new Marshall Plan' that would spur economic development in low-income nations (Yuan 2009). Similarly, Xu Shanda, deputy director of the State Administration of Taxation, submitted a policy proposal to the Ministry of Commerce entitled 'Chinese Marshall Plan' (Zhou et al. 2015). There were three key planks to Xu's plan: establish a sovereign wealth fund from which the Chinese government would issue infrastructure loans; provide government loans to aid Chinese enterprises with production surpluses to expand into the global market; and coordinate efforts to internationalize the *renminbi* as an acceptable form of payment and reserve currency (Ling 2015, p. 72).

Whatever the long-term advantages of joining an international economic and institutional order created under American auspices, it has not escaped the notice of policymakers in China that they are also exposed to its vicissitudes as well. There have been long-standing concerns in China about the merits of having the value of the *renminbi* decided by market forces (Vermeiren 2013), for example, and a determination to counter the advantages that accrue to the US as the provider of the world's de facto reserve currency (Chin 2014). Likewise, many Chinese policymakers, especially Xi Jinping, want to retain oversight—if not control of—'strategically important' state-owned enterprises (SOEs), as well as notionally independent companies (Szamosszegi and Kyle 2011). Such thinking was initially reflected in China's 'going out strategy,' in which SOEs played a prominent and coordinated role (Economy and Levi 2014). Indeed, although they might be loath to admit it, Chinese policymakers learned many lessons from Japan's state-led approach to domestic development and overseas expansion (Heilmann and Shih 2013). In fact, the CCP retains enormous power and influence over economic affairs and social relations (Ling 2020).

It is not only China's domestic ambitions and influence that has expanded under Xi's rule, however. As has been frequently noted, the 'hide and bide' approach to foreign policy advocated by Deng Xiaoping has been abandoned (Yan 2021). Xi appears determined to achieve a daunting set of economic and political reforms, in which the BRI plays an important practical and symbolic role. According to Jude Blanchette (2021, p. 10),

> Xi has consolidated so much power and upset the status quo with such force, because he sees a narrow window of 10–15 years during which Beijing can take advantage of a set of important technological and geopolitical transformations, which will also help it overcome significant internal challenges.

One of the factors that is encouraging Xi to transform China's mode of domestic governance and foreign policy is undoubtedly the declining fortunes and hegemonic status of the US. The global financial crisis (GFC) that developed in the US during 2008 saw America's loosely regulated form of capitalism subjected to intense internal and external criticism

(Whitley 2009). By contrast, the reputation of the so-called China model was significantly enhanced as its policymakers unleashed a highly effective stimulus package that not only saved the Chinese economy from going into recession but most of its regional neighbors, too (Breslin 2011). The consequence was that policymakers in China's immediate region and beyond were already looking to China for possible lessons and largesse even before the BRI was announced. This is especially the case in non-democratic states where the intrusive nature of reform packages sponsored by the BWIs was widely resented. As Micklethwait and Wooldridge (2014, p. 129) point out, as 'Asian countries generate clever ideas for reforming government, the West's greatest strength—representative democracy—is losing its lustre.'

4.4 Rolling Out and Financing the BRI

Even before the GFC, Chinese policymakers had not only been keen to play a more prominent role in the international institutional architecture that helped manage economic and even strategic relations, but they had begun experimenting with their organizations that reflected their norms and preferences (Beeson and Li 2016). This is entirely unsurprising: after all, one of the advantages of great power is the capacity to influence the way that international organizations (IOs) operate and the policy agendas they help to promote. As we have seen, the SCO, established in 2001, was one of the most important expressions of China's growing power and ambition. When attention turned toward Xi's even more ambitious plan for the BRI, one of its most noteworthy features was the simultaneous establishment of the Asian Infrastructure Investment Bank (AIIB). The original intention of the AIIB was, as the name suggests, to act as a vehicle for funding infrastructure development in parts of the world where the BWIs had previously been instrumental—and unpopular. In this context, the PRC saw an opportunity to build on its emerging 'soft power.' As Wang Zhen (2015) notes,

> Xi's strategy is a sophisticated and progressive one. Instead of directly challenging the current existing international institutions, the Chinese are trying to create new platforms that Beijing can control or substantially influence. Through these new initiatives, Beijing aims to create a new international environment that is more favorable to China, one that will limit strategic pressures from the United States.

In this context, former Premier Li Keqiang delivered a keynote speech at the opening ceremony of the Boao Forum for Asia in April 2014, where he indicated China's willingness to consult with relevant parties across Asia and beyond regarding the formal establishment of the AIIB (Li 2014). Significantly, and despite pressure from the Obama administration not to join, key US allies like Australia, South Korea, and the UK, as well as a number of other prominent European states, such as France and Germany, became founding members (Beeson and Xu 2019). While this was predictably seen as something of a diplomatic triumph in Beijing, the reality was more complex. To get Western states to sign on to the AIIB, the PRC had to dilute its influence somewhat and conform to extant international norms around transparency and 'good governance.' Indeed, according to some observers, 'despite all of the rhetoric from and about China that talks about the genesis of a new 'China model' of development, in reality China seems to have bought into 'business as usual' international development banking norms—and has spent relatively little money in doing so' (Babones et al. 2020, p. 333).

For all the attention they have garnered, both the AIIB and the New Development Bank (NDB), which was established in conjunction with the other BRICS countries [Brazil, India, Russia, and South Africa]), have had a relatively limited impact. In reality, China's state-owned banks, policy banks, and sovereign wealth fund are doing the heavy lifting for BRI lending. Xi (2014b) announced the creation of a $40 billion Silk Road Fund 'to provide investment and financing support for countries along the Belt and Road' at the APEC Dialogue on Strengthening Connectivity Partnership, so that they could carry out infrastructure and natural resources projects. The State Administration of Foreign Exchange would provide 65% of the fund's total capital, the China Investment Corporation and the Export–Import Bank of China would contribute 15% each, and the China Development Bank would account for the remaining 5% (SFR 2021). Whatever one thinks of the motivations for and implications of the BRI, there is no doubt that inadequate infrastructure is a major problem across much of Asia that hinders economic development (ADB 2017); anything that looks as if it might alleviate this problem is likely to be welcomed, all other things being equal.

4.4.1 Too Much of a Good Thing?

The BRI is expected to consist of six overland economic corridors radiating out from China: (1) the New Eurasian Land Bridge Economic Corridor (NELBEC) connecting Western China to Europe; (2) the China–Mongolia–Russia Economic Corridor (CMREC) connecting Northern China to Eastern Russia; (3) the China–Central Asia–Western Asia Economic Corridor (CCWAEC) connecting Western China to Turkey; (4) the China–Indochina Peninsula Economic Corridor (CICPEC) connecting Southern China to Singapore; (5) the Bangladesh–China–India–Myanmar Economic Corridor (BCIMEC) connecting Southern China to India; and (6) the China–Pakistan Economic Corridor (CPEC) connecting Southwest China to Pakistan. To achieve greater interconnectivity, the overland corridors would connect to the maritime corridor at strategic ports. The Maritime Silk Road (MSR) would run from China's coastal regions through the South China Sea down to Singapore and across the Indian Ocean through to the Arabian Sea, the Persian Gulf, and the Red Sea before finishing at the Mediterranean Sea.

Unlike the agreements issued by the WTO, however, China's BRI documents usually lack specific provisions, rights, and obligations for the signatories. For example, there is typically a clause near the end of the MoU that states that agreements are not legally binding (Walsh 2018). China expects participants to give 3 months' written notice, through the appropriate diplomatic channels, if they wish to terminate their agreement. An analysis of 100 Chinese debt contracts with foreign governments confirmed that cancelation, acceleration, and stabilization clauses in the contracts allow Beijing to influence the domestic and foreign policies of recipient states. More than 90% of the contracts analyzed had clauses that authorized Chinese officials to 'terminate the contract and demand immediate repayment' if there was a 'significant' change in the recipient state's laws or policies (Gelpern et al. 2021).

While there is a good deal of debate about how constraining or effective China's 'debt-trap diplomacy' actually is (Brautigam 2020), given significant pushback from countries such as Malaysia (Stromseth 2019), one thing is clear: China's approach to foreign infrastructure projects is strikingly different to the traditional Western approach (Hillman 2018).

China's domestic political structure allows it to bring together all of the state's key actors, including corporate leaders and government officials, when making an offer to a prospective recipient state. While the Chinese present a united front, the Western approach requires the recipient state to deal with an assortment of actors, including some who operate independently and others who actively compete with each other. The Chinese are also willing to engage in instrumental 'minerals-for-infrastructure' deals, such as the $6 billion infrastructure loans issued to the Democratic People's Republic of Congo in 2007, which were to be repaid with mining profits from the Sicomines copper and cobalt mine (Anonymous 2015).

The continuing evolution, scale, and status of some of the projects associated with the BRI makes it difficult to assign a definitive value on the rollout. Graham Allison (2017, p. 23) suggested that the BRI contained 900 projects at a predicted cost of more than $1.4 trillion. Jonathan E. Hillman (2020, p. 4), a specialist on infrastructure investment, estimated the total cost at $1 trillion. When adjusted for inflation, this estimate, which is at the lower end of educated guesses, would make the BRI nearly seven times larger than the Marshall Plan. According to Refinitiv (2020), a leading financial data-providing firm, there were 1,887 BRI projects planned or underway by August 2020, with a total value of $2.3 trillion. It is also important to note that in addition to financial wherewithal, China also boasts some of the world's best engineers and technical experts. China went from having less than 160 kms of motorways in 1989 to 64,000 kms in 2012, second only in length to the United States' inter-state highway system (Fenby 2012, p. 263). Indeed, domestic overcapacity in China's building sector generally has become a serious problem, for which outward investment and infrastructure development may provide an outlet (Beeson and Li 2016, p. 355).

As with the Marshall Plan, however, it is important to emphasize that the BRI has a major geopolitical rationale that reflects a distinct Chinese conception of the national interest. In this context, the perceived need to diversify energy supplies and secure key maritime supply routes is seen as critical. With 90% of all traded goods carried by sea, it is considered essential that the PLA Navy (PLAN) can secure key maritime routes between ports. These strategic considerations help to explain why the 21st Century Maritime Silk Road has received 60% of BRI project funding and the overland Silk Road Economic Belt only 40% (Balhuizen 2017). Such strategic considerations and the perceived vulnerabilities of Sea Lines of Communication (SLOCs) also help to explain its growing territorial assertiveness in neighboring waters.

In what has been described by one American strategist as a Chinese iteration of the Monroe Doctrine (Holmes 2012), China has sought to increase its foothold in the Yellow, East China, and the South China seas, and attempted to secure port access with a so-called string of pearls strategy around the Indo-Pacific (Brewster 2017). According to Brahma Chellaney (cited in Miller 2017, p. 169): 'Commercial penetration is the forerunner to political penetration, and the integration of economic and military power. First they use engineering companies to create projects; then they bring in their own labour; then they acquire diplomatic influence. And they finally acquire strategic leverage.'

Despite some rather conspiratorially minded commentary, it is also worth noting that precisely because of China's frequently prioritized long-term strategic calculations, it does not always do due diligence on potential partners and loan recipients. A UN Development Programme (2016, p. 6) report found 'huge discrepancies' in the reporting of China's funding streams to recipients had created 'an unbalanced picture of China's performance as a development partner and the scope of China's support.' China's 'fast and flexible' approach to infrastructure finance means that it does not follow the established methods of international development (Parks 2019).

As a direct consequence of the CCP's disdain for Western transparency and accountability practices, the BRI lacks the customary project appraisal standards; procurement guidelines; and environmental, social, and fiduciary safeguards. Some of these deficiencies were laid bare during the COVID-19 pandemic, which caused a dramatic global recession and forced heavily indebted developing countries to spend more on their beleaguered healthcare systems. Following the highly publicized defaults of recipient states like Sri Lanka and Zambia, China marked the BRI's tenth anniversary with a revamped debt appraisal framework that would provide 'a more prudent approach is assessing growth risks' (Cash 2023).

This followed the Center for Global Development's study of 100 Chinese debt contracts with foreign governments, which found that China's 'contracts contain more elaborate repayment safeguards than their [Western] peers in the official credit market' (Gelpern et al. 2021, pp. 5–6)—one of the reasons critics fret about possible 'debt-traps' and geoeconomic leverage, of course. Given the inherent complexity and ambition of the BRI rollout, however, it is entirely possible that such fears are exaggerated and simultaneously over-estimate the PRC's ability to control such a project in all its multifarious dimensions, and underestimate the capacity of potential partners to push back when it suits them.

4.5   Concluding Remarks

It is, perhaps, the perception that the BRI is designed to deliver tangible benefits and influence to the PRC as well as to recipients that distinguishes this project from the earlier American version. To be sure, the Marshall Plan undoubtedly reflected American norms and geopolitical goals, but the actual utilization and disbursement of aid from the US occurred at arms-length. Indeed, it is arguably one of the defining features of American hegemony that it has often operated at a distance through institutional intermediaries such as the BWIs. Such observations are not intended to downplay America's frequent direct and violent military interventions in international affairs, but this was not a feature of the postwar reconstruction effort; China has not demonstrated anything like a similar willingness to utilize its more traditional forms of geopolitical influence or domination. The big question is whether the PRC will be able to utilize the BRI to translate potential geoeconomic leverage into the sort of hegemonic influence that the US enjoyed.

Thus far, the answer to this question seems to be 'probably not.' Despite claims about the emergence of 'Cold War 2' (Kaplan 2019), there are major differences between the stand-of between the Soviet Union and the US and the current competition with China. Most importantly, perhaps, the level of economic interdependence between the US and the PRC remains very significant, and neither country can easily unpick a symbiotic relationship from which they have both benefited. Likewise, despite much excited talk about the Washington consensus versus the Beijing variety (Halper 2012), and the possible importance of different forms of capitalism (Peck and Zhang 2013), it is the fact that both countries are capitalist economies of some sort that is noteworthy: ideological differences are nothing like as great or potentially as insurmountable as they were during the Cold War. This matters, because the amount of pressure to conform, and the importance of ideas and values are necessarily reduced in such an environment. While much attention has been given to China's willingness to work with unattractive authoritarian regimes (Faiz 2019), it is also important to remember that the US was prepared to overlook the normative shortcomings of client states in the capitalist orbit. In principle, therefore, there is no reason the two superpowers might not develop a pragmatic modus vivendi.

This may not be as unlikely as it may seem. Whether the world actually needs the sort of hegemonic leadership that the US formerly offered, and which is such a foundational idea in much Western IR theory, is a moot point (Buzan 2011); but the idea that the US and the PRC have to cooperate on at least one issue looks less controversial. As Anatole Lieven (2020, p. xii) points out, 'the world's great powers are far more threatened by climate change than they are by each other.' Recognition of the immediacy of the threat posed by climate change does seem to be growing, although adequate action still seems a remote prospect. Joint leadership from the PRC and the US could transform international attitudes and outcomes more widely, however. While this may seem somewhat unlikely in light of the preceding discussion, if it were part of the sort of arms reduction treaties that distinguished the Cold War, and was tied to a commitment to invest the savings to restructure their economies along more sustainable lines (Beeson 2020a, b), it might provide the sort of 'win–win' outcome that Xi Jinping frequently invokes.

Western IR theory does not have a good record in predicting major turning points in international affairs; the supposed inevitability of 'hegemonic transitions' looks anything but certain at this point in history. In the meantime, long festering domestic problems have drifted to the surface in China, raising serious questions about the PRC's capacity to supplant the United States as the world's leading economic power. An unraveling property sector, unmanageable local government debts, growing deflationary pressures, and long-term demographic challenges will surely curtail China's capacity to fund big-ticket BRI projects (Ip 2023).

In recent years, both Xi and President Joseph R. Biden Jr. have recognized the importance of establishing some sort of working relationship—and the possible dangers of not doing so (Kanno-Youngs and Sanger 2021). The distinct possibility of a second Trump administration—led by the self-proclaimed 'Tariff Man'—augers an uncertain future for Sino-American relations on a number of fronts (Savage et al. 2023). The absence of 'G2' cooperation will have significant ramifications for trade and investment, climate policy, and strategic competition. If the US and China cannot find a way to manage their differences for the common good, then the discussions of comparative hegemony and the continuing rise of China will become theoretically irrelevant and empirically improbable.

REFERENCES

Asian Development Bank. 2017. *Meeting Asia's Infrastructure Needs*. Manila: ADB.

Agnew, John. 2005. *Hegemony: The New Shape of Global Power*. Philadelphia: Temple University Press.

Allison, Graham. 2017. *Destined for War: Can America and China Escape Thucydides's Trap?* Boston: Houghton Mifflin Harcourt.

Anonymous. 2015. China's "Infrastructure for Minerals" Deal Gets Reality-Check in Congo. *Reuters*. https://www.reuters.com/article/congodemocra tic-mining-china-idUSL8N0ZN2QZ20150708. Accessed 8 July 2015.

Babones, Salvatore, John H.S. Åberg, and Obert Hodzi. 2020. China's Role in Global Development Finance: China Challenge or Business as Usual? *Global Policy* 11 (3): 326–335.

Balhuizen, A. 2017. China's Belt and Road Initiative, Episode Two: A Vision Encased in Steel, *BHP*. https://www.bhp.com/media-and-insights/prospe cts/2017/09/belt-and-road-initiative. Accessed 26 Sep 2017.

Beeson, Mark. 2009. Hegemonic Transition in East Asia? The Dynamics of Chinese and American Power. *Review of International Studies* 35 (1): 95–112.

Beeson, Mark. 2014. Security in Asia What's Different, What's Not? *Journal of Asian Security and International Affairs* 1 (1): 1–23.

Beeson, Mark. 2020a. Southeast Asia and the BRI: Integrative or divisive? In *The Belt and Road Initiative and the Future of Regional Order in the Indo-Pacific*, eds. Michael Clarke, Matthew Sussex and Nick Bisley ,181–200. Indiana: Lexington Books.

Beeson, Mark. 2020b, Avoiding a Cold War and a Hot Planet. *The Strategist*, 10 September.

Beeson, Mark, and Fujian Li. 2016. China's Place in Regional and Global Governance: A New World Comes Into View. *Global Policy* 7 (4): 491–499.

Beeson, Mark, and Shaomin Xu. 2019. China's Evolving Role in Global Governance: The AIIB and the Limits of an Alternative International Order. In *Handbook of the International Political Economy of China*, ed. Ka Zeng, 345–360. Cheltenham: Edward Elgar.

Blackwill, Robert D., and Harris, Jennifer M. 2016. *War by Other Means: Geoeconomics and Statecraft*. Harvard University Press.

Blanchette, Jude. 2021. Xi's Gamble: The Race to Consolidate Power and Stave of Disaster. *Foreign Affairs* 100 (4): 10–19.

Brautigam, Deborah. 2020. A Critical Look at Chinese 'Debt-Trap Diplomacy': The Rise of a Meme. *Area Development and Policy* 5 (1): 1–14.

Bremmer, Ian. 2009. State Capitalism Comes of Age: The End of the Free Market? *Foreign Affairs* 88 (3): 40–55.

Breslin, Shaun. 2011. China and the Crisis: Global Power, Domestic Caution and Local Initiative. *Contemporary Politics* 17 (2): 185–200.

Brewster, David. 2017. Silk Roads and Strings of Pearls: The Strategic Geography of China's New Pathways in the Indian Ocean. *Geopolitics* 22 (2): 269–291.

Buzan, Barry. 2011. A World Order Without Superpowers: Decentred Globalism. *International Relations* 25 (1): 3–25.

Cash, Joe. China Revamps Debt Appraisal Framework for Belt and Road Programme. *Reuters*, October 20.

Cheng, Evelyn, and Lee, Yen Nee. 2021. New Chart Shows China Could Overtake the U.S. as the World's Largest Economy Earlier Than Expected. *CNBC*, https://www.cnbc.com/2021/02/01/new-chart-shows-china-gdp-could-overtake-us-sooner-as-covid-took-its-toll.html. Accessed 31 Jan.

Chin, Greg. 2014. China's Rising Monetary Power. In *The Great Wall of Money: The Great Wall of Money: Power and Politics in China's International Monetary Relations*, ed. Eric Helleiner and Jonathan Kirshner, 184–212. Ithaca: Cornell University Press.

Chung, Chien-Peng. 2004. The Shanghai Co-operation Organization: China's Changing Influence in Central Asia. *The China Quarterly* 180: 989–1009.

Clark, Ian. 2014. International Society and China: The Power of Norms and the Norms of Power. *The Chinese Journal of International Politics* 7 (3): 315–340.

Clarke, Michael. 2017. The Belt and Road Initiative: China's New Grand Strategy? *Asia Policy* 24 (1): 71–79.

Converse, Elliot V. 2011. *Circling the Earth: United States Plans for a Postwar Overseas Military Base System, 1942–1948*. Maxwell Air Force Base, AL: Air University Press.

Cox, Robert W. 1987. *Production, Power, and World Order: Social Forces in the Making of History*. New York: Columbia University Press.

Cumings, Bruce. 2009. *Dominion from Sea to Sea: Pacific Ascendancy and American Power*. New Haven: Yale University Press.

Curran, Enda. 2023. China's Difficult Challenge to Reach the Middle. *Bloomberg*, October 24.

Deng, Yong. 2001. Hegemon on the Offensive: Chinese Perspectives on US Global Strategy. *Political Science Quarterly* 116 (3): 343–365.

Economy, Elizabeth C. 2018. *The Third Revolution: Xi Jinping and the New Chinese State*. Oxford: Oxford University Press.

Economy, Elizabeth C., and Michael Levi. 2014. *By All Means Necessary: How Chinas Resource Quest is Changing the World*. Oxford: Oxford University Press.

Faiz, Abbas. 2019. Is China's Belt and Road Initiative Undermining Human Rights?, *The Diplomat*, June 7.

Fenby, Jonathan. 2012. *Tiger Head, Snake Tails: China Today, How It Got There and Why It Has to Change*. London: Simon & Schuster.

Gaddis, John L. 1982. *Strategies of Containment: A Critical Appraisal of Postwar American Security Policy*. Oxford: Oxford University Press.

Gelpern, Anna. 2021. How China Lends: A Rare Look into 100 Debt Contracts with Foreign Governments. *Center for Global Development*, March. https://www.cgdev.org/sites/default/fles/how-chinalends-rare-look-100-debt-contracts-foreign-governments.pdf. Accessed 1 Apr.

Glyn Andrew, Hughes Alan, Lipietz Alain, and Singh Ajit. 1990. The Rise and Fall of the Golden Age. In *The Golden Age of Capitalism: Reinterpreting the Postwar Experience*, ed. Stephen Marglin and Juliet Schor, 39–125. Clarendon Press.

Gries, Peter H., Qingmin Zhang, H. Michael. Crowson, and Huajian Cai. 2011. Patriotism, Nationalism and China's US Policy: Structures and Consequences of Chinese National Identity. *The China Quarterly* 205: 1–17.

Halper, Stefan. 2012. *The Beijing Consensus: How China's Authoritarian Model Will Dominate the Twenty-First Century*. New York: Basic Books.

Heilmann, Sebatian, and Lea Shih. 2013. *The Rise of Industrial Policy in China, 1978–2012*. Trier: University of Trier.

Hillman, Jonathan E. 2018. China's Belt and Road Initiative: Five Years Later. *Center for Strategic and International Studies*, https://www.csis.org/ana lysis/chinas-belt-and-road-initiative-fve-years-later-0. Accessed 25 Jan.

Hillman, Jonathan E. 2020. *The Emperor's New Road: China and the Project of the Century*. New Haven: Yale University Press.

Hogan, Michael J. 1987. *The Marshall Plan: America, Britain, and the Reconstruction of Western Europe, 1947–1952*. Cambridge: Cambridge University Press.

Holmes, James R. 2012. China's Monroe Doctrine. *The Diplomat*, June 22, 2012, https://thediplomat.com/2012/06/chinas-monroe-doctrine/. Accessed 23 June.

Ikenberry, G. John. 2011. The Future of the Liberal World Order. *Foreign Affairs* 90 (3): 56–68.

Ip, Greg. 2023. Why Xi Can No Longer Brag About the Chinese Economy. *Wall Street Journal*, November 14.

Kaplan, Robert. 2019. A New Cold War Has Begun. *Foreign Policy*, January 7.

Kang, David C. 2003. Getting Asia Wrong: The Need for New Analytical Frameworks. *International Security* 27 (4): 57–85.

Kanno-Youngs, Zolan and Sanger, David E. 2021. Biden Speaks with Xi Amid Low Point in U.S.-China Relations. *New York Times*, September 10.

Kindleberger, Charles P. 1973. The World in Depression 1929–1939. Berkeley: University of California Press.

Kirshner, Jonathan. 2006. Globalization and National Security. In *Globalization and National Security*, ed. Jonathan Kirshner, 1–33. London: Routledge.

Kissinger, Henry. 1994. *Diplomacy*. New York: Simon and Schuster.

Lardy, Nicholas R. 2002. *Integrating China into the Global Economy*. Washington: Brookings Institute.

Ling, Jin. 2015. The 'New Silk Road' Initiative: China's Marshall Plan? *China International Studies* 50: 70–83.

Lampton, David M. 2015. Xi Jinping and the National Security Commission: Policy Coordination and Political Power. *Journal of Contemporary China* 24 (95): 759–777.

Li, Keqiang. 2014. *Speech by H.E. Li Keqiang at the Opening Plenary of the Boao Forum for Asia Annual Conference 2014*. 10 April.

Lieven, Anotol. 2020. Climate Change and the Nation State: The Case for Nationalism in a Warming World. Oxford: Oxford University Press.

Lipset, Seymour M. 1996. *American Exceptionalism: A Double-edged Sword*. New York: W. W. Norton.

Luttwak, Edward. 1990. From Geopolitics to Geoeconomics. *The National Interest (Summer)*: 17–23.

Maddison, Angus. 2002. The Nature of US Economic Leadership: A Historical and Comparative View. In *Two Hegemonies: Britain 1846–1914 and the United States 1941–2001*, ed. K. Patrick, 183–197. O'Brien and Armand Cleese. Farnham: Ashgate.

Mardell, Jacob. 2017. The "Community of Common Destiny" in Xi Jinping's New Era. *The Diplomat*, October 25.

Mearsheimer, John J. 2001. *The Tragedy of Great Power Politics*. New York: W.W. Norton.

Micklethwait, John, and Adrian Wooldridge. 2014. The State of the State: The Global Contest for the Future of Government. *Foreign Affairs* 93 (4): 118–132.

Miller, Tom. 2017. *China's Asian Dream: Empire Building Along the New Silk Road*. London: Zed Books.

Ministry of Foreign Affairs (MoF). 2013. *President Xi Jinping Delivers Important Speech and Proposes to Build a Silk Road Economic Belt with Central Asian Countries*. Beijing: MoF, September https://www.fmprc.gov.cn/mfa_eng/topics_665678/xjpfwzysiesgjtfhshzzfh_665686/t1076334.shtml. Accessed 1 Oct.

Mosher, Steven W. 2000. *Hegemon: China's Plan to Dominate Asia and the World*. San Francisco: Encounter Books.

Owen, John M., and Michael Poznansky. 2014. When Does America Drop Dictators?'. *European Journal of International Relations* 20 (4): 1072–1099.

Parks, Brad. 2019. Chinese Leadership and the Future of BRI: What Key Decisions Lie Ahead? *Center for Global Development*, July 24. https://www.cgdev.org/publication/chinese-leadership-and-future-bri-what-key-decisions-lie-ahead. Accessed 25 July.

Peck, Jamie and Zhang, Juny. 2013. A Variety of Capitalism ... with Chinese Characteristics?', *Journal of Economic Geography* 13 (3): 357–396.

Pillsbury, Michael. 2015. *The Hundred-year Marathon: China's Secret Strategy to Replace America as the Global Superpower*. New York: Henry Holt.

Pollard, Robert A. 1985. *Economic Security and the Origins of the Cold War, 1945–1950*. New York: Columbia University Press.

Pyle, Kenneth B. 2007. *Japan Rising: The Resurgence of Japanese Power and Purpose*. New York: Public Affairs.

Qin, Y. 2011. Development of International Relations theory in China: progress through debates. *International Relations of the Asia-Pacific* 11 (2): 231–257.

Refinitiv. 2020. BRI Connect: Fighting COVID-19 with Infrastructure, November, https://www.refinitiv.com/content/dam/marketing/en_us/documents/reports/belt-and-road-initiative-in-numbers-issue-5.pdf. Accessed 1 Dec.

Ruggie, John G. 1992. Multilateralism: The Anatomy of an Institution. *International Organization* 46 (3): 561–598.

Savage, Charlie, Jonathan Swan, and Maggie Haberman. 2023. *A New Tax on Imports and a Split from China: Trump's 2025 Trade Agenda*. New York Times, December 26.

Sherwin, Martin J. 2020. *Gambling with Armageddon: Nuclear Roulette from Hiroshima to the Cuban Missile Crisis, 1945–1962*. New York: Alfred A. Knopf.

Silk Road Fund (SFR). 2021. About us, http://www.silkroadfund.com.cn/enweb/23775/23767/index.html. Accessed 12 May 2021.

Silver, Beverly J., and Giovanni Arrighi. 2003. Polanyi's "Double Movement": The Belle époques of British and US Hegemony Compared. *Politics and Society* 31 (2): 325–355.

Steil, Benn. 2013. *The Battle of Bretton Woods*. Princeton: Princeton University Press.

Steinfeld, Edward. 2010. *Playing Our Game: Why China's Rise Doesn't Threaten the West*. Oxford University Press.

Stromseth, Jonathan. 2019. *Don't Make Us Choose: Southeast Asia in the Throes of US-China Rivalry*. Washington: Brookings Institution.

Stubbs, Richard. 2005. *Rethinking Asia's Economic Miracle*. Basingstoke: Palgrave.

Szamosszegi, Andrew, and Cole Kyle. 2011. *An Analysis of State-owned Enterprises and State Capitalism in China*. Washington: Capital Trade.

Tabb, William K. 1995. *The Postwar Japanese System: Cultural Economy and Economic Transformation*. New York: Oxford University Press.

United Nations Development Programme. 2016. Demand-Driven Data: How Partner Countries are Gathering Chinese Development Cooperation Information. https://www.cn.undp.org/content/china/en/home/library/south-south-cooperation/demand-driven-data---how-partner-countries-are-gathering-chinese.html. Accessed 22 Sep.

Van Ness, Peter. 1970. *Revolution and Chinese Foreign Policy: Peking's Support for Wars of National Liberation*. Berkley: University of California Press.

Vermeiren, Mattias. 2013. Foreign Exchange Accumulation and the Entrapment of Chinese Monetary Power: Towards a Balanced Growth Regime? *New Political Economy* 18 (5): 680–714.

Walsh, Michael. 2018. China's Belt and Road Initiative and Just What it Means to Sign On. *ABC News*, December 1, 2018, https://www.abc.net.au/news/2018-12-01/china-belt-and-road-what-does-it-meanwhen-countries-sign-on/10562374. Accessed December 2.

Wang, Zhen. 2015. China's Alternative Diplomacy. *The Diplomat*, January 30.

Wei, Gu. 2009. China May Marshal Reserves to Fund African Demand. *Reuters*, August 12, https://www.reuters.com/article/column-china-idUSLB404562 20090812. Accessed 13 Aug.

Weldes, Jutta. 1996. Constructing National Interests. *European Journal of International Relations* 2 (3): 275–318.

Whitley, Richard. 2009. US Capitalism: A Tarnished Model? *Academy of Management Perspectives* 23 (2): 11–22.

Winter, Tim. 2019. *Geocultural Power: China's Quest to Revive the Silk Roads for the Twenty-First Century*. Chicago: University of Chicago Press.

Xi, Jinping. 2014a. New Asian Security Concept for New Progress in Security Cooperation. *Ministry of Foreign Affairs of the People's Republic of China*. http://www.fmprc.gov.cn/mfa_eng/zxxx_662805/t1159951.shtml.

Xi, Jinping. 2014b. Connectivity Spreadheads Development and Partnership Enables Cooperation. *Embassy of the People's Republic of China in the Republic of Indonesia*. https://www.fmprc.gov.cn/ce/ceindo/eng/jrzg/t12 11795.htm. Accessed 11 Aug.

Yan, Xuetong. 2021. Becoming Strong: The New Chinese Foreign Policy'. *Foreign Affairs* 100 (4): 40–47.

Yuan, Jirong. 2009. "Chinese Marshall Plan" a Sound Notion. *Global Times*, April 22, 2009, https://www.globaltimes.cn/content/427625.shtml.

Zhang, Feng. 2013. The Rise of Chinese Exceptionalism in International Relations. *European Journal of International Relations* 19 (2): 305–328.

Zhao, Tingyang. 2009. A Political World Philosophy in Terms of All-Under-Heaven (Tian-Xia). *Diogenes* 56 (1): 5–18.

Zhou, Jiayi, Hallding, Karl and Han, Guoyi. 2015. The Trouble with China's 'One Belt One Road' Strategy'. *The Diplomat*, June 26, https://thediplomat.com/2015/06/the-trouble-with-the-chinese-marshall-plan-strategy/

CHAPTER 5

The Maritime Silk Road Initiative and Its Implications for China's Regional Policy

Charles Chong-Han Wu

5.1 Introduction

Several case studies and datasets presented in multiple research designs have already identified salient issues regarding territorial integrity, and disputes over territory are more likely than other issues to be reciprocated, remain unsolved, cause fatalities, and even escalate to war. In light of previous findings and research, a central question has yet to be completely answered: Why do Association of Southeast Asian Nations

---

This chapter is an updated version of the journal article: Wu, C.CH. "The Maritime Silk Road Initiative and Its Implications for China's Regional Policy." *Chin. Polit. Sci. Rev.* 8, 63–83 (2023). https://doi.org/10.1007/s41111-022-00209-5

C. C.-H. Wu (✉)
Department of Diplomacy, National Chengchi University, Taipei, Taiwan, ROC
e-mail: chonghan@nccu.edu.tw

© The Author(s), under exclusive license to Springer Nature Switzerland AG 2025
K. G.Cai et al. (eds.), *China and Global Economic Governance, Volume I: China's BRI & AIIB and Global Economic Governance*, Politics and Development of Contemporary China,
https://doi.org/10.1007/978-3-031-73212-6_5

(ASEAN) members adopt conciliatory attitudes in maritime disputes and placate Beijing while the disputed sovereignty over the South China Sea (SCS) remains unsettled? A major example is the president of the Philippines, Rodrigo Duterte, who has set aside the unanimous rulings found against China and sought a more constructive bilateral relationship with Beijing. What is the driving force that encourages cooperative behavior among Beijing and Southeast Asian nations in these disputed waters? More specifically, how is it possible to identify if countries are sincere in reaching a new consensual position on the maritime issues and disputes in this region when studying states' behavior in Southeast Asia in light of China's "Belt and Road Initiative" (BRI)?[1]

This study employs empirical evidence to analyze the above questions, showing that even though territorial disagreements remain unresolved, both Beijing and ASEAN countries have switched their focus away from the roadblocks toward negotiated settlement. Because peace and security have been viewed as major concerns in the South China Sea, ASEAN has taken the leading role in proposing several initiatives aimed at decreasing tensions and constructing rules and norms among the claimant countries. Moreover, the Chinese government's message to ASEAN neighbors is that China, under Xi Jinping, remains dedicated to "peaceful and sustainable development."[2] More cooperative and peaceful foreign policy tools have been introduced between Beijing and ASEAN members to solve low-politics maritime disputes (such as fisheries) and high-politics disputes (such as territory).[3]

The Belt and Road Initiative, including the "Silk Road Economic Belt" (SREB) and "China's Maritime Silk Road Initiative" (MSRI), are popular projects involving broad infrastructure items and cooperative strategies. This paper attempts to demonstrate the pacifying effects provided by

---

[1] The author has attempted not to adopt the "Belt and Road Initiative" as a whole, but to separate the discussions of how "Maritime Silk Road Initiative" (MSRI) offers a peaceful mechanism for China and the Philippines to achieve a more corporative bilateral relation. For the political and economic implications of BRI and MSRI, please see (Blanchard 2018). For China's SCS policy, please see (Kuik 2017). For the increasing conflicts between the US and China in the SCS, please see (Hu 2021).

[2] Xi Jingping gave an important talk relating to foreign affairs in Beijing on November 29, 2014. Available at: https://www.fmprc.gov.cn/mfa_eng/zxxx_662805/t1215680.shtml.

[3] Cooperative management of international maritime disputes is a major theme of the "1982 United Nations Convention on the Law of the Sea" (UNCLOS).

MSRI to countries in Southeast Asia, especially focusing on the case of the Philippines, which has experienced the most continuous friction over maritime boundaries with China. The author also examines economic, political, and trade issues associated with China's proposals, exploring opportunities for aquaculture collaboration, and seeking to explain how joint development can solve territorial disputes.

5.2 Theoretical Arguments of Territorial Peace

Territorial disputes have been considered the most salient of all issues in the study of international conflict (Huth 1998, Senese and Vasquez 2008). There has been an increasing academic attention to the question of how states' territorial interests might influence interstate, and/or intrastate, conflict, and cooperation in modern world politics. Since territorial interests are viewed as incompatible interests with both tangible and intangible factors, state leaders become even more resistant and intolerant toward the issue of conflicted territories. States leaders show less willingness to make concessions over territorial threats and more resolved to use military force to settle territorial disputes (Hensel 1996). In other words, territorial disputes significantly raise the risk of militarized conflict, and leaders place higher utility on controlling disputed territory and mobilizing domestic support and military forces for disputed territorial claims (Huth and Allee 2002, p. 82).

Wars are also significantly correlated with territorial issues among states. John Vasquez mentioned in his early work that territorial disputes are a distinctly important factor in explaining both conflict and war (Vasquez 1995). Senese and Vasquez inform us that "pairs of states with an outstanding territorial claim are significantly more likely to engage in militarized disputes, while states that have territorial "Militarized Interstate Disputes" (MIDs) have a greater probability of going to war within five years" (Senese and Vasquez 2008, p. 88). They also point out that "non-contiguous foes are three times more likely to escalate territorial disputes to war than contiguous foes" (Senese and Vasquez 2008). The "steps-to-war" argument has been proved with empirical evidence by realists, who argue that territory should be viewed as a source of power in high politics, and decision-makers will defend their interests over what they view as sovereign territory.

By applying theoretical models to explain the steps-to-war phenomenon, it is possible to discover why states and decision-makers are inflexible on the intervention of territorial integrity and sovereignty issues. Most and Starr's model of "opportunity and willingness" helps us understand that bordering states face "greater uncertainty in their relations than more distant states, exacerbating the well-known security dilemma and leading to the outbreak of conflict" (Most and Starr 2015, pp. 23–46). The opportunity and willingness model helps explain the "nice law" that "joint necessary conditions should be considered when studying territorial disputes and wars" (Starr 2015, p. 42), because geographic proximity is correlated with various measures of conflict onsets and escalations (Diehl 1985, Senese 1996). For instance, geographically contiguous adversaries are more likely to become involved in armed conflict and escalate their disputes to more serious levels. In fact, countries "bordering a belligerent adversary in an ongoing war are more likely to go to war than are other states" (Siverson and Starr 1991, p. 73). The correlations between geographic proximity and conflict/war have notified us that "not only because of the link to military capabilities and opportunities to use force, but also because contiguous countries become involved in disputes over conflicting claims of sovereign rights to bordering territory" (Huth 2000, p. 96).

The second half of the literature on territorial peace theory aims to add more arguments related to domestic conditions while discussing the nuances of territorial peace theory. Scholars in the field also found that countries with peaceful and stable borders are more likely to have a less centralized government, thereby facilitating democratization. As a result of settling the borders, states may reduce the control of governments, switching from autocratic regimes, and becoming more democratic. If states do not fight each other, it is "because the borders between them had to be settled before democracy" (Hutchison and Starr 2017). Thus, previous studies also pointed out in their research that "the removal of territorial threat facilitates the democratization process within those countries" (Hutchison and Starr 2017).

Previous literature on the territorial peace theory also remarked on the significance of domestic political legitimacy when state leaders face potential territorial threats. In most cases, the government facing potential territorial challenges needs to deal with the rival, whether it is through more minimal increases in army personnel, or by pursuing mass conscription (Gibler 2012, p. 167). Hence, territorial threats embed the government with more legitimacy, including unified domestic politics with stronger support from the opposition party, a more centralized public opinion, a centralized party system and institutions, and even a more repressive state (Gibler 2012). Additionally, territorial conflicts also create a strong wave of internal cohesion within the states, and successful involvement in territorial conflicts bring more legitimacy and "rally around the flag" effect to the leaders (Gibler 2012, p. 91, Hutchison 2011). Based on the theoretical and empirical evidence, strong correlations exist between territorial threats and domestic political legitimacy, where the leaders of the state have to carefully handle relevant external influences. It is also important to realize that the failure to respond to threats from abroad risks domestic leader tenure by capture, and ineffective responses also pose inevitable risks for leaders (Starr 2015).

Finally, discussions of the territorial peace theory should also include the application of foreign policy options for secondary states in theoretical investigations. Alternative options among balance of power, bandwagon, or even the highly discussed concept of hedging have been highlighted in the relevant literature. When facing potential territorial challenges from China on SCS issues, it is important to explain the variations in foreign policy behavior by the Southeast Asian states because different foreign policy options will create different results to the territorial issues. What kind of policies will be adopted by the member states facing acute tensions in the SCS? During the last 50 years, most international relations scholars have claimed that balancing is far more common than bandwagoning (Walt 2013, Schweller 1994). However, scholars in this field have increasingly begun to challenge this balancing hypothesis. Research has shown that the theory is "incorrect in its claim for the repetitiveness of strategy and prevalence of balancing in international politics" (Powell 2020, p. 155). These scholars have proposed that in a system of steep hierarchy, bandwagoning replaces balance of power as the main strategy of secondary states, and has historically been the more common of the two (Kang 2007). Bandwagoning predominates in hierarchically ordered political realms, where functional differentiation is low, and influential resources are tightly concentrated in the hands of the dominant power. However, there are still open questions about bandwagoning, especially for the minor powers surrounding the great powers. When studying these issues of the territorial peace theory and the domestic legitimacy of leaders in Southeast Asia, the dichotomy of balancing and bandwagoning offers an overly simplified framework, which cannot be applied to the description of security issues between China and its neighboring states. Hence, there is a strong possibility of a third choice between the two traditional strategies mentioned above: hedging, which offers a timely and practical strategy for the Southeast Asian countries. In general, hedging demonstrates a clear policy of engagement and rapprochement by not choosing sides, and maintaining equal distance from the great powers (Ciorciari 2009, Kuik 2008, 2016, Lim and Cooper 2015, Tessman 2012).

5.2.1 Territorial Peace Theory in Asia

The study of territorial conflicts and peace contains another critical issue in relation to territorial salience and regime types. The territorial peace and regime type discussion has presented us with another interesting puzzle about how democracies maintain peace with each other.[4] A new approach can lead to a new understanding of the application of the democratic peace theory in East Asia. If it is not the regime type that has helped states in this region maintain peace, then there should be another salient issue that explains the peaceful environment among the region's countries. Territorial peace theory demonstrates useful theoretical and empirical validity, helping explain why East Asian countries have maintained a largely peaceful environment and have escaped large-scale conflicts. The explanation can be found in the fact that the removal of territorial issues from the state's agenda substantially changes international and domestic leverage. Hence, by settling territorial issues, states at territorial peace are also likely to have resolved the most dangerous issue on their agenda. States at territorial peace should, therefore, experience fewer, less-intense conflicts, especially over territorial issues with their neighbors.

Sharing a border with fourteen countries in Asia, China has been forced to contend with several issues arising from territorial and border disputes. The Chinese government has incorporated into its grand strategy the leveraging of influence via a hub-and-spoke structure, and the use of the MSRI as a cooperative mechanism to solve potential territorial and maritime disputes. Even though Southeast Asian countries have different concerns, they share common interests in maintaining peace and the uninterrupted flow of maritime trade. While a major war is unlikely, leaders in this region have worked to prevent maritime skirmishes

---

[4] Please see the discussions on the "zone of peace" theory which indicates that the relationship between democratic regimes and international peace might be spurious, and the issue of territorial threat should be considered in peace studies (Gleditsch 2009, 25).

involving patrol boats, fishing trawlers, and research survey vessels from sparking military clashes that may potentially escalate into an unplanned and dangerous crisis. Hence, preventing unwanted minor skirmishes has become the first step in maintaining peace between Beijing and ASEAN members.

There is a relationship between territorial claims and maritime disputes, and understanding the correlations between these two issues has become increasingly important. First, a more peaceful approach to maritime issues may contribute to the improvement of relations over territorial and boundary disputes. China's use of peaceful strategies to solve the SCS issues with claimant countries has effectively mitigated regional tensions. Multiple channels of communication and a sense of shared interests on how to resolve territorial disputes have been built slowly via the MSRI framework and other sustainable development initiatives among China and ASEAN members, especially between Beijing, the Philippines, and Vietnam. Similar approaches have been adopted by leaders in Southeast Asian countries. As the former Vietnamese Prime Minister Nguyen Tan Dung argued in 2015, "A single irresponsible action or instigation of conflict could well lead to the interruption of these huge trade flows, with unforeseeable consequences not only to regional economies but also to the entire world."[5]

Southeast Asia has become China's largest trading partner in 2020.[6] This important factor has spurred Beijing to adopt conciliatory policies in its effort to win the hearts and minds of the region. Many of these efforts fall under the framework of MSRI. In fact, there is a shortage of a specific list of MSRI projects, and the initiative encompasses a sweeping array of policies and projects adopted by Beijing (Blanchard 2018, p. 332). Aware of the limited development in Southeast Asian countries, Chinese policymakers have focused chiefly on building public transportation infrastructure, fueling economic growth through cooperative initiatives, and providing financial assistance to countries along the MSRI route through

---

[5] "Building strategic trust for peace, cooperation and prosperity in the Asia Pacific region," Nguyen Tan Dung, Prime Minister, Vietnam, Shangri-La Dialogue 2015 keynote address. Available at: https://www.iiss.org/en/events/shangri-la-dialogue/archive/sha ngri-la-dialogue-2013-c890/opening-remarks-and-keynote-address-2f46/keynote-address-d176.

[6] Please see "ASEAN becomes China's largest trading partner in 2020, with 7% growth." *Global Times*, January 14, 2021. Available at: https://www.globaltimes.cn/page/202101/1212785.shtml.

the issuing of grants and loans. For instance, Laos lacks basic infrastructure, and many roads and highways stop along the northern border. The government has experienced difficulties in allocating resources to poorer cities and villages. Laos has adopted a development strategy that makes use of Chinese foreign aid to upgrade infrastructure, which will facilitate inter-regional connectivity in the land-locked central regions and allow inland areas to have direct access to the cities near the Chinese border and port facilities in neighboring countries (Miller 2019). This plan can effectively diffuse economic activities across geographic spaces. Hence, the primary goal of the MSRI is to increase the flow of goods and people from China to Southeast Asia by building transportation infrastructure. By doing so, China hopes to establish new global value chains reliant on human capital and greater resources made available to the region. This Chinese policy blueprint is "helping the region quickly integrate with China and the world market" (Blanchard 2018, pp. 349–341).

As Karl Deutsch has shown, countries gradually form a "community" based on a process of integration, which shows a "learning" process with positive incentives to continue and expand such interactions (Deutsch 1957). As such interactions occur, the peoples/states involved become highly interdependent, and they create more mutual trust and reciprocal interests. Applying Deutsch's theoretical arguments, it becomes clear that the major appeal of the MSRI is to build a community and norms that are highly reliant on the hard and soft infrastructure established by the Chinese government, and to facilitate cooperative policies through which regional countries can address various issues.

Meanwhile, the MSRI will continue to propel economic development for countries in the region and provide economic assistance through the "Asian Infrastructure Investment Bank" (AIIB), which will bolster the credibility of regional governments with their own constituents. The AIIB will "facilitate and accelerate infrastructure improvement by providing loans and grants to regional partners" (Yu 2017). While all of the aforementioned arguments are pertinent, this introduces a useful explanation of how the MSRI mitigates strained relationships in the region.

Turning the problem around, it is evident that a more peaceful territorial or border environment may help resolve related fishery or maritime issues. The economic logic is simple enough: "Fishermen will follow fish as they swim across territorial boundaries into the waters of other sovereign states" (Hendrix and Roberts 2017). When a country tries to impose a maritime boundary which does not obtain the recognitions from its rivalries, the boundary issues will precipitate a naval standoff. Most of the resulting MIDs will become so famous in regions of substantial geopolitical imports, and countries will attempt to intervene to protect their national interests with naval forces. From 1993 to 2010, studies have shown that "in the maritime hotspots in the SCS, the Gulf of Aden, and Arabian Sea, countries will compete against each other for geopolitical prominence" (Hendrix and Roberts 2017). From the argument above, it is obvious to argue that territorial issues have a close link with fishery and maritime disputes. A more peaceful and settled boundary environment may create a more stable environment for fishing and maritime resources. It seems obvious that the cost of using force to solve disputes in the SCS issue will be very high, which makes the adoption of liberals' bilateral/multilateral negotiation mechanisms more appealing to countries in the region. In the next sections, evidence of maritime cooperation between Beijing and the Philippines will be illustrated through case studies. Overall, the explanatory mechanisms related to the territorial peace theory, along with the conflict-management rhetoric and bilateral/ multilateral negotiation strategies adopted by both governments, will help the audience of interest build a broader picture of the key aspects of how peaceful territorial/border scenarios lead to a more stable regional order among the major players in the region. In fact, it is important to realize that since territory is literally always of high value, salience, and importance to people, territory raises the possibility of conflict escalation. Recent research has shown that when countries do settle border disputes through treaties which establish agreed boundaries, such settlement will lead to peace (Starr 2013). The causal mechanism between the territorial claims and interstate disputes/peace is the key lesson from this study.

Based on the elaborations, the main concern of the study is the outline of structural effects brought by territorial peace, along with domestic political legitimacy and various foreign policy considerations, focusing on rigorous discussions on balancing, bandwagoning, and/or hedging. Applying the key concepts of the territorial peace theory with the empirical evidence in this study will prudently lead us to look into the nuanced development of maritime and territorial issues in the region.

5.3 The Maritime and Territorial Claims in Asia

In order to demonstrate the salient issues of territorial and maritime claims in this region, it is important to investigate the descriptive statistics of the "Issue Correlates of War" (ICOW).[7] The ICOW project started in 1997 and expanded to include all the territorial claims; it has since identified 618 territorial claims and 267 maritime claims. By comparing the frequency of territorial and maritime claims in Table 5.1 (from 1900 to 2001), it is evident that territorial claims were more common than any other claim in most of the world's regions. In addition, by comparing different regions, it caught our attention that the only area with more maritime claims than territorial claims is the Western Hemisphere, where the percentage of territorial to maritime claims was 134%. The Asia and Oceania regions had only 47 maritime claims, which accounts for about one-fourth of the total territorial claims during the period (28.4%). The percentage of territorial and maritime claims in the Asia and Oceania region is much lower than any other region in the world, and even lower than the average number of total territorial claims to maritime claims in general (28.4%/43.2%). The lower rate of maritime claims indicates that even when there have been tensions over territorial issues for several years in this region, China and other countries showed a certain degree of flexibility by finding peaceful resolutions and a corporative framework to work for joint development. The major reason is that both China and Southeast Asian nations have not contentiously raised the issues of SCS before early 2000, and territorial and maritime quarrels involving neighboring countries have not resulted in an overall confrontational stance, with most of the countries in this area embracing the strategy of maintaining the status quo.

Second, there were more militarized conflicts caused by territorial claims than maritime claims, and previous studies containing territorial and maritime information have also generated significant results regarding this phenomenon. Hensel and Mitchell (2017, p. 133) found that disputing parties "have been more reluctant to settle territorial disputes through international courts"; however, they preferred the use

---

[7] Dataset downloaded at "Issues of Correlate of War" dataset. Available at: http://www.paulhensel.org/icow.html.

Table 5.1 Territorial and maritime claims, 1900–2001

Region	Territorial Claims	Maritime Claims	T/M %
Western Hemisphere	50	67	134
Europe	182	75	41.2
Africa	127	50	39.3
Middle East	94	28	29.7
Asia and Oceania	165	47	28.4
Total	618	267	43.2

Source Dataset can be downloaded from the Issues of Correlates of War dataset. Available at: http://www.paulhensel.org/icow.html
The data for territorial and maritime claims were only available until 2001 from the ICOW webpage

of violent methods to solve territorial issues.[8] Most of the maritime disputes are just bloodless seizures of fishing boats, and most states opted for peaceful resolutions of fishery or maritime issues and sought to resolve disputes through the frameworks of transnational treaties and/or multilateral negotiations.

Fishery disputes have increased tensions among territorial claims. To the best of our knowledge, fishery issues are more likely to be one of numerous subjects at the heart of any major conflict escalation, but fishery disputes in Asia have not demonstrated certain political phenomena. It becomes clear that fishery issues have led to minimal armed conflicts (the number of cases was limited when compared to the overall militarized disputes in Asia), and neighboring countries reacted generally with self-constrained policies.[9] There was only one fishery dispute among 33 armed conflicts that occurred in 2002, while there were five incidents of

[8] Based on their findings, 41.8% of territorial claims from 1900 to 2001 have resulted in at least one militarized interstate dispute, and 28.9% resulted in at least one combat fatality. Nonetheless, only 27.3% of maritime claims resulted in violent MIDs, and only 4.1% of those claims produced fatalities. About their argument and data, please see (Mitchell and Prins 1999, p. 132).

[9] The reason to adopt MIDs 4.0 rather than ICOW is because the data on territorial and maritime claims by ICOW has not been updated yet, and the ratio of territory over maritime claims for the region of Asia and Oceania region is not completely clear. Besides, MIDs 4.0 has been recognized as the most available dataset of MIDs (Palmer et al. 2015).

fisheries-related MIDs among 51 cases of militarized disputes in 2003.[10] Theoretically speaking, fishery-related tensions could escalate to global maritime conflicts in the future, and are more likely to cause diplomatic rows and endanger border and trade relations; however, there is no clear evidence that shows that fishery-related disputes in Asia will lead to war in the future. Furthermore, countries are unlikely to risk interdependent trade and business interests or tear apart their integrated economic relationships due to trivial fishery disputes. Apparently, the huge economic benefits of MSRI to the Chinese government, along with the hard and soft infrastructure under the MSRI blueprint, will ease tensions among countries neighboring China.

While there might be an upward trend of territorial and maritime claims, Beijing has demonstrated a strong commitment to enhance mutual political trust and understanding since 2013 and has been supportive of important regional cooperation with countries in Southeast Asia. For instance, Premier Li Keqiang delivered a media interview to ASEAN countries, showing Beijing's willingness to develop more comprehensive cooperation on economic and trade relations with ASEAN countries.[11] Based on the cooperative framework, ASEAN countries became either more economically dependent on China or sought to accommodate a more corporative atmosphere under the MSRI framework. Even though the Philippines, which has unilaterally challenged the legality of China's expansive claims in the SCS and submitted the territorial case to the "Arbitral Tribunal" established under "UNCLOS Annex VII of the United Nations Convention on the Law of the Sea," withdrew from the lengthy and controversial process in 2017. As China-ASEAN relations reached a milestone on the 25th Anniversary of China-ASEAN dialogue, members of ASEAN began to adopt more cooperative attitudes toward China's BRI.[12]

---

[10] Fishery disputes are calculated by the author, using the codebook of the Correlates of War project (MIDs 4.0). All other data are adopted from MIDs 4.0. Dataset can be downloaded at http://www.correlatesofwar.org/data-sets/MIDs.

[11] Premier Li Keqiang gives joint written interview to media from ASEAN countries, *ASEAN-China Center*, Oct 9, 2013. Available at: http://www.asean-china-center.org/english/2013-10/09/c_133062698.htm.

[12] Scholars suggest that policymakers should expect less from the MSRI and not worry too much about MSRI's political implications. Please see (Blanchard 2018; Chen 2018). MSRI includes not only the hard infrastructure, but also institutions and personnel exchanges, policy exchanges, and trade and capital flows (Boden 2014; He 2015).

In fact, there are relations between territorial claims and fishery issues. Scholarly works have supported the relevant arguments that "effective cooperation on the issues of low politics—usually seen as 'soft issues'— such as fisheries management and marine environmental protection, could generate strategic trust which will be needed for cooperation on matters of high politics, and maritime disputes in general" (Zhang and Bateman 2017). This is called the *spillover effect*. Even through the lens of the complicated and hard-to-solve issue of territorial disputes, politicians and researchers have long considered cooperation on fishery disputes to be a matter of low politics, which might have a *spillover effect* on other areas of cooperation in the SCS.

Hence, it becomes more important to concentrate precisely on the MSRI's potential inferences for Southeast Asia, using fishery/maritime cooperation as a case study, but not exclusively considering other maritime issues, such as joint development or research. Fishery cooperation among countries is "not a choice but a necessity" when handling the relevant issues involved in territorial disputes (Zhang 2018). Regarding fishery cooperation, it is noteworthy that most of the fishery resources in the SCS are either highly transboundary or migratory species, such as tuna, mackerel, or scads. While many fishing grounds have disappeared, fishermen have to carry out offshore fishing or cross-border fishing. This has resulted in more frequent excessive enforcement and the use of force on cross-border fishing. Fishing disputes thus rise and become another major cause of territorial disputes. Countries with disputed maritime boundaries or fishing disputes are more likely to seek intensive bilateral relations and account for a high percentage of militarized interstate disputes in the region.

What best explains this connection between China's conciliatory fishery policies and the easing of territorial disputes with explanations of the spillover effects? From an international perspective, many observers have attributed this puzzle to Beijing's greater concerns in the region, arguing that Beijing's sovereignty and territorial interests in the SCS are of key importance. However, tensions between Beijing and ASEAN countries decreased after the initiation of the MSRI in 2013. Despite the Chinese government's repeated assertion of its historical fishery and territorial rights as "national interests," China contradictorily demonstrated no intention of confronting the US and other powers in the region. Kuik Cheng-Chwee explained that an assertive territorial policy by the Chinese government "would not be of benefit to China's reputation, and would ultimately lead to further involvement in the South China Sea by the United States and other regional powers, such as Japan, Australia, and India" (Kuik 2017). To prevent that scenario and to secure domestic legitimation and control, Beijing has managed territorial issues in a more amicable manner, such as the cooperative fishing policies. This approach also creates a better scenario for sustainable economic development in contested waters. Thus, it appears that Beijing prefers stable domestic politics along with a peaceful regional order to maintain legitimacy and political survival.

From an interstate perspective, even though China and the Philippines have signed the Memorandum of Understanding on Fisheries Cooperation and the Memorandum of Understanding on Broadening and Deepening Agriculture and Fisheries Cooperation in 2004 and 2007, both sides still encountered accidents related to fishery issues. However, this does not mean that coordination under the created rules and norms have no functions for peace between the two sides. After fishery disputes led to both the 1995 Mischief Reef Incident and the 2012 Scarborough Shoal Incident, Beijing has attempted to mitigate the tensions among China and neighboring countries and also gradually moderated its actions, including self-regulated fishery actions after the middle of 2012 in order to lower the structural pressures caused by varying territorial claims. For instance, the detention of foreign fishing vessels dropped drastically in 2012 (Fravel 2011, p. 305). Beijing has also attempted to repair relations with claimant states by adopting a more conciliatory approach. The recurring summer anti-China protests in Vietnam have prompted Beijing to seek to repair bilateral relations with Hanoi and to reaffirm its willingness to work with ASEAN states. Regional governments have responded positively to the new Chinese approach and have slowly integrated into a peaceful regional order.[13] Above all, the empirical evidence suggests that China's leadership has become aware of "the importance of the balance between its external sovereignty protection (weiquan) and its internal stability maintenance (weiwen)" (Kuik 2017, p. 180).

---

[13] Beijing has aimed to ratify the Port State Measures Agreement (PSMA), which is a UN treaty requiring countries to close their ports to illegal fishing vessels, and to share real-time information to make that possible. PSMA came into effect in 2016 and requires participating nations to restrict the entry of foreign fishing vessels to designated ports. To date, 62 nations plus the European Union are parties to the PSMA, at https://chinadial ogueocean.net/11135-china-psma-illegal-fishing/ [8 July 2020].

However, it is unlikely that the Philippines and other Southeast Asian countries will make major concessions to China in terms of territorial claims and disputes. In contrast, the continued presence of Chinese maritime militias during the Whitsun Reef Incident in April 2021 has urged the Philippine Department of Foreign Affairs' pledge to issue daily diplomatic protests while Chinese vessels appeared in the Philippines' maritime zones (Lendon 2021). Beijing responded that Chinese boats have been fishing near the reef for a long time, and recently some of the vessels have been sheltering in the area. Fortunately, the Whitsun Reef Incident that created minor tensions between Beijing and Manila did not lead to an overall interstate militarized dispute between the two nations. Beijing and the Philippines have urged both sides to "exercise self-restraint in the conduct of activities that would complicate or escalate the disputes and influence peace and stability" (ASEAN 2021). In addition, the bilateral and multilateral framework on fishery and maritime issues, combined with closer interstate communications between Beijing and the Philippines, have helped to stabilize the regional order. It is clear that both sides will use their wisdom to continue collaborations, lowering the tensions created by maritime issues. President Duterte disclosed to the nation for the first time that he had a "verbal agreement" with Chinese President Xi Jinping, allowing Chinese fishing vessels to fish in Philippine Exclusive Economic Zone (EEZ) in the West Philippine Wasters (WPS) immediately after ramming in the Reed Bank of the Filipino fishing vessel F/B Gem-Ver in 2019. Duterte mentioned that "As far as I'm concerned, I'm the owner, and I'm just giving the fishing rights" (Carpio 2021).

Fishing activities and cooperation are arguably less sensitive than other territorial disputes in the SCS, and most neighboring countries have adopted cooperative behavior in less sensitive areas. Making decisions to solve high-politics issues, such as territorial boundaries and disputed sea claims, would clearly be a time-consuming process; the exploitation of fish is less costly and sensitive than any other disputed issue, such as territorial integrity. Therefore, efficient fishery planning is more viable and quickly resolved among countries in the SCS. Cooperation might create more high-profile compliance, such as the joint development of maritime resources, especially when the overlapping area involves the issue of sovereignty claims over land. Using China and Japan as an example, Nguyen argued that "Beijing and Tokyo had concluded a fishery arrangement more than a decade before they reached a principled consensus on oil and gas exploitation in 2008" (Nguyen 2012). The area of joint development and defined consensus on oil and gas is located within the provisional measure zone, established by the agreement on fisheries between Beijing and Tokyo, which entered into force on June 6, 2000.[14] This convincing evidence has revealed how fishery/maritime collaboration can generate such *spillover effects* and trigger more cooperation in the field of territorial issues. In a broad sense, relative peace and stability can be ascribed to the peaceful mechanisms provided by the MSRI.

Within the China-ASEAN corporative framework, one of the most representative mechanisms that has made China more conciliatory is the concept of the Code of Conduct on the South China Sea (COC). Starting in the 1990s, ASEAN members learned how to engage China through multilateral negotiations under the COC framework, which committed all countries to the peaceful resolution of outstanding disputes. This mechanism aims to minimize the risk of a conflict spiral, which can lead to a conventional conflict. Even ASEAN has finally sought to obtain China's consent to a biding COC in the South China Sea in 2002, which is earlier than the employment of MSRI; the implementation can be seen with some causal effects from the COC to the reduction of conflict and improvement of regional relations. This political phenomenon can also be buttressed by the proposed project that all sides negotiate in good faith and abide by the COC framework. A further bilateral mechanism called the Declaration on the Conduct of Parties in the South China Sea (DOC) was agreed upon between Beijing and ASEAN members.

The DOC is intended to bring both China and ASEAN countries into a framework of international law, but no progress was made before 2010–2011. When the BRI and MSRI were first introduced in 2013, Beijing rephrased its position and adjusted its approach to the COC and the DOC. Four new points guided China's approach toward the COC, and Chinese Foreign Minister Wang Yi persuaded ASEAN countries that China would take the COC seriously. Beijing has sincerely demonstrated a good neighbor policy to calm discontent and suspicion in the region. One prominent example was that Beijing announced the end of a fishing blockade around the Scarborough Shoal in July 2016, allowing the access of Filipino fisherman. Furthermore, in order to preserve a peaceful regional order, the foreign ministers of ASEAN endorsed a framework for

---

[14] For more evidence for supporting the causal logic between the argument, please see (Kim 2004, pp. 338–347; Gao 2009).

a Code of Conduct on the South China Sea (COC) in Manila in August 2017.

An additional case study of China-Philippines maritime cooperation will be examined in the next section to support the argument above.

5.4 Beijing's Maritime Cooperation with Manila

Fishery disputes and maritime incidents in the SCS have created threats to regional stability, and the Chinese government has been keenly aware of these risks. The conflicts involve countries that do not often consider themselves in interstate competition; for example, the Philippines has assigned a higher salience value to fishery and maritime disputes in the SCS than to other issues. Empirical evidence demonstrates that the Philippines only engaged in 0.4 percent of total MIDs involving all other issues, but engaged in 5 percent of fishery MIDs from 1993 to 2001 (Hendrix and Roberts 2017). Most fishery MIDs are between the Philippine and Chinese fishermen. This is the chief reason why this project focuses on bilateral relations between China and the Philippines.

In addition, the China-Philippines conflict over marine fishery resources has been a growing security concern in recent decades. One of the critical examples of conflict was the Philippine Navy's detention of Chinese fishing vessels near the disputed Scarborough Shoal in April 2012. Due to the harassment of Chinese fishing vessels, the Philippines was threatened by China's provocative behavior in this area, and thus decided to proactively protect its security interests with a two-pronged strategy in the face of China's expansive claims and aggressive actions in the disputed SCS. Manila, on the one hand, continued bilateral negotiations with China; on the other hand, it actively multilateralized the maritime disputes within the ASEAN processes and beyond. Manila's most important step in internationalizing the maritime dispute was its application for a special Arbitral Tribunal, which ultimately gained international legitimacy by rebuking China after the verdict of the SCS Arbitration was issued on July 12, 2016 (Tseng 2017). Developments before and after the Award of the SCS Arbitration manifested Manila's two-pronged strategy in dealing with Beijing.

On June 14, 2016, China attempted to mitigate the potential negative impacts of the arbitration by hosting a special meeting with all ASEAN states in Kunming, but it was reported that diplomatic struggles had occurred during the meeting between China and ASEAN over whether the final joint statement, consented to by ASEAN states, with strong wording referring to recent and ongoing developments in the SCS would be read out on Chinese soil. Although China managed to force the statement to be withdrawn a few hours after its release, the statement explicitly outlined concerns on the impact of China's actions in the SCS; the statement was instead released by individual states after the meeting (Thayer 2016).

Although the arbitration results proved favorable to the Philippines, Manila responded in a restrained manner and signaled its willingness to continue bilateral talks with China over the SCS issues. Meanwhile, Manila attempted to include the arbitration ruling in the joint statement of the 49th ASEAN Foreign Minister's Meeting, held in Laos in 2016, to bolster its position in the international community and vis-à-vis China.[15] Since the president of the Philippines, Duterte, tried to extend an olive branch to China and advocated the shelving of the Hague rulings on the issue of the SCS, the possibility of a peaceful and cooperative approach to solving the maritime issues between Beijing and Manila increased.

Most of the recurrent maritime conflicts are related to cross-boundary fishing. For China, the high level of fishing subsidies offered by Beijing to offshore fishermen has led to an increasing number of fishing disputes involving Chinese fishermen in regional waters (Zhang and Wu 2017). Based on the data, China has a growing number of fishermen and vessels plying in the SCS, with 672,416 motorized fishing vessels, including 187,211 marine fishing vessels and 2,512 deep-water fishing vessels" (Bureau of Fisheries of China 2016). Before the MSRI was promoted, the transformation of the fishery industry trended away from inshore fishing to offshore fishing. In Guangzhou, for example, inshore fishing accounted for only 60 percent of the total catch in 2013. In fact, the increase in offshore fishing has been vigorously promoted and subsidized by the Chinese government. However, this increase has become one of the major causes of potential fishery disputes between China and neighboring countries.

---

[15] During the 23rd ASEAN Regional Forum, member states of ASEAN urged "all parties to work expeditiously for the early adoption of an effective Code of Conduct (COC)." Political leaders also indicated concerns about China's territorial reclamations and escalation of activities in the SCS. Please see Chairman's Statement of the 23rd ASEAN Regional Forum, *ASEAN Regional Forum,* July 26, 2016. Available at: https://asean.org/wp-content/uploads/2016/07/Chairmans-Statement-of-the-23rd-ASEAN-Regional-Forum_FINAL.pdf.

To reduce fishery disputes and maritime issues, Beijing has emphasized the importance of sustainable development in its maritime policy and made it a state strategy in the 12th and 13th National Five-Year Plans. Within the official documents, "marine fishery has been identified as one of the key areas for international cooperation, endorsed by officials from both central ministries and China's major fishing provinces" (Zhang and Wu 2017, p. 221). After the 12th National Five-Year Plan was announced, the State Council held its first meeting related to the fishery issues, and the Chinese government published an instruction on promoting healthy and sustainable marine development in 2013. This is the first time that the Chinese government presented a country-level document on marine policy (Zhang and Wu 2017, p. 221).

Beijing has repeatedly indicated its willingness to consider bilateral joint development. Except for the government policies implemented at the domestic level, China's marine governance also abides by international and regional agreements at the interstate level, such as the "Code of Conduct on Responsible Fishery" and over 20 bilateral fishery agreements. In fact, it is not the first time that Beijing has achieved successful cooperation under a joint maritime development framework. As early as 2005, the Philippine President Arroyo became the primary driver for ASEAN's coordinated efforts to maintain peaceful resolution, signing an agreement on "Joint Marine Seismic Undertaking" (JMSU) in certain areas of the SCS between the "China National Offshore Oil Corporation" (CNOOC) and the "Philippine National Oil Corporation" (PNOC).[16] Without primary consultation with other ASEAN members, the Philippines took the lead in joint development initiatives in the SCS with Beijing.[17]

---

[16] Based on the agreement, the JMSU between China and the Philippines was only valid for three years, which expired in 2008 and has not been renewed since (Santamaria 2016).

[17] President Duterte's abandoned the cooperation on oil and gas development project with China due to renewed conflicts over sovereignty in the South China Sea. However, Beijing expressed readiness to collaborate with the Marcos Jr. administration, aiming to advance negotiations and achieve meaningful progress (Khaliq 2022). Marcos Jr. cautioned against the significant challenges presented by an increasingly assertive China to collaborative oil exploration efforts, and expressed disappointment over the limited progress achieved in the talks (Lema et al. 2023).

However, the close collaboration between Beijing and Manila over the JMSU framework has not always been stable after the Arroyo administration. An opposition figure during the Arroyo administration, President Aquino criticized former President Arroyo's policy of tilting toward China, generating several high-level cases of shady deals, such as the JMSU and the controversial National Broadband Network Project with the Chinese-owned ZTE. The asymmetrical national capabilities and domestic concerns urged Aquino to adopt a more balancing strategy toward Beijing, especially on the South China Sea issues (Tran 2019). However, due to budget constraints, the difficulties in receiving arms sales from the US, and the strong commitments from the US military assistance in response to the potential conflicts in the SCS, the Aquino administration adopted a hardline stance on the South China Sea without harming its economic ties with Beijing (Tran 2019, p. 629). The up and down of the collaborations clearly demonstrated two major concerns for the Aquino administration. First, there are strong connections between foreign policy decision-making and domestic support. Leaders should focus on national support and domestic public opinion while modifying their foreign policy decision-making. Second, pure balancing or bandwagoning China's policies may not benefit the national interests of the Philippines, while a more practical hedging policy, economic ties with China, and strong security linkages with the US may help the leaders to achieve its goal of political survival.

In addition to bilateral coordination, China's preference to undertake and practice global fishery norms and regulations in global governance could mark a step forward for the ocean's protection. Beijing has begun the reform of fishery policies in a more multilateral manner since the announcement of MSRI, and the "China Maritime Surveillance" (CMS) was tasked with implementing the mission of protecting China's extensive EEZ. Several cooperative mechanisms have been implemented under CMS guidance, including a serious and detailed "zero growth" plan to control fishing capacity, along with a summer ban on fishing in both the Bohai and the SCS. Moreover, with more specific regulations, the "Fisheries Law Enforcement Command" (FLEC) has been established by the government in order to bring Chinese fisheries management in line with international standards with the domestic needs for fisheries management. China has attempted to lower its assertive conduct in regional and/or global fisheries, with the reduction of using fishery issues as a stick to compel the neighbors. China now has better transparency, publishing statistics, and official records, such as the annual Chinese Fisheries Yearbook, which helps the government and fisheries sectors fulfill their international responsibilities (Goldstein 2013).

The global community has long harbored doubts about China's MSRI and its significance to regional stability, even though scholars have demonstrated the stabilizing outcomes of MSRI. Bilateral cooperation between China and the surrounding countries has clearly shown the positive outcomes brought by the MSRI. For instance, Duterte announced his intention to compromise with China after he was elected president of the Philippines in May 2016. Duterte then accepted an invitation from the Chinese ambassador and chose China for his first state visit in October 2016. President Xi viewed the Filipinos as "brothers who could appropriately handle disputes," and Duterte replied positively, showing that the two countries have "entered a new spring" and that the two countries would seek a peaceful resolution of SCS disputes. Furthermore, Duterte sent out several friendly signals to Beijing, demonstrating that the Philippines intends to join China's MSRI. By accepting US$9 billion in low-interest loans from Beijing, Duterte announced that the Philippine fishermen will resume fishing at Scarborough Shoal in the SCS with Beijing's permission. These political developments demonstrate that Duterte has starkly different policies from his predecessor toward China's maritime behavior and bilateral relations. This notable cooperation between Beijing and Manila illustrates the key causal mechanisms and better empirical and logical support for asserted causal inferences in this project.

President Duterte has played down concerns over China's militarization in the SCS, and has opted not to pressure Beijing over its maritime activities in return for economic concessions from China, which has resulted in an increase in bilateral cooperation between Manila and Beijing. For example, the Chinese government agency tasked with aquaculture administration has signed an MOU on "China-Philippines Cooperation of Fisheries Technical Training and Exchange," and donated 100,000 Leopard Coral Grouper seeds to the Philippines between 2017 and 2019.

During the second meeting of the "China-Philippines Joint Committee on Fisheries" (JCF) held in Manila, Beijing and Manila reached preliminary consensus on carrying out "technical training and exchange activities, facilitating business cooperation, bolstering maritime culture, and strengthening aquatic product processing, among other things" (Ministry of Agriculture 2017). The second meeting of JCF also found success when negotiators reached a mutual understanding and maritime cooperation agreement. Various forms of fishery and maritime cooperation already existed between China and the Philippines, which eased tensions between the two countries. For instance, Duterte made a verbal agreement with Xi in 2016 that allowed fishermen from both the Philippines and China access to fishing areas in each other's waters. On July 15, 2019, Duterte announced in his fourth state of the nation address that he would allow Chinese fishermen to fish in Philippine waters, which has been viewed as the final confirmation that both sides were ready to move to a more stable and sustainable cooperative framework on fishing and maritime issues. On July 14, 2020, top diplomats from China and the Philippines held a teleconference reaffirming that both sides agreed to "continue to manage issues of concern and promote maritime cooperation in a friendly consultation" (Venzon 2020). The developments will encourage more investment and maximize gains, enhance deeper cooperation, and peaceful settlement on relevant territorial and maritime disputes. This is additional evidence showing how the MSRI can solve maritime disputes between Beijing and Manila.

The cooperation between Beijing and Manila experienced more or less hurdles during President Ferdinand Marcos Jr. In 2023, Marcos Jr. adopted a notable shift in its foreign policy, particularly in relations with China, as maritime disputes in the South China Sea intensified. This period witnessed a series of events that underscored the evolving dynamics between the Philippines and China, coupled with the Philippines' strategic alignment with the United States. The Philippines granted the United States expanded access to four military bases under the 2014 Enhanced Defense Cooperation Agreement (EDCA) (Vergun 2023). This move marked a clear strategic pivot, signaling the Philippines' intent to enhance its defense capabilities in response to regional security concerns, particularly those involving China (Renato 2022, 258). Most seriously, the Philippines accused China's coastguard of directing a "military-grade laser" at Filipino troops aboard a grounded warship in the disputed Second Thomas Shoal (Morales and Lema 2023). This issue led to the summoning of China's ambassador by President Marcos, highlighting a more assertive response to perceived threats. Even though the bilateral relations between the Philippines and China have experienced instabilities, the regional security and political atmosphere have still been under control by both sides.

5.5 Conclusion

The territorial peace theory is broad and applicable to many different regions and the literature. Even though China's maritime assertiveness creates instability in the system, Beijing has consistently employed technocratic cooperation with its neighbors through innovative bilateral and multilateral maritime cooperation in this volatile region. This study uses territorial peace theory to explain important changes in territorial issues between China and neighboring countries. This study has provided general discussions on the MSRI and aims to connect previous studies on how the MSRI's internal and external objectives have improved regional relations and order, including the implementation of fishery cooperation frameworks. The main argument illustrates the pacifying effects of the MSRI on countries in Asia, which has resulted in decreased tensions between China and neighboring countries. Finally, this study has also explained the implications of the MSRI, with a specific focus on the security impact of MSRI's aquaculture and maritime factors.

Based on liberalist thinking, the linkage between economic interdependence and peace has proved that more trade will bring more peace (Oneal and Russett 1999, Russett and Oneal 2001). If the liberal theoretical arguments are robust, the conditions for peace in Southeast Asia exist, since all states in the region are engaged in interdependent economic ties with Beijing, which provides economic benefits to its neighbors and in return, benefits from a peaceful regional order.

China fully understands the current economic situation and is seeking to reshape the operational landscape by creating a "new reality" in the region that requires careful management. Beijing's overall strategy offers economic incentives to establish a more harmonious economic environment, but maintains its territorial claims to secure legitimacy at home. This phenomenon probably explains why maritime disputes still occur occasionally in this region. Beijing's approach involves both carrots and sticks, but carrots have proven to be more important. Initiatives such as the BRI/MSRI have allowed Beijing to promote partnerships for "common prosperity" by building economic connections with the claimant states. In summary, China does not want regional chaos to disturb business opportunities and trade relationships.

Hence, facing the carrots and sticks strategies from Beijing, Southeast Asian countries will continue to use economic engagement to manage territorial issues with China. Regardless of whether countries in Southeast Asia are sincere in reaching a new consensus position on maritime issues and disputes, China's growing economic power has posed significant challenges to individual states' policy decisions, especially when they involve security issues related to territorial boundaries. Regional claimant states, including the Philippines and Vietnam, are not prepared to pursue a long-term policy of antagonism against China (Swe et al. 2017). As a result, a conciliatory stance is adopted. For instance, after the 2013 meeting between Xi Jinping and Vietnamese President Truong Tan Sang, both countries agreed to set up a hotline to alert each other of any fishery incidents within 48 h. In September 2015, President Truong Tan Sang visited Beijing, and both sides agreed to handle the South China Sea disputes through dialogue. Two months later, Beijing and Hanoi reached cooperation agreements to repair bilateral relations strained over disputes in the South China Sea, including a loan of US$200 million from the Chinese Development Bank during President Xi's visit to Vietnam. Similarly, the president of the Philippines, Rodrigo Duterte, coordinated with Beijing to set aside the decisions made by the Arbitral Tribunal and focus on economic cooperation and trade issues.

Economic interdependence has surpassed other factors that shape territorial issues. China's economic influence has had a tremendous impact on the region, and it is notable for its use of soft power through economic engagement. The MSRI is a major part of China's economic statecraft and its ability to create diplomatic space. It has helped build China's image as a benevolent power that brings economic benefits to neighboring countries.

China's newfound wealth and power have not only allowed for bilateral cooperation between Beijing and Southeast Asian states, but also for growing multilateral cooperation. The financial support of the AIIB has allowed China to pursue its grand strategy in the region, and the MSRI is a major part of that strategy, which also makes use of the framework of the Regional Comprehensive Economic Partnership (RCEP) among ASEAN members. The MSRI has been a major factor facilitating the process of RCEP negotiations (Ye 2015, Vines 2018), which leads to a high possibility of outward-looking liberalization as a result.

In order to provide a more comprehensive idea of the causal inferences of how the MSRI leads to benevolent effects on regional territorial tensions, one of the most promising aspects of studies for researchers of the MSRI would be to reinvestigate the relevant countries in the region. It would be helpful to collect data related to the political and/or economic cooperation among neighboring countries and China, which have been affected by the MSRI or BRI framework since they were announced. An overall empirical analysis with sufficient data collection may shed some light on the drivers, challenges, and potential policymaking considerations of whether China's global strategy has really been implemented. This is an intriguing area that deserves further academic attention. This study promises compelling insights that could be bolstered by detailed analysis of relevant territorial disputes, especially on how Beijing has reacted to the issues from both a theoretical and an empirical standpoint.

REFERENCES

ASEAN. 2021. Chairman's Statement of the 24th ASEAN-China Summit 26 October 2021.

Blanchard, Jean-Marc F. 2018. China's Maritime Silk Road Initiative (MSRI) and Southeast Asia: A Chinese 'Pond' Not 'Lake' in the Works. *Journal of Contemporary China* 27 (111): 329–343.

Boden, Christopher. 2014. China Pledges $40 Billion for New Silk Road. *AP News*, 9 November, 2014. Accessed 20 March 2019. https://apnews.com/article/68eba733e03946589ae463804fcdc103.

Bureau of Fisheries of China. 2016. *China Fisheries Year Books*. Beijing: China Agriculture Press.

Carpio, Antonio. 2021. Why Chinese Fishermen are in the WPS. *Inquirer.net*, April 22, 2021. https://opinion.inquirer.net/139537/why-chinese-fishermen-are-in-the-wps.

Chen, Shaofeng. 2018. Regional Responses to China's Maritime Silk Road Initiative in Southeast Asia. *Journal of Contemporary China* 27 (111): 344–361.

Ciorciari, John David. 2009. The Balance of Great-Power Influence in Contemporary Southeast Asia. *International Relations of the Asia-Pacific* 9 (1): 157–196.

Deutsch, Karl Wolfgang. 1957. *Political Community and the North American Area*. Princeton: Princeton University Press.

Diehl, Paul F. 1985. Contiguity and Military Escalation in Major Power Rivalries, 1816–1980. *The Journal of Politics* 47 (4): 1203–1211.

Fravel, M Taylor. 2011. China's strategy in the South China Sea. *Contemporary Southeast Asia*: 292–319.

Gao, Jianjun. 2009. A Note on the 2008 Cooperation Consensus Between China and Japan in the East China Sea. *Ocean Development & International Law* 40 (3): 291–303.

Gibler, Douglas M. 2012. *The Territorial Peace: Borders, State Development, and International Conflict*. Cambridge University Press.

Gleditsch, Kristian Skrede. 2009. *All International Politics is Local: The Diffusion of Conflict, Integration, and Democratization*. Ann Arbor, MI: University of Michigan Press.

Goldstein, Lyle J. 2013. Chinese Fisheries Enforcement: Environmental and Strategic Implications. *Marine Policy* 40: 187–193.

He, Yini. 2015. China to invest $900b in Belt and Road Initiative. *China Daily USA*, 28 May, 2015. Accessed 19 April 2019. http://usa.chinadaily.com.cn/business/2015-05/28/content_20845687.htm.

Hendrix, Cullen, and Paige Roberts. 2017. One in 10 Interstate Disputes are Fishy- and the Implications Stink. *New Security Beat*, 20 December, 2017. Accessed 10 October 2019. https://www.newsecuritybeat.org/2017/12/10-interstate-disputes-fishy-implications-stink/.

Hensel, Paul R. 1996. Charting a Course to Conflict: Territorial Issues and Interstate Conflict, 1816–1992. *Conflict Management and Peace Science* 15 (1): 43–73.

Hensel, Paul R., and Sara McLaughlin Mitchell. 2017. From Territorial Claims to Identity Claims: The Issue Correlates of War (ICOW) Project. *Conflict Management and Peace Science* 34 (2): 126–140.

Hu, Bo. 2021. Sino-US Competition in the South China Sea: Power, Rules, and Legitimacy. *Journal of Chinese Political Science*. https://doi.org/10.1007/s11366-020-09716-1.

Hutchison, Marc L. 2011. Territorial Threat, Mobilization, and Political Participation in Africa. *Conflict Management and Peace Science* 28 (3): 183–208.

Hutchison, Marc L., and Daniel G. Starr. 2017. The Territorial Peace: Theory, Evidence, and Implications. In *Oxford Research Encyclopedia of Politics*.

Huth, Paul K. 1998. Major power Intervention in International Crises, 1918–1988. *Journal of Conflict Resolution* 42 (6): 744–770.

Huth, Paul K. 2000. Why Are Territorial Disputes Between States a Central Cause of International Conflict. In *What Do We Know About War*, ed. John A. Vasquez, 94–99. Lanham: MD: Rowman & Littlefield.

Huth, Paul K., and Todd L. Allee. 2002. *The Democratic Peace and Territorial Conflict in the Twentieth Century*. Cambridge University Press.

Kang, David. 2007. *China Rising: Peace, Power, and Order in East Asia*. Columbia University Press.

Khaliq, Riyaz. 2022. Joint Energy Exploration 'Right Way' Ahead, China Says after Philippines Pullout. *Anadolu Ajansı*, June 24, 2022. https://www.aa.com.tr/en/economy/joint-energy-exploration-right-way-ahead-china-says-after-philippines-pullout/2621674?fbclid=IwAR1-t83ZRpq6FCQuHoG716 2MzxMylqYVOZLcWFTNCnkjT54VKu-UE5mUiDQ.

Kim, Sun Pyo. 2004. *Maritime Delimitation and Interim Arrangements in North East Asia*. Vol. 40. Martinus Nijhoff Publishers.

Kuik, Chengchwee. 2008. The Essence of Hedging: Malaysia and Singapore's Response to a Rising China. *Contemporary Southeast Asia: A Journal of International and Strategic Affairs* 30 (2): 159–185.

Kuik, Chengchwee. 2016. Malaysia Between the United States and China: What Do Weaker States Hedge Against? *Asian Politics & Policy* 8 (1): 155–177.

Kuik, Chengchwee. 2017. Explaining the Contradiction in China's South China Sea Policy: Structural Drivers and Domestic Imperatives. *China: An International Journal* 15 (1): 163–186.

Lema, Karen, Mallard William, and Perry Michael. 2023. Philippines Wants to Start New Energy Exploration Projects in South China Sea. *Reuters*, December 17, 2023. https://www.reuters.com/world/asia-pacific/philip pines-marcos-says-tensions-south-china-sea-have-increased-2023-12-17/?fbc lid=IwAR1T8AAH6_9NbCg_lte91OAZd8k9L3hK3m-7vJc3Uf6HUgwcVG 4pq4nGvr4.

Lendon, Brad. 2021. Beijing Has a Navy It Doesn't Even Admit Exists, Experts Say. And It's Swarming Parts of the South China Sea. *CNN*, April 13, 2021. https://edition.cnn.com/2021/04/12/china/china-maritime-militia-explainer-intl-hnk-ml-dst/index.html.

Lim, Darren J, and Zack Cooper. 2015. Reassessing Hedging: The Logic of Alignment in East Asia. *Security Studies* 24 (4): 696–727.

Miller, Tom. 2019. *China's Asian Dream: Empire Building Along the New Silk Road*. Zed Books Ltd.

Mitchell, Sara McLaughlin, and Brandon C. Prins. 1999. Beyond Territorial Contiguity: Issues at Stake in Democratic Militarized Interstate Disputes. *International Studies Quarterly* 43 (1): 169–183.

Morales, Neil, and Lema Karen. 2023. Philippines President Summons China Envoy Over Laser Incident. *Reuters*, February 14, 2023. https://www.reu ters.com/world/asia-pacific/philippines-files-protest-china-over-use-laser-agg ressive-activities-by-vessels-2023-02-14/.

Most, Benjamin A., and Harvey Starr. 2015. *Inquiry, Logic, and International Politics: With a New Preface* Columbia: University of South Carolina Press.

Nguyen, Dang Thang 2012. Fisheries Co-operation in the South China Sea and the Irrelevance of the Sovereignty Question. *Asian Journal of International Law* 2 (1): 59–88.

Oneal, John R, and Bruce Russett. 1999. Assessing the Liberal Peace with Alternative Specifications: Trade Still Reduces Conflict. *Journal of Peace Research* 36 (4): 423–442.

Palmer, Glenn, Vito d'Orazio, Michael Kenwick, and Matthew Lane. 2015. The MID4 Dataset, 2002–2010: Procedures, Coding Rules and Description. *Conflict Management and Peace Science* 32 (2): 222–242.

Powell, Robert. 2020. *In the Shadow of Power*. Princeton University Press.

Renato Cruz De Castro. 2022. Caught Between Appeasement and Limited Hard Balancing: The Philippines' Changing Relations With the Eagle and the Dragon. *Journal of Current Southeast Asian Affairs* 41(2): 258–278. https://journals.sagepub.com/doi/pdf/10.1177/18681034221081143.

Russett, Bruce, and John R Oneal. 2001. *Triangulating Peace: Democracy: Interdependence, and International Organizations*. New York, NY: Norton & Company.

Santamaria, Carlos. 2016. Times to Revive the Joint Maritime Seismic Undertaking in the South China Sea? *South China Sea Think Tank*, 2016. Accessed 3 July 2020. https://storage.googleapis.com/scstt/publications/Issue-Briefings-2016-15-Santamaria.pdf.

Schweller, Randall L. 1994. Bandwagoning for Profit: Bringing the Revisionist State Back in. *International Security* 19 (1): 72–107.

Senese, Paul D. 1996. Geographical Proximity and Issue Salience: Their Effects on the Escalation of Militarized Interstate Conflict. *Conflict Management and Peace Science* 15 (2): 133–161.

Senese, Paul D., and John A. Vasquez. 2008. *The Steps To War: An Empirical Study*. Princeton University Press.

Siverson, Randolph M, and Harvey Starr. 1991. *The Diffusion of War: A Study of Opportunity and Willingness*. Ann Arbor, MI: University of Michigan Press.

Starr, Harvey. 2013. On Geopolitics: Spaces and Places. *International Studies Quarterly* 57 (3): 433–439.

Starr, Harvey. 2015. *On Geopolitics: Space, Place, and International Relations*. Routledge.

Swe, Lim Kheng, Hailong Ju, and Mingjiang Li. 2017. China's Revisionist Aspirations in Southeast Asia and the Curse of the South China Sea Disputes. *China: An International Journal* 15 (1): 187–213.

Tessman, Brock F. 2012. System Structure and State Strategy: Adding Hedging to the Menu. *Security Studies* 21 (2): 192–231.

Thayer, Carl. 2016. Revealed: The Truth Behind ASENA's Retracted Kunming Statement. *The Diplomat*, 19 June, 2016. Accessed 17 June 2019. https://thediplomat.com/2016/06/revealed-the-truth-behind-aseans-retracted-kunming-statement/.

Tran, Bich T. 2019. Presidential Turnover and Discontinuity in the Philippines' China Policy. *Asian Perspective* 43 (4): 621–646.

Tseng, Hui-Yi. 2017. Fishing: A New Dimension to China's Engagement in Maritime Issues. *China: An International Journal* 15 (3): 184–200.

Vasquez, John A. 1995. Why Do Neighbors Fight? Proximity, Interaction, or Territoriality. *Journal of Peace Research* 32 (3): 277–293.

Venzon, Cliff. 2020. China and Philippines Affirm Ties After South China Sea spat. *Nikkei Asia*, July 15, 2020. https://asia.nikkei.com/Politics/Intern ational-relations/South-China-Sea/China-and-Philippines-affirm-ties-after-South-China-Sea-spat.

Vergun, David. 2023. New EDCA Sites Named in the Philippines. *U.S. Department of Defense*, April 3, 2023. https://www.defense.gov/News/News-Sto ries/Article/Article/3350297/new-edca-sites-named-in-the-philippines/#:~: text=The%20four%20new%20sites%20are,who%20briefed%20the%20media% 20today

Vines, David. 2018. The BRI and RCEP: Ensuring Cooperation in the Liberalisation of Trade in Asia. *Economic and Political Studies* 6 (3): 338–348.

Walt, Stephen M. 2013. *The Origins of Alliances*. Cornell University Press.

Ye, Min. 2015. China and Competing Cooperation in Asia-Pacific: TPP, RCEP, and the New Silk Road. *Asian Security* 11 (3): 206–224.

Yu, Hong. 2017. Motivation Behind China's 'One Belt, One Road' Initiatives and Establishment of the Asian Infrastructure Investment Bank. *Journal of Contemporary China* 26 (105): 353–368.

Zhang, Hongzhou. 2018. Fisheries Cooperation in the South China Sea: Evaluating the Options. *Marine Policy* 89: 67–76.

Zhang, Hongzhou, and Sam Bateman. 2017. Fishing Militia, the Securitization of Fishery and the South China Sea Dispute. *Contemporary Southeast Asia*: 288–314.

Zhang, Hongzhou, and Fengshi Wu. 2017. China's Marine Fishery and Global Ocean Governance. *Global Policy* 8 (2): 216–226.

CHAPTER 6

Building Blocks or Walls? BRI, Globalization, and the Future of East Asian Regionalization

Serafettin Yilmaz and Bo Li

This chapter is an updated version of the journal article: Yilmaz, S., Li, B. "The BRI-Led Globalization and Its Implications for East Asian Regionalization." *Chin. Polit. Sci. Rev.* 5, 395–416 (2020). https://doi.org/10.1007/s41111-020-00145-2

S. Yilmaz
Asia-Europe Institute, University of Malaya, Taiwan Center for Security Studies, Taipei, Taiwan, ROC
e-mail: shifanyao@sdu.edu.cn

B. Li (✉)
School of Political Science and Public Administration, Shandong University, Qingdao, China

© The Author(s), under exclusive license to Springer Nature Switzerland AG 2025
K. G.Cai et al. (eds.), *China and Global Economic Governance, Volume I: China's BRI & AIIB and Global Economic Governance*, Politics and Development of Contemporary China,
https://doi.org/10.1007/978-3-031-73212-6_6

6.1 Introduction

The relationship between globalization and regionalization has for long been a contested topic of scholarly interest. There is little agreement as to whether globalization undermines or reinforces regionalization and whether regionalization is a reaction to the (real or perceived) destructive side effects of globalization or simply a complementary process to it. However, it is generally agreed that, as historical models with distinct development patterns, outcomes, and prospects, they exert certain influence on each other, be it competitive or complementary. Both paradigms produce proponents and opponents with ideological attachments at varying degrees depending on the experience of individuals, groups, and nation-states with them.

In this research, we investigate the dynamics between globalization and East Asian regionalization process.[1] In that, we treat the China-led Belt and Road Initiative (BRI) as essentially a plan designed to promote a new type of globalization that is distinct in terms of its theoretical and practical vision of global economic and political governance from the US-led world order which is the dominant model ever since the end of the Cold War even though it has never been universally endorsed as there have been dissenting state actors such as China and Russia.[2] The new globalization is a complex set of ideas and institutions that seek to respond to the perceived shortcomings and negative aspects of the postwar international system. Some view it as an inherently benign and restorative phenomenon that aims to insert trust and confidence in the existing regimes by introducing reforms to contain the growing suspicions and counter the anti-globalization trend in some developed countries' increasingly populist political elites and fringe groups that rally

---

[1] While the term suffers definitional problems due to its loose economic and political structuring, in general, East Asia refers to the sub-regions of Northeast Asia and Southeast Asia (ASEAN). See Kim (2004).

[2] It must be noted here that the most authoritative document on the BRI, the Vision and Actions on Jointly Building Silk Road Economic Belt and 21st Century Maritime Silk Road does not explicitly refer to the Initiative as a model for global governance but states that, among others, the BRI "embrac[es] economic globalization..." (NDRC 2015). However, over the years, a growing literature generated by both strategy circles and academia (in China and elsewhere) has offered various interpretations on the Initiative, characterizing it as complementary to, alternative for, or even rival to the existing international system. See, for example, (Liu and Dunford 2016; Khan et al. 2018; Zhang et al. 2018; Ekman 2019; Fardella and Prodi 2017, p. 125; Zheng 2017, p. 29).

around nativist, protectionist, and conservative ideas (May 2018a, 2018b; Li 2016a, 2016b; Kellner 2018). Others, however, view the globalization program put into action by China through the BRI and the related programs such as the Global Development Initiative and the Global Security Initiative as efforts designed to eventually upend the established global order and promote a less liberal and more autocratic international system (Mandelbaum and Weiffen 2023; Osman 2023).

This is not to say that the BRI is a program designed for a literal imitation of the post-Cold War globalization along with all of its ideals and institutions such as democratization and removal of trade barriers. Quite the contrary, the alternative (or, at times, complementary) rules and norms envisioned under the BRI tend to uphold globalization only as an overarching structure under which it seeks to nurture a new or reformed set of regimes, which is popularly termed as "Globalization with Chinese characteristics" (Warner 2017; Kramer 2023). Thus, the BRI is as much about an approval of globalization as a historical phenomenon as it is about a critique of its many institutions and practices of governance. For example, the absolutist notion of non-intervention in domestic affairs of sovereign nations is firmly enshrined in the Constitution of the Asian Infrastructure Investment Bank (AIIB), which implies a critique of the liberal notions of humanitarian intervention and responsible sovereignty (Quinton-Brown 2023; Hathaway et al. 2013).[3]

Globalization and regionalization are two distinct but interrelated processes, which, in general, are viewed as either positive or negative in terms of the nature of their relationship. For some authors, the interplay between the two are positive in a way that they mutually facilitate and reinforce each other's conceptual and institutional development (Friedman 1990; Ruggie 1982). Others, on the other hand, view the two processes as having an antagonistic relationship, weakening each other in varying degrees (Hirst et al. 2015; Cox 1987). Through a reference to the interaction between the BRI-led new globalization and East Asian regionalization, we identify a third possibility which suggests that the development of one phenomenon leads to the weakening of the other.

---

[3] In Article 31(2) of the Asian Infrastructure Investment Bank's Articles of Agreement, it is explicitly stated that "The Bank, its President, officers and staff shall not interfere in the political affairs of any member, nor shall they be influenced in their decisions by the political character of the member concerned. Only economic considerations shall be relevant to their decisions." See AIIB (2015).

Thus, in this study, our objective is to explore the impact (or lack thereof) of China's globalization drive under the BRI on the country's participation in regional integration in East Asia through a survey of policies and academic and diplomatic discourses.

Accordingly, at a critical historical juncture in which China has mobilized a considerable amount of its national resources as part of a state strategy to reverse the downward pressure on globalization and to reshape it into its own image through the provision of new reformist and structuralist agendas and garnering international support, we detect a potential risk for the East Asian regionalism: too much emphasis on global may come at the cost of regional, leading to a situation in which globalization actually undermines regionalization in East Asia by dampening its institutionalization momentum and diluting its degree of regionness.

The primary objective of this study is to analyze the interaction between the two major contemporary processes by looking critically at the dynamic relationship between the BRI-driven globalization and the East Asian regionalization. We argue that, if China's efforts to promote its own version of globalization via the BRI results in a distracted and indifferent approach to (especially, political) regionalization, it may have a certain retarding effect on the region's integration. Therefore, we believe that a study on the efforts to rejuvenate and reform globalization may help throw illuminating light on the nature of the interplay between the processes of globalization and regionalization. However, we should note, with its focus on East Asia, this analysis does not claim to produce a blanket explanation of all individual cases (such as in Europe and Latin America) in which globalization and regionalization processes take place in their own particular socio-economic and political contexts.

As the world system goes through serious tribulations and challenges (such as the Russian invasion of Ukraine and the US-China rivalry) that affect the political and economic stability and development in many regions, a debate on regionalization becomes even more significant. Therefore, in the ensuing pages, we first provide a review on the nature of relationship between globalization and regionalization. Then, we offer a brief introduction to the Belt and Road Initiative, outlining its potential emerging role as one of the architects of the fourth wave of globalization (Robertson 2003). Here, we not only make a descriptive analysis of the Initiative, but also look analytically at the classical globalization as a system facing challenges and at its latent reproduction in a new form as envisioned by China under the BRI-led ideas and institutions. In the next section, we turn our attention to East Asian regionalization, analyzing historically the role China has played in promoting regional institutions and drafting new ideas. In the following section, we study critically the dynamics between the BRI-driven globalization and East Asian regionalization by investigating China's participation in and contribution to the community building efforts in East Asia since the BRI was launched in 2013. In the final section, we summarize our findings and conclude with a note on the future prospects and the potential courses of regionalization in East Asia and China's place in it.

6.2 The Debate on the Dynamics Between Globalization and Regionalization

Globalization is considered a fuzzy concept with no clear-cut delineation.[4] Among others, the difficulty to pinpoint a definition in which most agree upon results from the broad nature of the notion (Mills 2009). Still, numerous attempts have been made to define it. Aside from the general agreement that the term means different things to different social groups, when identifying the characteristics that make it stand out, scholars emphasize the density of connectedness and degree of sameness as the unique underlying features of the phenomenon (Hirst and Thompson 1996). Globalization, in this regard, is seen not only to be related to the intensification of trans-boundary connections helped by advanced communication and transportation technologies, but also to a fuller consciousness of it (Kacowics 1999, pp. 528–529).

Literature on globalization tend to put greater emphasis on economic connectivity and integration, and on its associated social, political, ideological, and cultural implications (Oman 1994). It is distinguished from globalism which is a process in which political, rather than economic, factors are dominant and markets are replaced by the state. Nevertheless, the anticipated outcomes in both processes are not incompatible, namely, greater integration and better connectivity among the related social forces. This taxonomy repeats itself in a similar fashion with respect to the relationship between regionalism and regionalization as far as the driving forces, processes and end goals of regional integration are concerned. The

---

[4] Held et al. (1999, p. 2) classify the varied approaches to globalization under three main categories: hyperglobalists, skeptics, and transformationalists. Also see Thompson (1998).

ontological connections between the two paradigms allow establishing conceptual linkages between globalism/globalization and regionalism/ regionalization. Similar agents such as the states, markets, and the individuals take part in these dual processes, although those forces differ in terms of the outcomes that they (aim to) lead to.[5] Globalization and East Asian regionalization are, too, processes that are inherently linked with each other even if the direction and nature of this interaction would be case-dependent.

First and foremost, both globalization and regionalization aim for connectivity and integration, and more than often their point of departure is the economic life of nations. Yet, the shared vision does not necessarily end in the same outcome. As has been widely debated in the literature, globalization is seen as an assembly line that produces identical products, whereas regionalization is perceived as a work station with a larger number of shops that churn out variegated products while maintaining their local identity. Regionalization is a less specific process than globalization because, in essence, and unlike the latter, the former thrusts toward multiplicity of institutions and multilateral relationships while, at the same time, seeking greater uniformity within the politically and economically defined institutional and geographic borders. Hence, a number of types of regions, regionalisms, and regionalizations are proposed informed by unique characteristics, formations, nature of interactions, and mutual perceptions (Thompson 1998, pp. 63–64; Nair 2008; Väyrynen 2003; Ba 2009; Kim 2004).

The multiple linkages that overlap between globalization and regionalization processes rule out any specific road map that may help detect a linear relationship in which dominating characteristics are identified. This adds to the multiplication of polarized approaches toward the nature of relationship between the two phenomena (Zhu 1997; Yin 2003). Broadly speaking, while for some, globalization and regionalization are mutually exclusive processes, for others, they are complementary in that one covers the shortcomings of the other. For a third group of analysts, globalization is the ultimate destination in that "the development of regionalism

---

[5] Although the concepts of regionalism and regionalization are distinguished (but not disconnected) in the literature, in this research, the two terms are used interchangeably to indicate the general mechanisms toward regional economic and political integration. For an in-depth analysis on the two processes and their relationship, see (Kim 2004, pp. 40; Pempel 2005; Ravenhill 2010).

is, to a certain extent, an integral part of the development of globalization" (Wei 2003, p. 51). A final line of thinking finds that it is impossible to imagine globalization and regionalization as either similar or diverse processes because there is no fixed route in which the two always converge or diverge (Therborn and Khondker 2006).

Those who imagine a more conflictual interaction between globalization and regionalization argue that when economies in a regional bloc initiate preferential trade policies with each other, it leads to a "trade diversion" due to the inefficiencies, thereby hampering global trade liberalization (Mehanna 2008, p. 297). Then, if regional economic integration encourages the stakeholders to "adopt closed or inward-looking policies," this may lead to a world economy that is divided into mutually exclusive regions in which "nationalism and protectionism" are widespread, "hindering the development of global economic marketization" (Zhu 1997, p. 44). For the second group, neither globalization nor regionalization are absolute phenomena. They are neither entirely good nor entirely bad; however, they can be conducive to economic growth, albeit in varying degrees (Mehanna 2008; Zhu 1997).

Functionalists, on the other hand, envision "globalization through regionalization"—those regions being either disparate growth areas within a nation (especially geographically large and diverse countries) or states that are organized into regional blocs (Valuev 2000). While globalization is seen as the ultimate destination, regionalization is considered a "related process" in which globalization eventually prevails even though the associated benefits from globalization may not be uniform across countries (Cook and Kirkpatrick 2010, p. 64). According to a similar approach, regionalization may actually act as a "regulator" between the nation-state and globalization, rendering the interaction between the two more harmonious (Wei 2003, p. 52). As a matter of fact, "regionalization is not only conducive to the integration of politics, economics and culture among the members of regional communities, but also objectively promotes globalization" (Liu and Lihua 2002, p. 158).

Others, in the meantime, hold that, globalization and regionalization overlap but this interaction, while "never harmonious," is not necessarily antagonistic or cooperative (Kacowics 1999, p. 528). That is to say, there cannot be a singular outcome. As historical precedence shows specific perspectives on these forces vary according to particular situations (e.g., developing and developed countries), nature of the agents (e.g., nation-states, minority groups, civil societies, multinational corporations, national elites), and perceptions (e.g., big powers, middle powers, small powers). As for the widely held argument that globalization undermines the nation-state and, for this reason, its outcome can be predicted, non-determinists stress the successful existence of states that are well integrated into the global economy and manage to maintain their essential sovereign authority. Globalization respects that peculiar authority. This mutual compromise is highlighted as a distinct trait of new regionalism and the accompanying global trade liberalism, which renders sweeping judgments on the merits of either phenomena a less feasible undertaking (Wang 2004).

6.3 The Belt and Road Initiative and New Globalization

Launched in 2013, the Belt and Road Initiative has generated debate on the question, among others, of the project's practicality, desirability, sustainability, and motives (Fleet 2017; De Graaff and Van Apeldoorn 2018; Miller 2017; Schulhof et al. 2022). Over the years, the Initiative has strived, with varying outcomes so far, to expand both quantitatively and qualitatively. Quantitatively, it has sought larger global coverage, involving in the scheme a multimodal communication network among public and private actors from various sectors such as business, diplomacy, and education, and spearheaded institutions such as the AIIB and the Silk Road Fund (SRF). Qualitatively, it promoted a number of historically charged political-economic lexicons—such as new type of major power relations, no-strings-attached development, and peaceful coexistence (Schortgen 2018). Both materially and ideationally, the BRI touts ideas on the economic, political, and cultural aspects of international governance, attempting to position itself a viable alternative to the existing globalization.[6]

The associations of the BRI with a new type of globalization rest, in large part, on the aspects of the existing international phenomena that are viewed as generating economic inequalities, power imbalances and

---

[6] In fact, drawing on the ancient Silk Road, which is "one of the first examples of globalization that became the first, largest, free-trade zone during the Mongol Empire," the BRI is considered by some authors as a contemporary but more extensive reformulation of the historical communication route (Qoraboyev and Mol- dashev 2018, p. 121).

dependencies (Ekman 2019; Wang 2016; Oman 1999). Even though, globalization, in general, is simply associated with growing connectivity and unobstructed movement of people, goods, and services, a plethora of contesting ideas exist on the distribution of its benefits and associated costs (Nef 2002; Therborn 2000; Giddens 1991; Harvey 1990; Robertson 1992). The difficulty in reaching an agreement on the economic, political, and cultural implications of globalization arises in large part from the fact that multiple overlapping historical variables are involved in the process of development, hence, it is difficult to point out a specific determinant and outcome for the associated success or failure through a cross-country comparison (Ravallion 2003). Nonetheless, those who propose a more cautious approach to globalization point out certain defects in the idea, involving economic, cultural, and political life of peoples and nations (Krasner 2009, p. 5).

Economically, contemporary globalization has been vindicated for generating vast inequalities between states and leading to uneven development (Rodrik 2001, p. 55; Wade 2004; Pritchett 1997). It is argued that most of the development brought about via connectivity and integration has been limited to coastal areas that are suitable for sea-faring trade, whereas geographically isolated inland regions have fallen outside the reach of most of the fast-moving capital and investment—which may also be true for most countries that experience deep wealth and development disparities between their inland and coastal regions. Also, even when connectivity is established between developed and underdeveloped areas, the relationship remains one of dependency created by a core–periphery arrangement in which the underdeveloped and developing nations continue to provide raw materials and other market advantages such as cheap labor while remaining dependent on the higher value-added products from developed nations (Daly 2001).[7] Such an arrangement generates a cycle in which poor nations experience immense difficulties in acquiring advanced production know-how and the required capital to lift themselves out of underdevelopment through investment in physical and social infrastructure (Hurrell and Woods 1999).

---

[7] It has been argued that the trade war between the US and China is more "about protecting the technological edge that has made the United States the world's dominant economic power" than about the US trade deficit with China (Huang 2018; Gros 2019; Obe and Sugiura 2018).

Culturally, globalization has been vindicated for phasing out cultural diversities that have been created throughout centuries out of experience, customs and practice, and molding cultural multitude into a singular form (Dupuy 1998, p. 57; Robertson 1995; Seabrook 2004). On this, critiques identify a hegemonic power relationship: those who are at the receiving end of ideas are required to take in whatever is being presented to them without any regard to the question of compatibility, feasibility, and long-term impact on local forms of living (Lomnitz 1994; McQuail 2000, p. 221). Also, culture is viewed as an instrument to help complete economic globalization: along with culture come products which themselves, in turn, shape the cultural life of the receiving groups (Ali 2005, p. 15). The culture–production dyad reinforces each other by generating a universal taste not only for cultural but also for industrial products.[8]

Finally, globalization is argued to create conditions of power imbalances in which economically and technologically advanced states dictate, shape and, at times, transform the political and economic life of less-developed countries—often by utilizing their advantages in information technologies. Once again, globalization facilitates easy access to the internal affairs of underdeveloped states and provides tools to influence national politics in target societies. When domestic conditions of such countries are exploited through such variegated means as gun-boat diplomacy, information dissemination or social engineering, little attention is paid whether those actions negatively affect people's well-being and development chances. In this regard, globalization is perceived as generating deep inequalities in political power and capacity (Kellner 2002).

Granted, the critique of globalization includes many subcategories of the three dimensions that we have outlined in a rather general fashion above (Falk 1999; Stiglitz 2002). Nevertheless, the criticisms levied against globalization allows to reflect comparatively on classical globalization and the alternative form promoted by the Belt and Road Initiative, which, albeit not without its critiques and skeptics, posits itself as a model with a new world view and related institutions (Zou and Qiu 2018). Below, we analyze the officially promoted normative and practical dimensions of the BRI as they relate to the globalization paradigm which not

---

[8] As opposed to the critiques, considerable literature exists on the positive correlation between the two processes of globalization and culture. See, for example, Rothkopf (1997), Clark (1990), and Dichter (1962).

only intends to integrate China more deeply into the existing global processes, "but also to create new standards for globalization" (Wang 2016, p. 19; Ekman 2019).

6.4 Belt and Road's Global Ambitions: Economics, Politics, and Culture

Covering over 150 states and 30 institutions (although the number of active participants is estimated to vary between 60 to 70), and involving related investments in more than 80 countries, the BRI is without a question a massive undertaking both in terms of its size and scale (Siu 2019; Ekman 2017; Du and Zhang 2017). The countries involved in the scheme at various levels represent over 70% of the world population, accounting for 70% of known global energy reserves and about one-third of global GDP and trade. Over the years, the project's outreach has extended to regions as diverse as Oceania, West, South and Central Asia, Eastern and Western Europe, Africa and Latin America, leading scholars into suggesting that the project "is probably the most ambitious Chinese international policy initiative in history" (Huang 2016, p. 320). Through the twin networks of belt (land-based) and road (sea-based) physical supra and infrastructure such as road and railway networks, ports, bridges, communication and grid lines, and airports, the project aims to establish transcontinental connectivity and integration between coastal and inland areas in a manner that allows faster and more convenient communication (Clifford 2017; Swaine 2015).

The land and maritime connections that have been set up or are in various phases of development suggest that the BRI may potentially provide answers to the questions raised by the critiques of globalization for the economic, political, and social inequalities it generates due, mainly, to the uneven distribution of economic resources across countries. This argument is further supported by the fact that almost all BRI-related programs are designed in a way to be "premised on the social and administrative beliefs of the less-developed countries" (Siu, 2019, p. 575). Thus, although disputed by various studies in recent years (Himaz 2021; Carmody and Wainwright 2022), an initial assessment by Zhai (2018, p. 92) on the anticipated impact of the BRI on economic development of the related countries held that:

With a moderate assumption of BRI investment in the coming 15 years, the simulation results find that the annual global welfare gains would be about US$1.6 trillion in 2030, accounting for 1.3% of the global GDP. More than 90% of this gain is expected to be captured by BRI countries. The BRI is also expected to boost global trade by 5% in 2030.

Furthermore, at the most fundamental level, the BRI is viewed "as the turning point from marine-based globalization to comprehensive globalization, integrating the inland and marine economies" (Zheng 2017, p. 29). Due to its emphasis on connectivity among developed, developing and underdeveloped regions, the BRI is argued to impact infrastructure development, trade growth, and economic performance of the participant countries by ensuring better access to the previously less accessible regions, facilitating transportation, reducing transaction costs, and upgrading critical infrastructure (Enderwick 2018, p. 451; Herrero and Xu 2017; Kohl 2019; Ramasamy and Yeung 2019). For instance, in partner countries, the BRI-related "infrastructure projects [have] driven the growth of industrial output from the transportation and the energy sectors... by 7.9% and 13.1% respectively" (Siu, 2019, p. 575). BRI countries have also seen their trade with China grow (Mao et al. 2019).

On the cultural and political plane, too, the BRI attests to provide space for cultural self-expression, and to tolerate political and governance differences (Andornino 2017). Within the BRI discourse generated by the Chinese policymakers and the academia, there are plenty of references that suggest a vision to improve the way traditional globalization approaches cultures and politics (Khan et al. 2018, pp. 8–13; Rimmer 2018). Indeed, it has long been argued by its critiques that globalization has failed to take into account the reality of cultural and political systems that do not fit in the dominant liberal democratic narrative. It is held in this regard that the BRI is more tolerant to such differences, respects alternative sets of values, appreciates diversity, and refrains from intervention in others' domestic affairs (Yin 2003; Li 2016a, 2016b). These long-held political, economic, and cultural principles are firmly embedded in the BRI's key documents.[9]

---

[9] Others, however, have disputed the non-intervention doctrine in BRI as both ingenuine and conducive to creating numerous economic and social problems. For example, Himaz (2021) found that BRI projects can lead to increased corruption, income disparities at sub-national levels, and environmental degradation due to lack of effective oversight, regulations and viable institutions. It has also been argued that "those countries involved

The BRI-driven new globalization is informed, naturally, by China's approach to global governance. First and foremost, China considers global governance as an area in which, in line with its growing economic and political clout, it is entitled for greater participation. Scholars and decision-makers in China also recognize the various sources of general dissatisfaction with the way globalization have negatively impacted people's economic and political life in developing and underdeveloped countries (Zeng 2019; Beijing Review 2018). Thus, strongly conditioned by historical circumstances, China's perspective on global governance is argued to be as much novel as it is complementary in that it is based on the country's "cultural DNA" consisting of such values as "integrity and connectivity; tolerance and inclusiveness; harmony and peace; and a holistic approach to world affairs" (He 2017, p. 350). This, however, does not mean that China's view on global governance is not controversial at all. As observed in the growing negative perception of the BRI in some countries such as Italy, which has recently withdrawn from the initiative by declining to renew the MOU signed in 2019, the China-led conceptualization generates tensions due to its potential geopolitical and economic implications.

Nevertheless, the BRI is not positioned to function as a systemic alternative to the existing global model, especially considering the fact that China has begun to reconsider and restructure its development commitments (Jones 2019; Zhou and Esteban 2018; Callahan 2016),[10] nor is it poised to decouple from the established international structures and norms not the least because of the well-set interdependencies (Lairson 2018, pp. 36–40). Rather, it represents a new stage within the context of globalization which is a long-winding process with phases that relate

in BRI projects are prone to a diminishment of certain democratic freedoms and labour rights" because "BRI… consist of huge infrastructure projects that are easier to plan and implement when labour rights and criticism from the media or civil society are kept to a low level." This can be corrected by getting, "international actors, including multi-national companies, non-governmental organizations, and international organizations, and the Chinese government itself" involved to ensure the implementation of good governance practices (Jerabek 2023, p. 357).

[10] Nevertheless, one can locate plenty of arguments to the contrary, which characterize the BRI as a major challenge to the Western international order on both normative and material levels. The suspicion, in this regard, is particularly reinforced by the vague language in the BRI-related statements and the lack of substantive data on its key aspects such as the total spending, the amount of loans, and "even an officially agreed-upon list of BRI countries" (Jones 2019, pp. 2–4).

to varying levels of global interconnectivity. Even though the evolving BRI-led paradigm has a different vision of global political, economic, and cultural relations from the existing one, it still builds on the progress that has been made so far and seeks to utilize the regimes that have long dominated the global economics and politics under the contemporary globalization (Ekman 2019, p. 120). Essentially, the BRI-led new globalization aims at "leveraging the benefits of the first phase of globalization to generate new momentums over the decades ahead" (Zheng 2017, p. 29). It, as neatly summarized by the Chinese scholars, aims to offer a new blueprint that complements and/or restores what traditional globalization is seen as having difficulty in providing for due to its now "fragmented, unbalanced and one-dimensional" characteristics which has led to, among others, "the slowdown in global economic growth and unbalanced global development" (Chen and Xiaoying 2017, p. 73).[11]

6.5   China and East Asian Regionalization

It follows that the BRI, and the ensuing initiatives on development, security, and culture that "add some conceptual backbone to a more globally engaged China," are designed to promote a Chinese vision of globalization (Osman 2023). The analysis in the previous two sections demonstrates that the BRI's global vision claims to address at least some of the fundamental criticisms directed at the brand of globalization influenced largely by the Western norms and values. This requires, as we proceed below, an investigation on the real and potential (negative) implications of the BRI-led globalization for East Asian regional development.[12] We, in this regard, identify two particular risks associated with China's push for globalization under the BRI framework. The first is a potential retarding impact on the regional institutional buildup and integration in East Asia due to the country's prioritization of a more globalist diplomacy and the associated negligence of regional processes.

---

[11] The typology developed by Chen and Gong (2017, p. 75) contrasts the BRI-led globalization with the traditional form, delineating a number of sharp differences.

[12] Although in this study we focus on the relationship between new globalization and East Asian regionalization within the context of China's approach to these two historical paradigms and seek to analyze the negative implications of the former for the latter, other scholars identify broader and geopolitically informed factors (such as China–Japan rivalry, China's extensive territorial claims in the SCS, and the US-China competition) that have had destructive effects on regionalization process in East Asia. See Yeo (2019).

The second is the risk of dilution of economic and political regionalism as China places all the East Asian participants in various BRI institutions under the broader umbrella of the Initiative along with the rest, thereby blurring the regionness of East Asia as a distinct category.[13]

The BRI signals a trend in China's push for a new type of globalization, connecting, in this respect, more "with globalization," than with "regionalism" (Tu 2018, p. 202). This brings forward an intriguing puzzle as to whether or not the slow-moving (or frustrated) East Asian regionalism may face yet another challenge in which much less attention is paid to it by the largest economy in the region (Nair 2008). This is especially important given the fact that China has relatively smaller stake in East Asian integration due to its emphasis on open regionalism, economic multilateralism and non-formalism (Wang 2011a, 2011b, p. 627). Indeed, whereas China has taken part in a number of regional and sub-regional institutions such as the ASEAN Regional Forum (ARF), East Asia Summit (EAS), and the Trilateral Cooperation Secretariat (TCS), its participation in those regional institutions falls short of the country's overall size and scale (Kang 2007).[14] Although China has been active in all East Asian regional institutions and sought to increase its influence in them, traditionally, it has refrained from taking initiative, rather it only claimed stake in the existing or newly proposed regimes such as the Regional Comprehensive Economic Partnership (RCEP). Furthermore, as has been recently the case with a number of BRI frameworks, when China proactively introduced new institutions, it avoided advocating deeper regionalism. Instead, it chose to propose wider institutional regimes surpassing the East Asian regional boundaries (such as the AIIB and the SRF), which can hardly be considered as regional. In fact, at times, as was the case with the Japanese proposed Asian Monetary Fund (AMF) or the proposal for an East Asian FTA, it openly opposed such initiatives in an effort to prevent an institution heavily influenced by another state such as Japan (Dent 2009, p. 167).

[13] Here, we also recognize that East Asia is only weakly defined as a region due to lack of meaningful institutionalization and integration both economically and, more so, politically. Hence, East Asia's regionness remains more of an abstract idea than a tangible reality.

[14] One notable exception is the ASEAN Plus Three (APT) in which China actively sought to sign a regional trade agreement with the ASEAN in 2001 in the aftermath of the Asian Financial Crisis of 2007. For a debate on "China and East Asian Regionalism," see Wang (2011a, p. 623).

Essentially, China's participation in regionalism in East Asia has been stronger economically but much weaker politically (Wang 2011a, 2011b, p. 623). On the economic front, albeit historically a late-comer, especially from the early 2000s onward, it took interest in (especially bilateral) regional trade agreements (Tu 2018, p. 196). More recently, Beijing has sought to promote a multilateral trade regime in the sub region of Northeast Asia (China–Japan–Korea FTA) and in the wider geographical context under the RCEP. Politically, China's contribution to East Asian regionalism has been minimal at best even after, at the end of the Cold War, China moved to forsake communist international ideology that previously hampered the chances for a meaningful stake in political regionalism in East Asia. At the instances when China seemed to be competing (often with Japan) and vying for a leading position in the region, "cooperative competition" has often led to a situation in which the rivaling sides consented for ASEAN to control and lead the East Asian regional discourse and lead its multilateral institutions (Park 2012, p. 304).

Still, there is no denying that, over the last few decades, China's involvement in regional multilateral regimes, both economic and political, has grown qualitatively and quantitatively. The country has begun to put greater importance on the relations with ASEAN and took important steps for this end. Among the recent developments were the conclusion of the upgrade in the China–ASEAN FTA and the launch of the China–ASEAN Defence Ministers' Informal Meeting in 2015 (Chuang 2015). Under the ASEAN Plus Three (APT) framework, China supported the Chiang Mai Initiative Multilateralization (CMIM) and also took part in all APT-related forums. In Northeast Asia (NEA), negotiations on a trilateral FTA continued with the 16th round of talks completed in January 2022. Furthermore, the three NEA countries have been engaged in a multitude of dialogues and consultations under various forums on issues ranging from disaster management and counter-terrorism to agricultural and scientific cooperation (Breslin 2010, pp. 722–727).

China has been involved in security-related frameworks in East Asia, too, including the ARF and EAS, hosting various workshops and forums. In 2016, it participated for the first time in the ASEAN Defence Ministers' Meeting Plus (ADMM-Plus) peacekeeping and demining joint exercise in India and, in 2018, held the first ever maritime exercise with ASEAN (Searight 2018). China also launched the Lancang-Mekong

Cooperation (LMC) framework in 2014, bringing together the six countries along the Lancang-Mekong River for regular consultations and meetings at the leaders and ministers' level. Thus, since 2013, China's participation in non-traditional security frameworks in East Asia has grown both in depth and scope, including disaster relief, anti-terrorism, transnational crimes, cybersecurity, maritime security, and nuclear non-proliferation (Atanassova-Cornelis 2010, p. 407).

Furthermore, as shown in Table 6.1, trade between China and the East Asian states has seen sustained growth over the past decade. Especially the China–ASEAN trade increased exponentially, accounting for more than 12% in China's total trade in 2017. Japan and Korea, in the meantime, saw their share decrease in relative terms from a high of 17.69% in 2008 to 14.20% in 2017. Yet, in absolute terms, the China–Japan–Korea trilateral trade rose to nearly $600 billion in 2017. In terms of China's extra-regional trade, the weight of the EU in the country's total trade decreased slightly, while the China–NAFTA trade increased both in relative and absolute terms. Thus, so far, the BRI-led emphasis on globalization does not appear to have slowed down China's primary role in regional trade. In fact, considering the central position of Southeast Asia in both maritime and land connectivity schemes under the BRI, the increase in China–ASEAN trade since 2013 may in part be attributed to the Initiative.

As far as institutional buildup is concerned, China has demonstrated greater efficiency in creating institutions with global outreach around the BRI, which differs radically from the country's weak track record in launching institutions with a particular focus on East Asia—a reality which also coincides with the region's general weakness in security-related institutionalization (Segal 1996, p. 114). One of the early global institutions is the AIIB, a multilateral financial lender to support infrastructure projects in developing countries. The membership structure of the Bank and the projects that have been approved reflect its global scope.[15] Another BRI-led institution that serves as a convention to bring together a diverse audience from across the world is the Belt and Road Forum for International Cooperation (BRFIC). First held in May 2017, the forum has a clear focus on promoting China's brand of globalization. Finally, although not originally a China-proposed framework, the BOAO Forum for Asia

---

[15] To view the investment structure of the AIIB, visit the official website at: https://www.aiib.org/en/index.html.

Table 6.1   China's trade with major partner regions and their share in China's total trade (2008–2017)

Year	China–ASEAN total trade—(Million USD)	ASEAN share in China's foreign trade (%)	China–CJK total trade—(Million USD)	CJK share in China's foreign trade (%)	China–NAFTA total trade—(Million USD)	NAFTA share in China's foreign trade (%)	China–EU28 (Total Trade)	EU28 share in China's foreign trade (%)
2017	518,121	12.60	583,905	14.20	688,561	16.74	534,964	13.01
2016	460,376	12.36	530,144	14.23	614,325	16.44	471,512	12.65
2015	465,296	11.99	554,330	14.28	647,502	16.68	482,029	12.42
2014	479,784	11.14	602,825	14.00	645,860	15.00	528,174	12.27
2013	442,707	10.64	586,187	14.09	608,557	14.63	482,538	11.60
2012	399,651	10.33	583,472	15.09	568,730	14.71	479,044	12.39
2011	362,326	9.95	596,297	16.10	624,177	14.40	504,410	13.85
2010	292,581	9.84	503,400	16.94	447,320	15.05	427,490	14.38
2009	212,711	9.64	385,113	17.40	344,924	1564	324,160	14.69
2008	231,155	9.03	453,064	17.69	386,624	15.10	379,264	14.81

Source Data compiled by the authors at Trilateral Cooperation Secretariat website (https://www.tcs-asia.org/?doc_id=statistics_chart) 2013 indicates the year in which the BRI was officially launched

(BFA) is a global event on security issues that are of significance for Asia and the rest of the world. Indeed, even though both the AIIB and BFA are not regional institutions in the strict sense of the word, they still aim to engage in regional multilateral communication and dialogue (Wang 2017).

When it comes to the official discourse on globalization and regionalization (which we believe indicates the level of enthusiasm for the related phenomena) at various levels of the government, the two paradigms continue to be emphasized at disparate rates (Table 6.2).[16] A brief survey on the website of the State Council of the People's Republic of China, in this respect, provides interesting insights. Comparatively speaking, whereas the word 'globalization' was repeated 2863 times in official documents between 2004 and 2012, 'regionalization' was displayed only 396 times. The number for 'globalization' reached to 6699 in the period from 2013 to 2023, while for 'regionalization,' it fell to 333 during the same time span. Similarly, academic interest in the two notions displays big discrepancies, too (Table 6.3). For example, a survey on the China National Knowledge Infrastructure (CNKI), a platform that collects academic data generated in China, produces about 256 thematic results for a search that uses the terms 'regionalism' and 'East Asian regionalism,' covering a period between 2008 and 2012. 'Globalization' on the other hand generates 2194 thematic results for the same period. From 2013 to 2023, academic research on the themes of 'regionalism' and 'East Asian regionalism' increased only incrementally to 711, whereas research on the themes 'One Belt One Road and globalization' and 'globalization' rose to a cumulative number of 8291.

---

[16] It is possible to identify a number of reasons for the discrepancy. The first, and perhaps primary, reason lies in the fact that China is a continental-sized country in terms of its geographic scope stretching well into Central Asia. The second reason is the major power nature of the country, which requires that its interest calculation extend globally. In this respect, China's relationship with the US, the present superpower, appears to be a major determinant. Recent US policies toward China, including the Obama-era Pivot to Asia and the Trump-era economic measures, lead to an impression of encirclement against which China attempts to develop counter strategies. Indeed, BRI itself can be seen, in part, as an outcome of such concern. Finally, it may be that the decision-makers and academic community in China do not hold a view that globalization and regionalization are mutually exclusive processes. Rather, they see the two as interrelated but corresponding to different areas of policymaking. Thus, one can promote both paradigms at the same time, provided that national resources are adequate.

142   S. YILMAZ AND B. LI

Table 6.2   Official discourse on globalization and regionalization

Theme	Years	Result	Years	Result
Globalization	2004–2012	2863	2013–2023	6699
Regionalization	2004–2012	396	2013–2023	333

Internet survey on the diplomatic discourse carried out by the authors on the internet platform of the State Council of the People's Republic of China (www.gov.cn)
Source Authors

Table 6.3   Academic discourse on globalization and regionalization

Theme	Years	Result	Years	Result
Globalization	2008–2012	2194	2013–2023	8291
Regionalism/East Asian Regional-ism	2008–2012	256	2013–2023	711

Internet survey on the epistemic community carried out by the authors on the CNKI database with the following areas selected to narrow down the research scope: Marxism, Chinese Communist Party, Political Science, Chinese Politics and International Politics, and International Law (https://www.cnki.net)
Source Authors

It is seen that whereas scholarly research on the East Asian regionalization (outnumbered by research on globalization even before the launch of the BRI) increased only incrementally in the post-BRI period, interest in globalization within the context of the BRI has almost doubled. This suggests that academic interest in regionalization has been retarded by the growing number of studies on globalization under the momentum generated by the BRI even though other factors (such as funding support by the related public and private institutions, which, also reflects a preference) may have been influential in this outcome, as well.[17]

---

[17] It should be noted that these surveys are only intended to give a general insight into the phenomena under study. Also, the fact that globalization has received more academic and political debate than regionalization may not always indicate that the cause for the discrepancy is the BRI. The causal uncertainty is further emphasized by the fact that even before the launch of the BRI, the regionalization discourse was secondary to globalization in terms of scholarly and political interest even though it is also obvious that the interest discrepancy has further widened ever since the establishment of the BRI.

6.6 Conclusion

It is understood from the analysis above that the emphasis on the BRI-driven globalization discourse may have certain retarding and diluting effects on China's regionalization policy in terms of active promotion of deep and viable channels of communication in East Asia. Yet, especially from economic perspective, the regression is relative since there has not been a noticeable decline in the country's commitment to and participation in the existing regional frameworks through bilateral and, even more so, multilateral agreements. Essentially, China's regionalism remains "economic-centered" and increasingly displays a more confident "economic engagement with others" (Wang 2011a, 2011b, p. 203 and 205). The retarding impact here is mostly related to a lack of momentum in the East Asian regionalization in terms of China's foreign diplomacy activism and contribution by academic circles, which are likely caused in part by the heavy emphasis on globalization under the BRI, thus, a loss of potential progress in regional integration. In other words, diplomatic and scholarly attention paid to the various processes of globalization under the BRI framework may have undermined the already slow-moving regionalization in terms of China's participation in it by further sidelining the debate on regional integration and cutting down on its momentum.

The negative implications appear to be greater on the institutional aspects of regionalization rather than that of economics. We identify two negative (real and potential) implications at this level. The first is the dampening effect of the BRI on the prospects of China's participation in regional institution buildup. Obviously, China has generally been more of a participant than a builder in East Asian institutionalization, which well predates the BRI. Nevertheless, greater focus on the global dynamics of connectivity and integration seems to have had an impact on China's role in the regional dimensions of institution-making and identity construction. To avoid such pitfalls as having a regressive effect on East Asian regionalism, China may need to draw a clearer idea of its vision of East Asia as a region by formulating a more precise conceptual and diplomatic framework, since, at the moment, and unlike many other regional stakeholders, China appears to still have "no clear idea about regionalism" (Wang 2011a, 2011b, p. 210).

The second implication, on the other hand, is less explicit and more consequential. In what may be called a diluting effect, by creating areas of overlaps across global and regional integration processes under globalization and regionalization, the BRI may risk obscuring the line between the two paradigms, thereby endangering regional institutions and the associated political, economic, and social identities. In this case, globalization may transgress the regional realm more than vice versa. For instance, by emphasizing Southeast Asia as an integral component, the BRI risks undermining the regionness of East Asia as a whole. To avoid the dampening effect, China may increase its feedback into the formalization process of East Asian regionalization by introducing new institutional frameworks with enough capital and human resources to ensure sustainable regional integration. Similarly, the risk of diluting regionalization may be precluded by ensuring that the BRI recognizes and supports regions and sub-regions by giving them space to express themselves as distinct units and interacting with them in their collective capacity.

In the final analysis, even though the BRI is still a relatively recent project that continues to unfold and evolve, it is significant to be aware of the potential implications and proactively develop strategies to ensure that East Asian regionalism stays on the course of its development in which the BRI gradually becomes both a partner and a reinforcing actor in all regional settings. As a matter of fact, if a positive synergy between the various mechanisms of the BRI and regionalism cannot be established, it would first and foremost impact the Initiative itself since the starting point and a significant component of the BRI is East Asia even though its main strategic direction is Eurasia (Yilmaz and Liu 2018). In a sense, the BRI as a program needs to "take-off" in East Asia first, hence the requirement for comprehensively understanding the interaction between the global (BRI-led globalization) and regional (East Asia regionalism) paradigms (Qoraboyev and Moldashev 2018, pp. 116–117).[18]

---

[18] Whereas, in this research, we emphasized the global characteristics of the BRI, it should be noted that there is hardly a consensus on this matter. For instance, Gimmel and Li maintains that the BRI shares certain features from both the state-driven old regionalism and market-driven new regionalism processes, thus, embodying a "hybrid model of regionalism" in which it "takes on ideas and follows trajectories of both traditions" (Gimmel and Li 2018, p. 14). The authors, however, also indicate that the BRI is more than what the two types of regionalisms suggest, thereby containing some globalization features, as well. Kaczmarski, on the other hand, points out to China's interpretation of regionalism, which is both broader in terms of territorial outreach and inclusive. Hence, the author does not see any potential friction between the BRI and regionalism as Chinese regionalism process is seen as very much integrated in globalization (Kaczmarski 2017).

Still, certain caveats apply in this analysis. Most importantly, perhaps, the question remains whether or not the dampening and diluting effects on China's participation in the processes of East Asian regionalization would entirely be ascribed to the BRI-led new globalization drive. What seems to be a causation could only be a correlation as there may be other factors that impact the process of East Asian regionalization and China's role in it. Internal variables such as diverse political and economic systems in East Asia ranging from authoritarian such as China to democratic such as Japan, complex historical relations and geopolitical tensions such as disputes over sovereignty over maritime and land territories, and external variables such as formal (Japan and the US) and informal (China and Russia) security alliances, and competition over resources certainly have negative implications for the pace and direction of regionalization in East Asia. Nevertheless, with those factors held as constant, it is obvious that, within the context of regionalization, the BRI-driven globalization seems to have had certain retarding and diluting effects on China's participation in and contribution to the region-making processes in East Asia. Further research, in this respect, is needed to gauge the relationship between globalization and regionalization within the context of the BRI by including in the analysis variables such as the long shadow of history in inter-regional relations, territorial disputes, incompatibilities between democratic and non-democratic regimes, development disparities, and geopolitical and economic rivalries that play a critical role in the regional strategic landscape, affecting the pace and direction of regionalization in East Asia.

References

AIIB. 2015. Articles of Agreement. Published May 22 2015. https://www.aiib.org/en/about-aiib/basic-documents/_download/articles-of-agreement/basic_document_english-bank_articles_of_agreement.pdf.

Ali, Ashraf H.M. 2005. Globalization as a Generator of Cultural and Economic Hegemony: A Postmod- ern Perspective. *Canadian Social Science* 1 (3): 11–20.

Andornino, Giovanni B. 2017. The Belt and Road Initiative in China's Emerging Grand Strategy of Con- nective Leadership. *China & World Economy* 25 (5): 4–22.

Atanassova-Cornelis, Elena. 2010. Dynamics of Japanese and Chinese Security Policies in East Asia and Implications for Regional Stability. *Asian Politics & Policy* 2 (3): 395–414.

Ba, Alice D. 2009. Regionalism's Multiple Negotiations: ASEAN in East Asia. *Cambridge Review of International Affairs* 22 (3): 345–367.

Beijing Review. 2018. Views on Global Governance, May 3. https://www.bjreview.com/Opinion/201804/t20180428_800128142.html.

Breslin, Shaun. 2010. Comparative Theory, China, and the Future of East Asian Regionalism(s). *Review of International Studies* 36: 709–729.

Callahan, William A. 2016. China's 'Asia Dream': The Belt Road Initiative and the New Regional Order. *Asian Journal of Comparative Politics* 1 (3): 226–243.

Carmody, Pádraig and Joel Wainwright. 2022. Contradiction and Restructuring in the Belt and Road Initiative: Reflections on China's pause in the 'Go world'. *Third World Quarterly* 43 (12): 2830–2851.

Chen, Jian, and Gong Xiaoying. 2017. 'Yi Dai Yi Lu' Zhanlue Kaiqi Juyou 'Renlei Mingyun Gongtongti' yishi de quanqiuhua fazhan de xinshidai [The 'One Belt, One Road' Strategy Opens a New Era of Globalization with the Consciousness of 'Human Destiny Community']. *Economist* 7 (7): 73–79.

Chuang, Peck M. 2015. Asean, China Seal Free Trade Agreement Upgrade. *The Business Times*, November, https://www.businesstimes.com.sg/node/77599.

Clark, Terry. 1990. International Marketing and National Character: A Review and Proposal for an Inte- grative Theory. *Journal of Marketing* 54 (4): 66–79.

Clifford, Tom. 2017. China: From the Treasure Fleet to One Belt, One Road. Counter Punch, December, https://www.counterpunch.org/2017/12/15/china-from-the-treasure-fleet-to-one-belt-one-road/.

Cook, Paul, and Colin Kirkpatrick. 2010. Globalization, Regionalization and Third World Development. *Regional Studies* 31 (1): 55–66.

Cox, Robert W. 1987. *Production, Power, and World Order: Social Forces in the Making of History*. New York: Columbia University Press.

Daly, Herman E. 2001. Globalization and Its Discontents. *Philosophy and Public Policy Quarterly* 21: 17–21.

De Graaff, Naná, and Bastiaan van Apeldoorn. 2018. US–China Relations and the Liberal World Order: Contending Elites, Colliding Visions? *International Affairs* 94 (1): 113–131.

Dent, Christopher M. 2009. Japan, China and East Asian Regionalism: Implications for the European Union. *Asia Europe Journal* 7: 161–178.

Dichter, Ernest. 1962. The World Consumer. *Harvard Business Review* 40 (4): 113–122.

Du, Julan, and Yifei Zhang. 2017. Does One Belt One Road Initiative Promote Chinese Overseas Direct Investment? *China Economic Review* 47: 189–205.

Dupuy, Alex. 1998. Thoughts on Globalization, Marxism, and the Left. *Latin American Perspectives* 25 (6): 55–58.

Ekman, Alice (ed.). 2019. *China's Belt & Road and the World: Competing Forms of Globalization*. IFRI: Center for Asian Studies, Paris. Published April 2019.

Ekman, Alie. 2017. China's New Silk Roads: A Flexible Implementation Process. In *The Years of China's New Silk Roads: From Words to (Re)action?*, 9–17. IFRI: Center for Asian Studies, Paris. Pub- lished February 2017.

Enderwick, Peter. 2018. The Economic Growth and Development Effects of China's One Belt, One Road Initiative. *Strategic Change* 27: 447–454.

Falk, Richard. 1999. *Predatory Globalization: A Critique*. Cambridge, UK: Polity Press.

Fardella, Enrico, and Giorgio Prodi. 2017. The Belt and Road Initiative Impact on Europe: An Italian Perspective. *China & World Economy* 25 (5): 125–138.

Fleet, Michael. 2017. China's Belt and Road Initiative: Harnessing Opportunities for Canada. In *Cracks in the Liberal International Order: 2018 Global Trends Report*, 95–100. Waterloo: Balsillie School of International Affairs.

Friedman, Jonathan. 1990. Being in the World: Globalization and Localization. *Theory, Culture & Society* 7 (2–3): 311–328.

Giddens, Anthony. 1991. *Modernity and Self Identity*. Oxford: Polity Press.

Grimmel, Andreas, and Yuan Li. 2018. The Belt and Road Initiative: A Hybrid Model of Regionalism. Working Papers on East Asian Studies, Institute of East Asian Studies, University of Duisburg- Essen, Duisburg, 122: 1–22.

Gros, Daniel. 2019. This is not a Trade War, It is a Struggle for Technological and Geo-strategic Domi- nance. *Centre for European Policy Studies (CEPS)* 1: 21–26.

Harvey, David. 1990. *The Condition of Postmodernity: An Enquiry into the Origins of Cultural Change*. Cambridge, MA: Blackwell.

Hathaway, Oona A., Julia Brower, Ryan Liss, Tina Thomas & Jacob Victor. 2013. Consent-Based Humanitarian Intervention: Giving Sovereign Respon- sibility Back to the Sovereign. *Cornell International Law Journal* 46: 499–568.

He, Yafei. 2017. China's New Role in Global Governance Shaping the Emerging World Order. *China Quarterly of International Strategic Studies* 3 (3): 341–355.

Held, D., Anthony G. McGrew, David Goldblatt, and Jonathan Perraton. 1999. *Global Transformations*. Stanford: Stanford University Press.

Herrero Alicia, G., and Xu Jianwei. 2017. China's Belt and Road Initiative: Can Europe Expect Trade Gains? *China & World Economy* 25 (6): 84–99.

Himaz, Rozana. 2021. Challenges Associated with the BRI: A Review of Recent Economics Literature. *The Service Industries Journal*, 41: 7–8, 512–526.

Hirst, Paul, and Grahame Thompson. 1996. Globalisation: Ten Frequently Asked Questions and Some Surprising Answers. *Soundings* 4: 47–66.

Hirst, Paul, Grahame Thompson, and Simon Bromley. 2015. *Globalization in Question*. Germany: Polity Press.

Huang, Yiping. 2016. Understanding China's Belt & Road Initiative: Motiva- tion, framework and assess- ment. *China Economic Review* 40: 314–321.

Huang, Yukon. 2018. Opinion: China's Trade War with U.S. is About Technological Dominance. Caixin Global, May 16. https://www.caixinglobal.com/2018-05-16/opinion-chinas-trade-war-with-us-is-about-technological-domina nce-101250670.html.

Jerabek, Marketa. 2023. Democracy and Human Rights in the Context of the Belt and Road Initiative. In *Securitization and Democracy in Eurasia*, eds. A. Mihr, P. Sorbello, B. Weiffen, 345–359. Springer, Cham. https://doi.org/10.1007/978-3-031-16659-4_24.

Jones, Lee. 2019. Does China's Belt and Road Initiative Challenge the Liberal, Rules-Based Order? *Fudan Journal of the Humanities and Social Sciences* 10000: 1–21. https://doi.org/10.1007/s40647-019-00252-8.

Kacowics, Arie M. 1999. Regionalization, Globalization, and Nationalism: Convergent, Divergent, or Overlapping? *Alternatives* 24: 528–529.

Kaczmarski, Marcin. 2017. Non-western Visions of Regionalism: China's New Silk Road and Russia's Eurasian Economic Union. *International Affairs* 93 (6): 1357–1376.

Kang, Davd C. 2007. *China Rising: Peace, Power, and Order in East Asia*. New York: Columbia University Press.

Kawai, Masahiro, and Ganeshan Wignaraja. 2011. Asian FTAs: Trends, Prospects and Challenges. *Journal of Asian Economics* 22 (1): 1–22.

Kellner, Douglas. 2002. Theorizing Globalization. *Sociological Theory* 20 (3): 285–305.

Kellner, Douglas. 2018. Donald Trump as Authoritarian Populist: A Frommian Analysis. In *Critical Theory and Authoritarian Populism*, ed. Jeremiah Morelock, 71–82. London: University of Westminster Press.

Khan, Muhammad K., Imran Ali Sandano, Cornelius B. Pratt, and Tahir Farid. 2018. China's Belt and Road Initiative: A Global Model for an Evolving Approach to Sustainable Regional Development. *Sustainability* 10 (11): 4234.

Kim, Samuel S. 2004. Regionalization and Regionalism in East Asia. *Journal of East Asian Studies* 4: 39–67.

Kohl, Tristan. 2019. The Belt and Road Initiative's Effect on Supply-Chain Trade: Evidence from Structural Gravity Equations. *Cambridge Journal of Regions, Economy and Society* 12 (1): 77–104.

Kramer, Franklin D. 2023. China and the New Globalization. *Atlantic Council*. February. https://www.atlanticcouncil.org/wpcontent/uploads/2023/02/China_and_the_New_Globalization_IB_Digital_v2-1.pdf.

Krasner, Stephen D. 2009. *Power, The State and Sovereignty: Essays on International Relations*. New York, NY: Routledge.

Lairson, Thomas D. 2018. The Global Strategic Environment of the BRI: Deep Interdependence and Structural Power. In *China's Belt and Road Initiative: Changing the Rules of Globalization*, ed. Wenxian Zhang, Ilan Alon, and Christoph Lattemann, 35–55. New York, NY: Palgrave Macmillan.

Li, E.X. 2016a. The End of Globalism. *Foreign Affairs*, December 9.

Li, Ming. 2016b. Guoji fa yu 'yidai yilu [International Law and 'One Belt, One Road']. *Law Science Mag- azine* 37 (1): 11–17.

Liu, Yuan, and Yang Lihua. 2002. Quanqiuhua Quyuhua yu Guojia Zhuyi [Globalization, Regionalization and Globalism]. *Journal of Literature, History & Philosophy* 1: 156–161.

Liu, Weidong, and Michael Dunford. 2016. Inclusive Globalization: Unpacking China's Belt and Road Initiative. *Area Development and Policy* 1 (3): 323–341.

Lomnitz, Claudio. 1994. Decadence in Times of Globalization. *Cultural Anthropology* 9 (2): 257–267.

Mandelbaum, H.G., Weiffen, B. (2023). The Belt and Road Initiative and Autocracy Promotion as Elements of China's Grand Strategy. In *Securitization and Democracy in Eurasia*, ed. Mihr, A., Sorbello, P., Weiffen, B., Springer, Cham. https://doi.org/10.1007/978-3-031-16659-4_25..

Mao, Haiou, Guanchun Liu, Chengsi Zhang, and Atif Rao. 2019. Does Belt and Road Initiative Hurt Node Countries? A Study from Export Perspective. *Emerging Markets Finance & Trade* 55: 1472–1485.

May, Clifford D. 2018a. Give Anti-Globalism a Chance. *The Washington Times*, April 4. https://www.washingtontimes.com/news/2018/apr/3/give-anti-globalism-a-chance/.

May, Hongmei G. 2018b. Globalization 5.0 Led by China: Powered by Positive Frames for BRI. In *China's Belt and Road Initiative: Changing the Rules of Globalization*, eds. Wenxian Zhang, Ilan Alon and Christoph Lattemann, 321–337. New York, NY: Palgrave Macmillan.

McQuail, Denis. 2000. *McQuail's Mass Communication Theory*. London, UK: SAGE Publications.

Mehanna, Rock-Antoine. 2008. Globalization Versus Regionalization: And the Winner Is.... *Journal of Transnational Management* 13 (4): 287–317.

Miller, Tom. 2017. *China's Asian Dream: Quiet Empire Building along the New Silk Road*. London: Zed Books.

Mills, Melinda. 2009. Globalization and Inequality. *European Sociological Review* 25 (1): 1–8.

Nair, Deepak. 2008. Regionalism in the Asia Pacific/East Asia: A Frustrated Regionalism? *Contemporary Southeast Asia* 31 (1): 110–142.

NDRC. 2015. "Vision and Actions on Jointly Building Silk Road Economic Belt and Twenty-first century Maritime Silk Road," https://eng.yidaiyilu.gov.cn/p/1084.html.

Nef, Jorge. 2002. Globalization and the Crisis of Sovereignty, Legitimacy and Democracy. *Latin American Perspectives* 29 (6): 59–69.

Nylund, Katarina. 1990s. Cultural Analyses in Urban Theory of the 1990s. *Acta Sociologica* 44 (3): 219–230.

Obe, Mitsuru, and Eri Sugiura. 2018. Five Things to Know About 'Made in China 2025'. *Nikkei*, April 04. https://asia.nikkei.com/Economy/Tradewar/Five-things-to-know-about-Made-in-China-20252.

Oman, Charles. 1994. *Globalisation and Regionalisation: The Challenge for Developing Countries*. Paris: OECD Development Centre Studies.

Oman, Charles. 1999. Globalization, Regionalization, and Inequality. In *Inequality, Globalization, and World Politics*, ed. Andrew Hurrell and Ngaire Woods, 36–66. Oxford: Oxford University Press.

Osman, Ruby. Bye Bye BRI? Why 3 New Initiatives Will Shape the Next 10 Years of China's Global Outreach. *Time,* October 2023. https://time.com/6319264/china-belt-and-road-ten-years/.

Park, Jinsoo. 2012. Regional Leadership Dynamics and the Evolution of East Asian Regionalism. *Pacific Focus* 27 (2): 290–318.

Pempel, TJ. 2005. Introduction: Emerging Webs of Regional Connectedness. In *Remapping East Asia: The Construction of a Region*, ed. T.J. Pempel, 1–28. Ithaca, NY: Cornell University Press.

Pritchett, Lant. 1997. Divergence, Big Time. *Journal of Economic Perspectives* 11 (3): 3–17.

Qoraboyev, Ikboljon, and Kairat Moldashev. 2018. The Belt and Road Initiative and Comprehensive Region- alism in Central Asia. In *Central Asia: Rethinking the Silk Road*, ed. Maximilian Mayer, 115–130. Singapore: Palgrave Macmillan.

Quinton-Brown, Patrick. 2023. Two Responsibilities to Protect. *Millennium: Journal of International Studies*, 1–25.

Ramasamy, Bala, and Matthew Yeung. 2019. China's One Belt One Road Initiative: The Impact of Trade Facilitation versus Physical Infrastructure on Exports. *The World Economy* 42 (6): 1673–1694.

Ravallion, Martin. 2003. The Debate on Globalization, Poverty and Inequality: Why Measurement Matters. *International Affairs* 79 (4): 739–753.

Ravenhill, John. 2010. The 'New East Asian Regionalism': A Political Domino Effect. *Review of Interna- tional Political Economy* 17 (2): 178–208.

Rimmer, Peter J. 2018. China's Belt and Road Initiative: Underlying Economic and International Relations Dimensions. *Asia Pacific School of Economics and Government, The Australian National University* 32 (2): 3–26.

Robertson, Robbie T. 2003. *The Three Waves of Globalization A History of a Developing Global Conscious- ness*. New York: Zed Books.

Robertson, Roland. 1992. *Globalization: Social Theory and Global Culture*. London: Sage.

Robertson, Roland. 1995. Glocalization: Time-Space and Homogeneity-Heterogeneity. In *Global Moderni- ties*, ed. Scott Lash, Roland Robertson, and Mike Featherstone, 25–44. London: Sage.

Rodrik, Dani. 2001. Trading in Illusions. *Foreign Policy* 123: 54–62.

Rothkopf, David. 1997. In Praise of Cultural Imperialism? *Foreign Policy* 107: 38–53.

Ruggie, John G. 1982. International regimes, transactions, and change: embedded liberalism in the postwar economic order. *International Organization* 36(2): 379–415. https://doi.org/10.1017/S0020818300018993.

Schortgen, Francis. 2018. China and the Twenty-First-Century Silk Roads: A New Era of Global Economic Leadership? In *China's Belt and Road Initiative: Changing the Rules of Globalization*, ed. Wenxian Zhang, Ilan Alon, and Christoph Lattemann, 17–35. New York, NY: Palgrave Macmillan.

Seabrook, Jeremy. 2004. *Consuming Cultures: Globalization and Local Lives*. UK: New International Publications.

Searight, Amy. 2018. ADMM-Plus: The Promise and Pitfalls of an ASEAN-led Security Forum. *CSIS*, November 1. https://www.csis.org/analysis/admm-plus-promise-and-pitfalls-asean-led-security-forum.

Segal, Gerald. 1996. East Asia and the 'Constrainment' of China. *International Security* 20 (4): 107–135.

Siu, Ricardo C.S. 2019. China's Belt and Road Initiative: Reducing or Increasing the World Uncertainties? *Journal of Economic Issues* 53 (2): 571–578.

Stiglitz, Joseph E. 2002. *Globalization and Its Discontents*. New York: W.W. Norton & Company.

Swaine, Michael D. 2015. Chinese Views and Commentary on the "One Belt, One Road" Initiative. *China Leadership Monitor* 47: 3–27.

Therborn, Göran. 2000. Globalizations: Dimensions, Historical Waves, Regional Effects, Normative Govern- ance. *International Sociology* 15 (2): 151–179.

Therborn, Göran, and Habibul Haque Khondker (eds.). 2006. *Asia and Europe in Globalization: Continents, Regions and Nations*. Leiden and Boston: Brill.

Thompson, Grahame. 1998. Globalisation Versus Regionalism? *The Journal of North African Studies* 3 (2): 59–74.

Tu, Xinquan. 2018. Is the Belt and Road Initiative a Chinese-style Regionalism? Korea Economic Institute of America (KEIA), August 3. https://www.keia.org/sites/default/files/publications/jukas_3.1_is_the_belt_and_road_initiative_a_chinese_style_regionalism.pdf.

Valuev, Vasiliy. 2000. Globalization Through Regionalization. *International Journal of Political Economy* : 21–43.

Väyrynen, Raimo. 2003. Regionalism: Old and New. *International Studies Review* 5 (1): 25–51.

Vera Schulhof, Detlef van Vuuren, and Julian Kirchherr. 2022 The Belt and Road Initiative (BRI): What Will it Look Like in the Future? *Technological Forecasting and Social Change*, 17 (5): 1–17. https://doi.org/10.1016/j.techfore.2021.121306

Wade, Robert H. 2004. Is Globalization Reducing Poverty and Inequality? *International Journal of Health Services* 34 (3): 381–414.

Wang, Hongying, and James N. Rosenau. 2009. China and Global Governance. *Asian Perspective* 33 (3): 5–39.

Wang, Jiangyu. 2011a. China and East Asian Regionalism. *European Law Journal* 17 (5): 611–629.

Wang, Yuzhu. 2011b. China, Economic Regionalism, and East Asian Integration. *Japanese Journal of Politi- cal Science* 12 (2): 195–212.

Wang, Mingguo. 2017. The Logic of Institutions of the Belt and Road Forum for International Cooperation. *Teaching and Research* 8: 58–66. [In Chinese].

Wang, Xueyu. 2004. Xin Diqu Zhuyi—Zai Guojia yu Quanqiuhua Zhijian Jiaqi Qiaoliang [New Regional- ism: Bridging the Gap between Nation-States and Globalization]. *World Economics and Politics* 1: 36–40.

Wang, Yiwei. 2016. *The Belt and Road: What Will China Offer the World in Its Rise*. Beijing: New World Press.

Warner, Malcolm. 2017. On Globalization 'with Chinese Characteristics'?, *Asia Pacific Business Review* 23: 3, 309–316, https://doi.org/10.1080/136 02381.2017.1304400.

Wei, Min. 2003. Quanqiuhua yu Diqu Zhuyi [Globalization and Regionalism]. *The Journal of International Studies* 40 (4): 46–53.

Yeo, Andrew. 2019. China's Rising Assertiveness and the Decline in the East Asian Regionalism Narrative. *International Relations of the Asia-Pacific*. https://doi.org/10.1093/irap/lcz013.

Yilmaz, Serafettin, and Changming Liu. 2018. China's 'Belt and Road' Strategy in Eurasia and Euro-Atlanti- cism. *Europe-Asia Studies* 70 (2): 252–276.

Yin, Mu. 2003. Guo Jia Zhu Yi Qu Yu Zhu Yi Yu Quan Qiu Zhu Yi De Xiang Hu Guan Xi [The Relation- ship Among Nationalism, Regionalism and Globalism]. *Guangxi Social Sciences* 5: 21–23.

Zeng, Jinghan. 2019. Chinese Views of Global Economic Governance. *Third World Quarterly* 40 (3): 578–594.

Zhai, Fan. 2018. China's Belt and Road Initiative: A Preliminary Quantitative Assessment. *Journal of Asian Economics* 55: 84–92.

Zhang, Wenxian, Ilan Alon, and Christoph Lattemann (eds.). 2018. *China's Belt and Road Initiative: Chang- ing the Rules of Globalization*. New York, NY: Palgrave Macmillan.

Zheng, Bijian. 2017. China's 'One Belt, One Road' Plan Marks the Next Phase of Globalization. *New Perspectives Quarterly* 34 (3): 27–30.

Zhou, Weifeng, and Mario Esteban. 2018. Beyond Balancing: China's Approach towards the Belt and Road Initiative. *Journal of Contemporary China* 27 (112): 487–501.

Zhu, Feng. 1997. Guanyu quyu zhuyi yu quan qiu zhuyi [Regionalism and Globalism]. *Contemporary Inter- national Relations* 9: 42–47.

Zou, Keyuan, and Wenxian Qiu. 2018. The Belt and Road Initiative and the Common Heritage of Mankind: Some Preliminary Observations. *Chinese Journal of International Law* 17 (3): 749–756.

CHAPTER 7

Infrastructure and the Politics of African State Agency: Shaping the Belt and Road Initiative in East Africa

Frangton Chiyemura, Elisa Gambino, and Tim Zajontz

7.1 INTRODUCTION

Infrastructure development has experienced a political renaissance in Africa and is again at the center of national, regional, and continental development agendas, with the African Union's *Agenda 2063* striving to "[c]onnect Africa with world-class infrastructure" (African Union 2015).

This chapter is an updated version of the journal article: Chiyemura, F., Gambino, E. & Zajontz, T. "Infrastructure and the Politics of African State Agency: Shaping the Belt and Road Initiative in East Africa." *Chin. Polit. Sci. Rev.* **8**, 105–131 (2023). https://doi.org/10.1007/s41111-022-00214-8.

F. Chiyemura
Open University, Milton Keynes, UK
e-mail: frangton.chiyemura@open.ac.uk

© The Author(s), under exclusive license to Springer Nature Switzerland AG 2025
K. G.Cai et al. (eds.), *China and Global Economic Governance, Volume I: China's BRI & AIIB and Global Economic Governance*, Politics and Development of Contemporary China,
https://doi.org/10.1007/978-3-031-73212-6_7

155

Much of Africa's infrastructure was inherited from the colonial era, during which it served the dual purpose of economic exploitation and territorial control. After independence and in light of 'modernisation' discourses and practices, infrastructure development in sub-Saharan Africa surged in the 1960s and 1970s, largely driven and financed by the Bretton Woods institutions (Mold 2012). Yet, many of these infrastructure projects were "regarded as too expensive and unsuited to African requirements" (Nugent 2018, p. 22). For instance, before the turn of the twenty-first century, around 30% of the roads built in the 1970s were not in use anymore (Zawdie and Langford 2002). In light of structural adjustment and austerity policies, the continent witnessed a 'prescribed' retrenchment of African governments from large-scale infrastructure development throughout the 1980s and 1990s (Zajontz and Taylor 2021).

Currently, Africa's "re-enchantment with big infrastructure" (Nugent 2018) is part and parcel of a global "emergent regime of infrastructure-led development whose ultimate objective is to produce functional transnational territories that can be 'plugged in' to global networks of production and trade" (Schindler and Kanai 2021, p. 40). Infrastructure has again become central to global development discourse and practice. The narrative that infrastructure needs to be built, upgraded, and rendered more efficient to increase African states' ability to deliver economic and social development is now hegemonic (see Schindler and Kanai 2021; Cissokho 2022). Over the past two decades, African governments, regional organizations, the private sector, as well as multilateral and bilateral development financiers have mainstreamed infrastructure in their development planning and mobilized resources to close the so-called infrastructure gap, which the African Development Bank (AfDB) estimates at $68–108 billion per year (AfDB 2018, p. 63).

E. Gambino (✉)
University of Manchester, Manchester, UK
e-mail: elisa.gambino@manchester.ac.uk

T. Zajontz
University of Freiburg, Freiburg Im Breisgau, Germany

Stellenbosch University, Stellenbosch, South Africa

T. Zajontz
e-mail: post@tim-zajontz.de

Against this background, China has been identified by African policymakers as a particularly suitable strategic partner, becoming Africa's largest bilateral source of infrastructure funding. According to the Infrastructure Consortium for Africa (ICA), infrastructure finance totaled at $100.8 billion in 2018, with China contributing about a fourth thereof ($25.7 billion) (ICA 2018, p. 7). As infrastructure has become a main pillar of Sino-African cooperation, there has been growing analytical interest in the role of African actors in shaping the terms and conditions and, by extension, the distribution of costs and benefits of infrastructure projects with Chinese participation (Taylor 2020; Wissenbach 2019; Zajontz 2020a, forthcoming; Mohan and Tan-Mullins 2019; Chiyemura 2019a, 2019b; Gambino 2021). This follows a more general African "agency turn" in China-Africa studies which has shifted the research focus to the myriad ways in which African state and non-state actors shape the continent's engagements with China (Alden and Large 2019, p. 13; see for instance, Gadzala 2015; Carmody and Kragelund 2016).

This article speaks to this growing body of literature by exploring different 'spheres' of African state agency, namely the agency of political elites in negotiating Tanzania's planned Bagamoyo port, bureaucratic agency in the context of Ethiopia's Adama wind farms and agency of local governance actors in the case of Kenya's Lamu port. As Mohan and Lampert (2013, p. 93) underline, "the ability of African actors to exercise [...] agency is highly uneven and can have as much to do with African politics as it does with the politics of China-Africa relations." In this paper, we thus respond to recent calls for a "contextual approach [...] that considers the contours and specificities of African agency" (Links 2021, p. 124). Our context-sensitive analytical approach toward various spheres of state agency focuses on ways in which African state actors are embedded in and interact with specific political, legal, institutional, and economic contexts.

As such, we seek to transcend reductionist and generalizing assumptions about a lack of African agency in light of power asymmetries between Africa and China—commonly understood to be tilted in the latter's favor. Certainly, China's economic and political clout in global affairs gives Chinese actors leverage in their engagements with their African counterparts. However, as this paper shows, the distribution of material capabilities and soft power at the international level is by far the only determinant for the degree of African agency in concrete Sino-African encounters. We show that, notwithstanding existing power asymmetries, African state actors shape the development of infrastructure projects with Chinese involvement in myriad ways and at different scales (see Nantulya 2021). Our analysis demonstrates that political, economic, and legal-bureaucratic contexts within African states do matter and crucially condition infrastructure projects with Chinese involvement.

The article draws on primary data collected through extensive field research on Sino-African cooperation in the infrastructure sector in China, Ethiopia, Kenya, and Tanzania. This data was triangulated with relevant secondary literature and primary textual sources, notably media reports and official documents, such as government and company reports and press statements. Semi-structured elite interviews were conducted in Tanzania throughout 2019 with over thirty Tanzanian government officials (including senior civil servants and top officials from relevant ministries and state agencies), civil society representatives, and academics. Passive observation was undertaken in both Dar es Salaam and Bagamoyo. The Ethiopian case study is based on over fifty elite and ethnographic interviews with Ethiopian federal and sub-national state officials, as well as representatives of the Chinese government and Chinese enterprises. Interviews in Ethiopia were conducted between April 2017 and January 2018. The Kenyan case study draws on interview data and ethnographic observations with Chinese government officials, representatives from Kenyan national and sub-national state agencies, and Chinese state-owned enterprises, conducted between June 2018 and July 2019 with over forty participants.

The article proceeds in five sections. First, we outline Africa's current Chinese-backed infrastructure boom and Africa's gradual integration into the Belt and Road Initiative (BRI) and situate this work within the recent literature on Sino-African relations. Here, we propose an explicitly non-reductionist understanding of agency which does justice to the variety of African actors involved in negotiating and mediating Chinese infrastructure projects in East Africa. Section two analyses Tanzanian developmentalist state agency in negotiating the Bagamoyo port and Special Economic Zone. Section three discusses Ethiopian bureaucratic agency in the planning processes of Adama I and Adama II wind farms. Section four deals with Kenya's Lamu port, highlighting the agency of local governance actors vis-à-vis Chinese contractors in the context of pre-existing center-periphery relations. Lastly, the paper concludes by underlining the key findings and suggesting future avenues for research.

7.2 THE BELT AND ROAD INITIATIVE, INFRASTRUCTURE, AND THE ROLE OF 'THE' STATE

Infrastructure is central to the BRI. Initially aimed at closing infrastructure gaps in China's immediate regional neighborhood, the initiative has now developed into a trans-regional—if not global—project which promotes multi-sectoral connectivity across Asia, Europe, Africa, South America, and even the Arctic. Although African countries were formally included in the BRI only in 2017, many already existing infrastructure projects have now been incorporated in this connectivity initiative (see Gambino 2022). For instance, the Lamu Port–South Sudan–Ethiopia Transport (LAPSSET) Corridor, a regional project initiated by East African governments, is now branded as a BRI 'project catalysing connectivity' (Belt and Road Forum 2019).

Even though Chinese financing is marketed as having 'no strings attached,' it is often accompanied by a stringent set of requirements, particularly with regard to the choice of contracting firms (Alden and Jiang 2019; Mohan and Tan-Mullins 2019). China Export Import Bank (China Exim Bank), for example, requires 70% of contract procurements (such as machineries and materials) to originate from China, and it was estimated that 89% of Chinese-funded projects are implemented by Chinese contractors (Hillman 2018). A growing number of Chinese firms are also constructing non-Chinese funded infrastructure projects, as in the case of the port of Lamu in Northern Kenya discussed below. A 2017 McKinsey report estimates that Chinese firms won about half of all international Engineering-Procurement-Construction (EPC) contracts and, by value, 42% of World Bank tenders in sub-Saharan Africa (Sun et al. 2017, p. 39). In East Africa, Chinese firms have constructed 41.9% of all infrastructure projects (Deloitte 2016, p. 21). Between 2009 and 2015, the revenues of Chinese construction companies from projects in Africa almost doubled—from $28 billion to $54.7 billion (CARI 2021).

While Chinese involvement in Africa's infrastructure sector has been considered as potentially transformative by decision-makers and scholars alike (see Bräutigam 2019; Soulé-Kohndou 2020), it has prompted lively debates around the social, economic, and financial impacts of certain Chinese-funded projects (Taylor 2020; Carmody et al. 2021). Increasingly unsustainable sovereign debt levels—partly related to Chinese loans for large-scale infrastructure—in countries like Djibouti, Ethiopia, Kenya, and Zambia have caused controversies and fiscal pressures for

African governments (Zajontz 2021a). Moreover, poor employment and working conditions in Chinese-built infrastructure projects have also caused contestation from governmental agencies, civil society actors, and workers (see Oya 2019; Gambino 2020a; Chiyemura 2021). In light of public controversies about some infrastructure projects with Chinese involvement, it is paramount to scrutinize the role played by African state actors in their negotiation, planning, and implementation.

In the context of Africa's recent infrastructure boom, "the state as the driver and promoter of development is now back on the agenda" (Wethal 2019, p. 492; see also Péclard et al. 2020). As Schindler and Kanai (2021, p. 40) underline, "infrastructure-led development" has brought back state-led spatial and development planning with the ultimate aim of "getting the territory right" for smooth and seamless integration into global trade and value chains. As the state plays a pivotal role in the provision, operation, and regulation of a country's infrastructure, a myriad of state agencies and institutions (at various levels of governance) are involved in the development of said projects. These range from central government institutions, such as presidencies, treasuries, line ministries, specialized agencies, and state-owned corporations, to authorities at the sub-national and local scales, for example provincial administrations, townships, and community assemblies. In other words, state agency in the infrastructure sector unfolds in various spheres.

7.2.1 Spheres of African State Agency: State Actors and Their Contexts

Our 'working definition' of African agency is the ability of Africans (as individuals or as collectives) to shape their engagements with external actors in ways subjectively seen as safeguarding and advancing actors' interests and objectives. We root our analysis in a dialectical understanding of the agency-structure relationship. As Wight (2006, p. 281) argues, "[t]he idea of an agent acting in a structural vacuum, or structures acting without agents, is logically impossible." This also applies to state actors. To transcend reifying and voluntarist conceptions of the state, our analysis of state agency—or rather state agenc*ies*—is rooted in a social-relational ontology of the state according to which state actors and institutions are firmly embedded in and interrelated with structural contexts (Jessop 2016, pp. 53–59; in China-Africa studies see Lampert and Mohan 2015;

Ziso 2018, pp. 37–39). As Zajontz (forthcoming) cautions, "if not appropriately conceptualised, there is a risk to reduce African state agency to elite agency and to misconstrue actions of political elites and officials as detached from state-society relations, historically specific state forms and wider political-economic structures."

A more nuanced understanding of (African) state agency requires us to first transcend the "'state-as-agent' thesis" (Wight 2006, pp. 177–178), which mistakes a highly complex entity for an anthropomorphic and unitary subject. Jessop (1990, p. 367) rightly reminds us that "it is not the state which acts, it is always specific sets of politicians and state officials located in specific parts of the state system." The state is thus to be understood as a dynamic and multilayered "institutional ensemble" which provides "a set of institutional capacities and liabilities" necessary to exert state power (Jessop 1990, pp. 269–270, footnote 13).

A social-relational ontology of the state implies that the ways in which state officials and agencies act are conditioned by historically specific state-society relations (see Migdal 2001). We concur with Hagmann and Péclard's (2010, p. 550) suggestion that statehood (in Africa) is constantly (de)constructed and 'negotiated' by a variety of actors in a host of "negotiation arenas and tables." In Migdal's (1994, p. 8) words, "[w]e need to break down the undifferentiated concepts of the state—and also of the society—to understand how different elements in each pull in different directions, leading to unanticipated patterns of domination and transformation." A nuanced analysis of state agency in China-Africa relations must acknowledge the multiscalarity and multifacetedness of the state. For one, it must account for "the manifold moves and efforts made at local, national and international levels to arrive at new arrangements towards the organisation of public authority" (Doornbos 2011, p. 201). Secondly, it must account for the complex spatio-temporality of 'the' state that entails myriad modalities of governance across time and space (see for instance Boone 2003; Olivier de Sardan 2011; Jessop 2016).

This paper sheds closer analytical attention on three (out of many) 'spheres' in which state agency is exerted by different state actors, namely the agency of political elites, bureaucratic agency, and agency of local governance actors. The first sphere in which African state actors shape the terms and conditions of Chinese projects and investments are the top echelons of the state. The agency of political elites in Sino-African relations has received increasing scholarly attention (see, for instance, Hodzi 2018; Mohan and Tan-Mullins 2019). Indeed, state leaders play a pivotal role in "defining and mediating the external expression of state preferences" (Brown 2012, p. 1892). Especially at an early stage, negotiations with Chinese financial institutions, investors, or contractors are usually headed by cabinet ministers and other top officials. As Soulé-Kohndou (2020) argues, delivering infrastructure is a key means of gaining electoral support and, hence, consolidating political power for leading politicians, both in democratic and less democratic contexts. Moreover, it is usually the presidency, the prime ministerial office, and relevant top officials which—in consultation with various social groups and organized interests—set the (political) agenda in the infrastructure sector. It is also these top-level politicians who crucially determine the political context for the bureaucracies and state agencies to see infrastructure projects through.

Hence, Mohan and Tan-Mullins underline that "the agency of Southern political elites shapes how infrastructure is financed, funded and utilised, which are ultimately questions of 'who benefits?'" (2019, p. 1370). For instance, throughout the 2010s, Zambia's ruling party has strategically used Chinese loans to advance its ambitious 'development-through-infrastructure' agenda (Zajontz 2020a). The keen interest of Chinese banks and firms to fund and construct infrastructure was strategically employed by Zambian elites to pursue infrastructure-led development, while simultaneously furthering certain vested interests with the help of 'not so public' procurement processes (Zajontz 2020b, pp. 123–130). The case study of the negotiations over a Chinese investment in a mega-port and Special Economic Zone in Bagamoyo, Tanzania, reveals how political elites—by means of the powers vested in their offices, or more abstractly put "positioned-practice-places" (Wight 1999)—can set the tone for negotiations of infrastructure projects. As will be shown, the agency of state actors in the sphere of political elites is thereby not autonomous but very much constrained or enabled by the balance of political powers within the state, hence the wider political context in Tanzania (see Jessop 2016, p. 54).

The second sphere where African state actors exert agency when dealing with Chinese stakeholders is that of African bureaucrats, interchangeably understood as government officials, civil servants, as well as technical and administrative experts. Such actors, by means of their access to various forms of institutional and regulatory power, are able to exercise "control over the process and outcome of negotiations with China in accordance to their country's national regulations" (Soulé-Kohndou 2019, p. 191). They do so by interpreting and applying the 'rules of the game,' including (in)formal laws, standards, norms, procedures, routines, and conventions. Therefore, political decision-making in the infrastructure sector is highly dependent on bureaucratic expertise and practices. Recent studies are recognizing the role of bureaucrats in enacting African agency in the context of Africa-China relations. In her study of Benin-China engagements in infrastructure development, Soulé-Kohndou (2019, p. 202) concludes that "bureaucrats located in ministerial departments in charge of reviewing calls for tenders, monitoring the execution of public works and closing projects" are able to exercise agency by applying (or potentially bending) procedural standards and legal-bureaucratic norms.

In the case of Ethiopia, as shown by Chiyemura (2020), bureaucrats, at various governance levels, are accorded with responsibilities to 'officially' plan, broker, coordinate, negotiate, agree, implement, and manage infrastructure projects in line with and conforming to the values, beliefs, and interests of political forces with access to the state. In this paper, we will show how Ethiopian government officials were able to exercise agency through planning of the arrangements around the finance and development of the wind farms in ways subjectively seen to advance the political and economic interests of their country. The bureaucratic sphere of state agency is thereby firmly embedded in the politics of broader political and governance structures of the Ethiopian authoritarian developmental state.

While political elites and state officials, by means of their (often unhinged) access to state institutions and resources, are certainly key actors in shaping their countries' relations with China, they are evidently not the only actors involved. The third sphere through which African actors exert agency and (re)shape their encounters with Chinese actors is local governance. As an analytical category, governance can be defined as "any organised method of delivering public or collective services and goods according to specific logics and norms, and to specific forms of authority" (Olivier de Sardan 2011, p. 22). In the African context, political decentralization and devolution—driven by endogenous and exogenous forces, such as structural adjustment programs (see for instance D'Arcy and Cornell 2016; Kanyinga 2016)—caught pace in the 1980s and 1990s when centralization was seen as a leading cause for inequality, marginalization, and conflict. Although sub-national authorities in devolved systems play a key role in the provision of goods and services (including infrastructure), the decision-making processes for the development of large-scale infrastructure remain highly centralized (Péclard et al. 2020).

In Kenya, since the 2010 constitutional reform, the newly formed county government, as well as social and political actors at the local level of governance, have constantly renegotiated their relations with the national government. This dynamic has also affected infrastructure projects with Chinese participation. At the same time and in light of the growing participation of Chinese actors in Kenya's development agenda, local governance actors are also engaging and negotiating with Chinese stakeholders directly (Wang and Wissenbach 2019; Gambino 2020b). Both these dynamics unfold in the Chinese-built port of Lamu, where the local administration and communities of fishers and mangrove farmers are shaping the decision-making and implementation processes for this port. The sphere of local governance thus refers to the critical juncture of 'layers' of power across time and space, which add to and intersect with one another when a 'local' political authority is formed (Bierschenk and Olivier de Sardan 1998). As will be shown below, the devolved system in Kenya has "created multiple opportunities for a diverse range of actors" (Chome 2020, p. 4), who reshape the development of infrastructure projects so as to include their 'local' interests.

7.3   Marking the Territory for Bagamoyo Port: Elite Agency and Tanzania's Autocratic Developmental State Under Magufuli

In September 2012, a memorandum of understanding was signed between the Tanzanian government of former President Kikwete and China Merchants Port Holdings (CMPort)[1] over the construction of a mega-port and a Chinese-run special economic zone (SEZ) in Bagamoyo (60 km north of Dar es Salaam). A framework agreement followed during Chinese President Xi's Tanzania visit in March 2013, with an implementation agreement being entered in January 2014. Oman's State General

---

[1] CMPort is publicly listed and headquartered in Hong Kong. Until August 2016, its name was China Merchants Holdings International. The Chinese government holds a majority share in CMPort through China Merchants Group. As one of China's biggest port developers and operators, CMPort is involved in several overseas ports, such as Sri Lanka's Hambantota port and Pakistan's Gwadar port.

Reserve joined the project in October 2014 by means of a tripartite agreement (Interview, former Tanzanian senior official, 27th November 2019). Bagamoyo has since been branded as a flagship project of the BRI with a promulgated total investment sum of $10 billion. The 3000 ha site is planned to be linked to Tanzania's new Standard Gauge Railway and the Tanzania-Zambia Railway Authority (TAZARA). This section briefly recounts the transformation of the Tanzanian state under the late President Magufuli, followed by an analysis of how these changing political and institutional contexts have engendered what we call autocratic developmental state agency, leading to a reappraisal of the conditions of the Bagamoyo project on the part of the Magufuli government and ultimately to a temporary cessation of negotiations with the Chinese investor.

7.3.1 Transforming the State from the Top: The 'Bulldozer Effect'

Magufuli's election in 2015 followed a period of waning popular support for the ruling party *Chama cha Mapinduzi* (CCM) and growing levels of dissatisfaction within the electorate regarding widespread corruption and sluggish economic development (Tsubura 2018; Paget 2021). The 2015 presidential race was marked by fierce political debates about overdue developmental benefits from foreign investment and by demands for an indigenization of Tanzania's economy (Schlimmer 2018). Having campaigned on a populist platform that promised higher public revenues from foreign investment and a resolute fight against corruption and tax avoidance, Magufuli, once in office, pursued a "[c]onfrontational and authoritarian approach towards the private sector" (Andreoni 2017, p. 37). This applied not least to foreign investment, including investments from the 'all-weather friend' China. A Tanzanian scholar suggested that Magufuli tried to capitalize on growing negative public sentiment toward Chinese investments, which had become manifest in a popular narrative that "this country is going to be colonised again" (Interview, M. Shangwe, 15th November 2019; see also Kinyondo 2019). In a foreword to the book *Tanzania's Industrialisation Journey, 2016–2056*, Magufuli wrote: "Most importantly, we must seize control of our economy and destiny. This will require courageous leadership, self-confidence, ingenuity, hard work and economic patriotism" (Magufuli 2017, p. viii).

The "resource nationalism" (see Jacob and Pedersen 2018) and state-steered developmentalism pursued by the Magufuli administration took on increasingly autocratic forms, as national development was stylized as an overarching goal that should not be compromised by political debate and contestation (Paget 2021). Magufuli earned himself the nickname 'Bulldozer' due to his uncompromising anti-corruption campaign, radical government interventions in the economy, and repressive measures vis-à-vis the political opposition, the media, and civil society. Institutionally, he worked toward transforming the Tanzanian state apparatus into an autocratic developmental state. His tenure was characterized by centralization of decision-making power in the presidential office, a tightening of control and oversight of the treasury, line ministries, and state agencies, as well as a rigid scrutiny of public spending, borrowing, and procurements. Magufuli aligned his cabinet and newly installed top bureaucrats with his 'economic patriotism,' with frequent dismissals of top officials creating an atmosphere of the constant threat of the president's zero-tolerance approach toward negligence and malfeasance (Polus and Tycholiz 2019; Andreoni 2017). This was passed on along the 'line of command,' with senior officials and bureaucrats in relevant ministries and state agencies swiftly subscribing to Magufuli's economic-nationalist rhetoric and practices.

A former Tanzanian senior official, for instance, acknowledged that the government had previously failed to maximize developmental benefits of infrastructure projects in negotiations with Chinese investors:

> With the Chinese, sometimes you have to open your eyes and look beyond the curtains because they might be speaking, but at the back of their mind, it's something very different. […] We were not good in negotiations. That we admit. […] And we are happy that we have a president who is focused and sees all this. […] So, negotiation, negotiation, negotiation is where we fail. (Interview, former Tanzanian senior official, 27th November 2019)

The political and institutional changes leading up to and following Magufuli's election in 2015 caused the Tanzanian government to reassess the Bagamoyo project and to pursue a confrontational strategy vis-à-vis the main investor CMPort.

7.3.2 *'Win–Win' Contested: Autocratic Developmental State Agency*

The Bagamoyo project is an instructive case that documents how (changing) political contexts condition the agency of African state actors vis-à-vis Chinese financiers, investors, or contractors. Once lauded by both sides as a transformative BRI project, the Magufuli administration pursued a confrontational strategy by fiercely contesting the terms and conditions put forward by the investors. In June 2019, Magufuli himself outspokenly criticized that.

This project has very difficult conditions. They are exploitative and awkward. We can't allow it. [...] In fact, the investors wanted to tie our hands in developing Tanga port, which is very crucial for the oil pipeline from Uganda and others in Mtwara and Kilwa. These are our oldest ports. (quoted in The Citizen 2019).

Here, Magufuli referred to so-called stabilization or adverse action clauses, *i.e.,* contractual provisions that protect the investor from revenue losses as a result of changing legislation/regulation or competing projects. Such clauses have become standard state-backed guarantees in investment agreements and public–private partnerships and intend to minimize risks and secure returns for investors (Hildyard 2016, pp. 37–38). A former senior government official confirmed that CMPort expected the government not to develop ports within a radius of 300 miles, which would affect all of Tanzania's current major seaports in Dar es Salaam, Kilwa, Mtwara, and Tanga (Interview, 27th November 2019).

The Tanzanian government was also apprehensive of a loss of sovereignty rights with regard to the authority over ports operations as well as over customs and taxation, since, according to the Director of Tanzania Ports Authority (TPA), "taxes, calculations and audits were set to be undertaken in China" (Kakoko, quoted in Musa 2019). A former senior official confirmed that "they [CMPort] wanted to collect revenue themselves" (Interview, 27th November 2019). A Tanzanian academic suspected that the question of who would be in control of the port could have been decisive for the government's hitherto suspension of the project: "one of the things China is interested in, worldwide, is ports and control of major ports. So, it is not just a question of assisting to construct a port but eventually who owns it and who controls it." The interviewee conjectured that relinquishing the operation of Bagamoyo port to a foreign corporation was incompatible with the "kind of nationalism" pursued by the Magufuli administration (Interview, N. Kamata, 5th February 2019).

Another point of contention has been the terms of the envisaged Build-Operate-Transfer (BOT) contract. While CMPort sought a duration of 99 years, the Tanzanian government wanted to limit the contract period to 33 years (Interview, former Tanzanian senior official, 27th

November 2019). The investors furthermore expected state-guaranteed compensations of any losses incurred during the implementation of the project—according to Kakoko a "demand [that] can render the country bankrupt" (quoted in Musa 2019). In addition, CMPort sought substantial tax exemptions, based on the argument that projected cargo volumes were still too low for the port to run profitably. Former TPA Director Kakoko revealed that the investors called for exemptions from land tax, workers compensation tax, skills development levy, customs duty, and value-added tax (The Citizen 2019). He justified the government's stance as follows: "Even [if] it was agreed that some taxes be waived, we would have to examine the percentage of exemptions. However, it seems they wanted to invest for free, which would be akin to selling our freedom" (Kakoko, quoted in Musa 2019). Demands for regulatory exemptions caused further controversy. An interviewee confirmed that "they [CMPort] wanted not to be touched by the labour laws, not to be touched by immigration laws. [...] We said: 'No, this is a country— you can't be given that freedom'" (Interview, former Tanzanian senior official, 27th November 2019).

Tanzanian officials emphasized that the government's initial intention was the establishment of a SEZ to boost manufacturing and related service industries, with the port providing supplementary infrastructure (Interview, Tanzanian top official, 15th November 2019; Interview, former Tanzanian senior official, 27th November 2019; Interview, senior official Tanzanian Ministry of Works, Transport and Communication, 15th November 2019). Yet, at the instigation of CMPort, "the port became the major—and the Special Economic Zone the minor" in the course of the negotiations (Interview, former Tanzanian senior official, 27th November 2019). The Tanzanian government remained adamant and requested detailed projections as to how the investment sum would be used to establish manufacturing and production sites and create jobs within the SEZ (*Ibid*). As a top official explained,

> Bagamoyo becomes only attractive if we have that industrial city there. If that matures, they [the SEZ and the port] will go together and it doesn't matter who will get the project for doing the same [the construction of the port]. [...] So now we are looking at things objectively, we want to discuss – it is not as desperate so that we are not taken for a ride. [...] The issue is here: This set of conditions we are still not agreeing [with]. If you [the investors] have another idea on them, you can come and we'll

continue discussing. We are not in a hurry. (Interview, 15th November 2019)

While overall the 'grand power asymmetry' between China and Africa (with which much research and commentary remains preoccupied) has evidently not changed, the shifting balance of forces in Tanzanian politics has caused the government to strategically reassess and clearly demarcate the conditions under which a mega-port and SEZ in Bagamoyo are deemed to serve Tanzanian national interests. Magufuli's autocratic developmentalism and related adjustments of governance procedures prompted a contestation of the omnipresent "notion of 'win–win' which is argued to have predominantly benefited associated Chinese contractors and suppliers in the past" (Makundi et al. 2017, p. 346).

The Bagamoyo project has shown that the 'sphere' of the elite agency is deeply embedded in dynamic state-society relations. The changing balance of political forces that had swept Magufuli into the presidential office led to the gradual transformation of Tanzania into an autocratic developmental state under his aegis. Following the systematic centralization of political power and control in the presidency and informed by populist-nationalist calculus, rhetoric, and action, Magufuli and his inner circle pursued a confrontational approach *vis-à-vis* the Chinese investor. The Magufuli administration thus effectively shelved the project over terms that were deemed detrimental to Tanzania's national interests. While negotiations have resumed under Magufuli's successor, President Samia Suluhu Hassan, it seems likely that certain terms that were initially proposed by the investor will remain taboo for the Tanzanian government. The territory for Bagamoyo port has been marked.

7.4 Planning Adama Wind Farms: Bureaucratic State Agency in Practice

This section uses Adama I (53 MW) and Adama II (151 MW) wind farms as case studies to expand the work of Soulé-Kohndou (2019) and that of others (see Chiyemura 2019a; Phillips 2019) to characterize and contextualize how Ethiopian state and government officials have exercised agency throughout the planning processes of these Chinese-backed wind farms. We believe a focus on planning is essential in the sense that the possibility of exerting agency is gained, maintained, or lost at this stage. As noted by an Ethiopian government official involved in the planning processes of the two wind farms, "if you fail to plan, you are planning to fail, it's high time we take care of our infrastructure development processes" (Interview, former Ethiopian ambassador to China 1999–2004, former member of the EPRDF-Executive Council, 12th May 2017).

This section begins by accounting for the authoritarian developmental state model adopted by the Ethiopian government aimed at bringing about 'positive' change to the lives of ordinary Ethiopians through infrastructure-led development. Doing so allows us to understand structural dynamics related to the centralization of state power and how governance modalities enable or constrain the exercise of agency. The second part of this section will then discuss how the Ethiopian bureaucracies exercised agency seen through the lens of planning and brokering processes around the Adama wind farms.

7.4.1 Electricity Infrastructure Development in Ethiopia

Ethiopia, like the rest of the African continent, has a huge population without access to electricity. According to the Ethiopian Ministry of Water, Irrigation and Electricity (MOWIE) (2019), only 44% of the 110 million Ethiopians have access to electricity, of which 33% are covered by the grid network and 11% by off-grid sources. By the end of March 2017, Ethiopia Electric Utility (EEU) had 2.3 million customers, and only 6,000 towns had access to electricity (Federal Democratic Republic of Ethiopia 2017). Access to electricity is particularly limited in rural areas. Although more than 85% of the Ethiopian population resides in rural areas, about 90% are without electricity supply (*ibid*). This is mainly caused by the lack and shortage of electricity infrastructure. Developing electricity infrastructure was therefore identified by the then ruling coalition, Ethiopian People's Revolutionary Democratic Front[2] (EPRDF), as a priority sector (Lavers et al. 2021).

At least until 2018, the EPRDF-led government pursued an authoritarian approach to development by centralizing decision-making powers in the hands of top party leadership, which tightly controlled the state and government at different governance levels (Bayu 2019). In this context, the ruling party was subjectively seen to have hegemony of value creation,

---

[2] EPRDF was disbanded in 2018 and replaced with the Prosperity Party.

and relative embedded autonomy to independently formulate and implement policies against contending social and market forces (Zenawi 2012). This period was marked by a top-down approach to the formulation of development policies and plans. The Council of Ministers—in consultation with the Prime Minister and members of the EPRDF coalition—set the development strategy and direction, while the design and implementation of development projects were decentralized to relevant bureaucracies which were constitutionally and legally mandated to do so.

Several policy instruments, such as the Growth and Transformation Plan (GTP) I (2010/11–2014/15) and II (2015/16–2019/20), were formulated and implemented to improve public infrastructure in the energy, transport, and communication sectors, as well as to establish export-oriented industrial zones. In the GTPs, electricity infrastructure was identified as a key driver and enabler of set development targets. The government planned to increase electricity generation capacity from 2000 to 8000 MW (MOFEC 2010). However, only 4180 MW were installed by the end of GTP I. In GTP II, the goal was to increase the energy generation capacity to 17,208 MW (MOFEC 2016, p. 179). To achieve these targets, the Ethiopian government outlined an implementation framework, as shown in Fig. 7.1.

Between 2004 and 2018, the Ethiopian economy grew at an average Gross Domestic Product (GDP) growth of 10.44% and reached over $80 billion in 2018 (World Bank 2018). The magnitude of Ethiopia's

Fig. 7.1 Energy projects implementation framework (*Source* Authors' compilation from field data)

economic performance considerably improved its economic clout in East Africa. Despite poor performance in the 'good governance' indicators, Ethiopia has continued to attract investment from both the West and the East regardless of the government's disapproval of "economic policies ostensibly favoured by the principal Western donors" (Clapham 2018, p. 1157). This all comes from the government's ability to proficiently play one donor against the other to its advantage and also the ability to show value for money through high and "visible returns on their investments" (Clapham 2018, p. 1157). As Furtado and Smith (2007, p. 24) remark, "this gives the [Ethiopian] government substantial bargaining power, which it exercises at times by refusing to compromise on its policy agenda." As explained by a MOWIE bureaucrat, "although we are collaborating with the Chinese in many sectors, the selection and prioritisation of the wind farms was […] and will remain an Ethiopian initiative" (Interview, Ethiopian government official from MOWIE, 11th November 2017).

The authoritarian developmental approach by the EPRDF-led government translated into a rigid implementation ecosystem, which provided the context for Ethiopian bureaucrats to exercise agency in the planning processes for infrastructure development.

7.4.2   Planning as Agency

Planning for the development of wind farms in Ethiopia can be traced back to 2001. At the time, the Ethiopian government—faced with erratic climatic conditions that were adversely impacting its hydropower-dominated generation capacity—demonstrated interest in deploying alternative energy sources, such as solar and wind. Yet, the government repeatedly cited a lack of adequate information and data to translate this interest into concrete policy frameworks. Consequently, upon the initiative of then Prime Minister Meles Zenawi, MOWIE lobbied for the country to be selected to participate in the Solar and Wind Energy Resource Assessment (SWERA) program funded by the United Nations Environment Programme (UNEP) and Global Environment Facility (GEF). In 2004, the SWERA program concluded that Ethiopia was endowed with wind resources to the tune of 100GW (Ethiopian Rural Energy Development and Promotion Centre 2007). The proactive engagement with international development partners by relevant state agencies is a concrete example of the ability of the Zenawi government to exercise agency resulting in the country being selected as one of the beneficiaries.

The participation in the UNEP-GEF allowed the Ethiopian government to undertake further planning and thus alter the bureaucratic context in which the country's planned energy transition was to take place. MOWIE subsequently invited the German Society for International Cooperation (GTZ, now GIZ)-Technical Expertise for Renewable (TERNA) to conduct feasibility studies for the deployment of wind energy in Ethiopia. Ashegoda, Harena, and Adama were highly recommended among 11 suitable sites (GTZ-TERNA. 2005), resulting in the development of the Ashegoda wind farm. Following complications related to logistics as well as the capacity of turbines in the context of Ashegoda—implemented by the French firm Vergnet (Economic Consulting Associates 2018)—bureaucrats swiftly reassessed the situation and pressed for contractual changes to reach agreed targets.

At the same time, EEP and MOWIE, strategically reoriented and diversified their engagements with international partners to avoid further delays in implementing the government energy transition agenda. As part of these efforts, in 2007–2008, the Ethiopia-China Development Cooperation Directorate in the Ministry of Finance and Economic Cooperation (MOFEC) approached the Chinese government seeking financial and technological assistance to develop further wind farms (Interview, Ethiopian government in the Ethiopia-China Development Cooperation Directorate at MOFEC, 30th June 2017). This resulted in a multisectoral $1 billion infrastructure cooperation agreement signed in 2009 and financed through a preferential buyer's credit facility by China Exim Bank (Ethiopia Electric Power 2017).

In the energy sector, the two sides agreed on a new Wind and Solar Master Plan to be fully financed by Chinese counterparts. The Master Plan found that Ethiopia had a wind energy potential of 3.03 TW; 51 wind farm sites were identified and proposed for development with a potential installed capacity of 6720 MW (Hydrochina Corporation 2012). Out of these 51, MOWIE—in collaboration with EEP—selected eight wind warms to be incorporated in the GTP I (Interview, Ethiopian government in the Ethiopia-China Development Cooperation Directorate at MOFEC, 30th June 2017). Subsequently, the Ethiopia-China Development Cooperation Directorate in MOFEC—under the auspices of the Prime Minister's office—concluded an EPC + Financing agreement for Adama wind farms with China Exim Bank (Interview, Ethiopian government official from MOWIE, 11th November 2017). In line with China Exim Bank's common practice, the project was tendered in a closed bidding process that involved only Chinese firms and the technology needed to be sourced from China. HydroChina Corporation[3] (HydroChina) and China Geo-Engineering Corporation Overseas Construction Group (CGCOC) won the contracts (see Table 7.1 for more details). Nevertheless, by adopting an EPC + Financing scheme, the Ethiopian government—informed by their previous (negative) experiences in the development of Ashegoda—shifted the project delivery risks from MOWIE, a public authority, to the contractor (Interview, Ethiopian government official from MOWIE, 11th November 2017; Interview, Ethiopian government in the Ethiopia-China Development Cooperation Directorate at MOFEC, 30th June 2017).

From the government's initial proactive outreach to UNEP-GEF to the awarding of the Adama contract, the planning process was marked by strategic learning and regular adjustments by the relevant Ethiopian bureaucracies. Planning is therefore crucial because "structures of thought and action may be creatively reconfigured in relation to actors' [...] desires for the future" (Emirbayer and Mische 1998, p. 971). Such creative reconfigurations also took place in the context of Ethiopia's energy transition. Reflective of their country's structural limitations, bureaucrats in EEP, MOWIE, and MOFEC successfully negotiated an EPC + Financing agreement with "a favourable 2% interest rate and a loan repayment plan of 13 years and a grace period of 7 years" (Chiyemura 2019b, p. 1). Furthermore, as an official in MOWIE highlighted, the SWERA and the Chinese-sponsored Master Plan significantly increased the government's planning capacity and, by implication, their ability to make informed decisions (Interview, 11th November 2017).

In an interview, the former Ethiopian ambassador to China underscored the importance of "proper project preparations" for the success of development projects (Interview, 17th May 2017). In the case of the energy sector, the Ethiopian government's political and development priorities were crucially co-determined by bureaucrats within relevant state institutions. The case study of the Adama wind farm has shown that Ethiopian bureaucracies crucially influence project implementation by planning, setting, and strategically reformulating development targets, leveraging necessary data and technical capacity, as well as initiating the

---

[3] HydroChina Corporation also known as Sinohydro—a subsidiary of Power Construction Corporation of China (PowerChina).

Table 7.1 Adama wind farms project terms and conditions. From: Infrastructure and the Politics of African state agency: Shaping the belt and road initiative in East Africa

Descriptor	Adama I	Adama II
Capacity	51 MW	153 MW
Unit power cost	$2314/KW	$2254.9/KW
Interest incurred during construction	$0.9945 m	N/A[a]
Interest rate	2%	2%
Project cost	$117 m	$345 m
Source of financing	15% Ethiopia and 85% C-EXIM	15% Ethiopia and 85% C-EXIM
Finance modality	Preferential Export Buyer's Credit	Governmental Concessional Loan[b]
Loan payment	13 years	13 years
Grace period	7 years	7 years
Loan maturity	20 years	20 years
Total investment cost	$117.9945 m	$345 m

[a] By the time of conducting fieldwork, the project capitalization report was not yet completed so the interest incurred during construction is not factored in. Total investment cost may be more if interest incurred during construction is added

[b] Official data does not state whether it was Preferential Export Credits, Export Sellers Credits or Mixed Credits. Simply it is recorded as a government concessional loan. For more details about the financing models, see (Massa 2011; OECD 2015) and also Export and Import Bank of China Preferential Facilities on http://english.eximbank.gov.cn/tm/en-TCN/index_640.html

development cooperation with Chinese actors. Thus, despite existing power asymmetries between Ethiopia and China, the specific political-institutional contexts in which Sino-African engagement occurs enable and condition the exercise of (bureaucratic) agency.

7.5 Reshaping Lamu Port: the Centrality of Local Governance

Since 2016, the Chinese state-owned contractor China Road Bridge Corporation (CRBC) has been building Phase I—the first three berths—of Lamu port in Northern Kenya. This infrastructure project, valued at $480 million, is envisioned to become one of the largest ports in East Africa (LCDA 2020). Phase I is currently being financed by the Kenyan government, which, despite seeking funding from international organizations, prioritized the construction of the port to kick-start the development of the transport corridor initiative planned for the Northern regions of Kenya, and beyond (see Gambino 2020b). In fact, Lamu port is part of a broader project, the LAPSSET Corridor, which aims to connect Kenya to South Sudan and Ethiopia through cross-border infrastructure, such as brand-new highways and a railway. This regional corridor is expected to not only connect Northern Kenya to neighboring countries, but also to global capital through Lamu port.

Lamu port is one of the flagship projects of Kenya's development agenda, Kenya Vision 2030, which heavily relies on the construction and refurbishing of infrastructure to lead the country to "a rapidly industrialising middle-income nation" (Government of Kenya 2007, p. i). This is in line with the development agendas of many other African nations, as well as those of regional and continental organizations (Nugent 2018; Péclard et al. 2020; Zajontz 2021b). Beyond its overarching goal of 'transforming' Kenya's economy, the country's development agenda also envisions that "[b]y 2030, it will become impossible to refer to any region of [the] country as 'remote'" (Government of Kenya 2007, p. viii). The development of LAPSSET Corridor in Northern Kenya fits within this objective, as this region has historically been a marginalized space since resources have often been redirected toward the development of regions considered to be 'productive.'

In the colonial era, connectivity initiatives were concentrated in the regions inhabited by or related to the activities of white settlers (Kanyinga 2016), particularly in the Central Region and Rift Valley of Kenya. In the racialized visions of the British colonial administration, "there were no outside economic reasons to break the underdevelopment loneliness of Northern Kenya" (The National Christian Council of Kenya 1972, p. 29). This trend of disregard toward the 'pastoral' North persisted after independence, as these regions are home to agricultural and pastoral communities regarded by the national government as 'backwards,' inhabiting 'remote' regions, and often "an inconvenience" (Mosley and Watson 2016, p. 453; see also Cormack and Kurewa 2018). In the blueprint of Kenya Vision 2030, the implementation of infrastructure and other development initiatives in these spaces (see Odhiambo 2013), is expected to "turn history on its head" (Government of Kenya 2011, p. 12). For instance, during the inauguration speech of Lamu port in May 2021, President Kenyatta made clear: "marginalisation... you don't want that word ever again" (Kenyatta 2021). This exemplifies the (at least rhetorical) shift from the abovementioned patterns of marginalization.

The Lamu port project is being implemented against the background of said pre-existing contextual dynamics. As will be shown below, mirroring existing imbalances of power in center-periphery relations, the institutional and legal authority for project implementation and agenda-setting are concentrated in the hands of national-level state actors. This impacts the ways in which and the extent to which 'local' actors engage with Chinese contractors participating in infrastructure projects in the periphery. The following subsections will highlight how, despite contextual power asymmetry that characterize center-periphery relations and broader China–Africa relations, local governance shapes infrastructure projects with Chinese participation.

7.5.1 Local Governance in the Context of Centre-Periphery Relations

Centre-periphery relations are a crucial factor determining the room for maneuver and degree of influence of local governance actors in reshaping Sino-African infrastructure projects. Concerning center-periphery relations, Boone (2003, p. 9) suggests that "rulers operate within different structural or strategic contexts," the dynamics of which are to be understood through the analysis of socio-political (and economic) trajectories in the periphery (see also Nugent 2019). This points to the need to bring politics of the 'periphery' to the center of analysis in the study of infrastructure projects with Chinese participation.

The 2013 elections saw the formation of the first county governments in Kenya, following the promulgation of a new constitution in 2010, which represented an "ambitious and rigorous experiment in democratic decentralisation" (Subera 2013, p. 32). The extent to which these reforms have addressed the unequal allocation of state resources and legal competencies remains questionable. This is particularly true for (mega)infrastructure projects 'at the margins,' as the mandate for their agenda-setting, planning, and implementation remains in the hands of the central government. Against this background, the rhetorical focus on 'opening up' of the Northern part of Kenya and 'connecting' these territories to the national market and the global economy not only speaks to a trend of *respacing* (Engel and Nugent 2010) through the construction of physical infrastructure (see for instance Lesutis 2019), but also to the reshaping of people's perceptions of their futures (Enns and Bersaglio 2020) and their identities (Kochore 2016).

It is important here to remember that, as much as infrastructure projects are envisioned to promote 'connectivity' and 'integration,' they also imply disconnection and dispossession. Indeed, some might "end up being marginalised by the 'modernity' to come" (Lesutis 2019, p. 605; see also Appel et al. 2018; Harvey 2018). For instance, some members of the county government in Lamu argue that the LAPSSET Corridor still leaves Lamu residents as "mere spectators," as opposed to participants of development initiatives. For them, the parameters and conditions of 'development' continue to be negotiated in Nairobi (Interview, Senior Official, County Government, Lamu, 13th July 2019). Different 'economies of anticipation' (Elliott 2016; Greiner 2016; Chome 2020; Chome et al. 2020; Aalders et al. 2021; Müller-Mahn et al. 2021) are thus emerging vis-à-vis the development of infrastructure projects in the Northern regions of Kenya, which, in turn, has affected projects with Chinese involvement. On the one hand, in anticipation of the construction of the Lamu port project, political and business elites at the 'center' moved to acquire land in Lamu, speaking to the not uncommon practice of lucrative land grabbing in the (previously 'untapped') peripheries. On the other hand, Lamu communities, the county government, and other local governance actors are attempting to reshape these infrastructure projects so as to comprise their own agendas and interests.

7.5.2 Centering 'Peripheral' Agency

In the broader Kenyan context, local governance actors have often engaged with Chinese contractors. For instance, popular demands and protests in the context of the construction of the Nairobi-Mombasa Standard Gauge Railway resulted in negotiations between CRBC and different county governments along the railway route (Wang and Wissenbach 2019). Similarly, in Lamu, negotiations take place between the current county government (2017–) and CRBC with regard to job openings and other opportunities in the construction site as they become available (Gambino 2020b). This followed calls from community leaders to include laborers from the Swahili groups inhabiting the Lamu archipelago in the soon-to-be port. Even though the centralized LAPSSET Corridor Development Authority has the (presidential) mandate to oversee and implement the Lamu port project, these examples show that local governance actors have carved room for maneuver. Such 'peripheral' agency has prompted Chinese companies to formulate and then redeploy risk mitigation strategies with regard to controversies around local content requirements.

This implies that project implementation of large-scale infrastructure with Chinese participation is highly contingent upon the local political context. In 2012, Lamu elders and LAPSSET officials formed the LAPSSET Steering Committee—chaired by the County Commissioner—with the aim of increasing support for the project (Interview, Secretary, County Government, Lamu, 19th March 2019). This committee was a response to community protests (SaveLamu 2011) and a court case submitted against the national government by Lamu communities (High Court of Kenya, 2012; see below). While it did not initially prove conducive to increasing the agency of local governance actors, it provided a platform for engagement among different stakeholders. The LAPSSET Steering Committee, however, was short-lived, being dismantled soon after the election of the first county governor of Lamu Issa Timamy (2013–2017). This decision was likely motivated by party politics (Chome 2020), as the sitting members of this committee had been associated with the benefactor—or patron—of Timamy's political opponent Fahim Twaha, who would eventually win the 2017 elections.

Timamy's time in office was characterized by struggles with the national government over land allocation for LAPSSET Corridor components, which exposed Twaha as a benefactor of land deeds re-allocation (Nema 2017). This further embittered in-county resentment, particularly among the Timamy-Twaha factions, the latter of which, in the meantime had been "edged out of the instruments of local governance" (Chome 2020, p. 15). In 2017, however, Twaha emerged as the winner of the county electoral race, becoming the second governor of Lamu. Twaha's government represented a shift from that of Timamy's. On the one hand, Twaha pursued a less confrontational approach toward the central government due to his affiliation with the ruling party in Nairobi. On the other hand, in his role as Lamu county governor, Twaha also faced the necessity to address the concerns and demands of his constituency.

In 2018, following the *Petition n22 of 2012* discussed above, the High Court of Kenya ruled that, in the Lamu port project inception, there had been a violation of the new 2010 Constitution due to lack of inclusion of the county government. The court also ordered to compensate fishers for the disruption caused by the port construction and its future operations. Overall, the ruling recognized the exclusion of the county government and called for more inclusive forms of community participation in the planning and implementation of the Lamu port. Consequently, calls for participation in the national development agenda regained prominence in Lamu politics. In 2019, Twaha's government initiated a committee aimed at promoting the inclusion of specific (and at times diverging) 'local' interests in the development of the Lamu port project (Interview, state official, 17th March 2019). In contrast to the previous LAPSSET Steering Committee, the new Lamu port committee also includes the Chinese contractor CRBC. The decision to include CRBC in the new Lamu port committee signals the establishment of direct and more formal channels of engagement for local governance actors to raise their concerns and interests.

In the context of the Lamu port projects, by raising, voicing, and manifesting concerns and grievances, local governance actors have successfully renegotiated the insertion of community interests in the national development agenda. This has happened with the support of civil society organizations, vocal individuals, and by means of resistance in the form of public protests or litigation. Local governance actors have gained some room for maneuver to promote their specific (and at times diverging) interests in development projects that are otherwise largely characterized by centralized and top-down decision-making processes. Indeed, most of the negotiations in the agenda-setting, planning, and implementation phases of infrastructure projects with Chinese participation are undertaken by national-level actors. The case of Lamu has shown that the agency of supposedly 'peripheral' actors is not so peripheral after all. As discussed with regard to labor relations, local governance actors can, under certain conditions, influence the implementation of large-scale infrastructure projects with Chinese participation.

7.6 Conclusion

Inspired by Links' recent call for a "contextual approach [...] that considers the contours and specificities of African agency" (2021, p. 124), this article explored different spheres of African state agency in the context of three African infrastructure projects with Chinese participation. Rooted in a social-relational ontology of the state which sees the state as a multifaceted and multi-scalar 'institutional ensemble' (see Jessop 1990), our analysis has shown that infrastructure projects with Chinese participation are shaped by various actors in three (out of many) highly dynamic 'spheres' of the state. We have shown that the extent and forms of state agency exerted are inherently interrelated with and, thus, highly contingent upon concrete institutional, economic, political, and bureaucratic contexts in which African state actors are firmly embedded.

First, in the case of Tanzania's envisaged Bagamoyo mega-port and special economic zone, Tanzania's transformation toward an autocratic developmental state under late President Magufuli has resulted in a thorough reappraisal of the project and a confrontational negotiation strategy toward the investor. Second, the Ethiopian case study revealed that the EPRDF-led authoritarian developmental state model created a political and institutional context which allowed the state bureaucracies to crucially influence project implementation by planning, setting, and strategically reformulating development targets, leveraging necessary data and technical capacity, as well as initiating the development cooperation with Chinese actors. Third, the case of the Kenyan port of Lamu showed that the agency of local governance actors reshapes the implementation of infrastructure projects with Chinese participation. Indeed, local governance actors negotiate the inclusion of their (at times diverging) interests vis-à-vis the implementation of the national development agenda.

There are broader conclusions for the study of African agency—or rather agenc*ies*—in Africa-China relations (and beyond). The extent to and the ways in which African state actors exert agency is conditioned but not determined by undeniable power asymmetries between China and Africa that are all too often invoked. For an assessment of African agency (or the lack thereof) the concrete contexts in which actors find themselves matter profoundly. This finding calls for further theory-informed empirical investigations into the complex politics of African agency vis-à-vis China and other external actors.

References

Aalders, J.T., et al. 2021. The Making and Unmaking of a Megaproject: Contesting Temporalities along the LAPSSET Corridor in Kenya. *Antipode* 1–21 (ahead of publication)

African Development Bank. 2018. *Africa's Infrastructure Great Potential but Little Impact on Inclusive Growth*. Abidjan: African Development Bank.

African Union. 2015. *Agenda 2063: The Africa We Want*. Addis Ababa: African Union Commission.

Alden, C., and L. Jiang. 2019. Brave New World: Debt, Industrialization and Security in China-Africa Relations. *International Affairs* 95 (3): 641–657.

Alden, C., and D. Large. 2019. Studying Africa and China. In *New Directions in Africa-China Studies*, ed. C. Alden and D. Large, 3–35. London: Routledge.

Andreoni, A. 2017. *Anti-corruption in Tanzania: A Political Settlements Analysis* (No. 1; Working Paper).

Appel, H., N. Anand, and A. Gupta. 2018. Temporality, Politics, and the Promise of Infrastructure. In *The Promise of Infrastructure*, ed. N. Anand, A. Gupta, and H. Appel, 1–38. London: Duke University Press.

Bayu, T.B. 2019. Fault Lines Within the Ethiopian People Revolutionary Democratic Front (EPRDF): Intraparty Network and Governance System. *International Journal of Contemporary Research and Review* 10 (02): 20592–20602.

Belt and Road Forum. 2019. 第二届"一带一路"国际合作高峰论坛圆桌峰会联合公报 *di er jie 'yi dai yi lu' guoji hezuo gaofeng luntan yuanzhuo fenghui lianhe gongbao* [Joint Communique of the Leaders' Roundtable of the Second Belt and Road Forum for International Cooperation], *Xinhua News*. Available at: https://bit.ly/2VCuqM9. Accessed 22 May 2019.

Bierschenk, T., and J.P. Olivier de Sardan. 1998. Les arènes locales face à la décentralisation et à la démocratisation. Analyses comparatives en milieu rural béninois [Local arenas facing decentralization and democratization. Comparative analysis in rural Benin], 11–51.

Boone, C. 2003. *Political Topographies of the African State*. Cambridge: Cambridge University Press.

Bräutigam, D. 2019. Chinese Loans and African Structural Transformation. In *China-Africa and Economic Transformation*, ed. A. Oqubay and J.Y. Lin, 129–146. Oxford: Oxford University Press.

Brown, W. 2012. A Question of Agency: Africa in International Politics. *Third World Quarterly* 33 (10): 1889–1908.

Carmody, P., and P. Kragelund. 2016. Who is in Charge? State Power and Agency in Sino-African Relations. *Cornell International Law Journal* 49 (1): 1–24.

Carmody, P., I. Taylor, and T. Zajontz. 2021. China's Spatial Fix and 'Debt Diplomacy' in Africa: Constraining Belt or Road to Economic Transformation? *Canadian Journal of African Studies/revue Canadienne Des Études Africaines* 56: 1–21.

China Africa Research Initiative. 2021. CARI Contract Database, CARI. https://bit.ly/2xbzL4c. Accessed 14 Jan 2021.

Chiyemura, F. 2019a. The Winds of Change in Africa-China Relations? Contextualising African Agency in Ethiopia-China Engagement in Wind Energy Infrastructure Financing and Development. The Open University. PhD thesis.

Chiyemura, F. 2019b. Chinese Infrastructure Financing: Is Ethiopia Naïve? Addis Fortune Newspaper, Addis Ababa. https://addisfortune.news/chinese-infras tructure-financing-is-ethiopia-naive/. Accessed 23 Mar 2020.

Chiyemura, F. 2020. Contextualising African Agency in Ethiopia-China engagement in wind energy infrastructure financing and development. *Innovation, Knowledge and Development Working Series,* Number 88.

Chiyemura, F. 2021. Chinese Firms—And African Labor—Are Building Africa's Infrastructure. https://www.washingtonpost.com/politics/2021/04/02/chi nese-firms-african-labor-are-building-africas-infrastructure/.

Chome, N. 2020. Land, Livelihoods and Belonging: Negotiating Change and Anticipating LAPSSET in Kenya's Lamu County. *Journal of Eastern African Studies* 14 (2): 310–331.

Chome, N., et al. 2020. "Demonstration Fields", Anticipation, and Contestation: Agrarian Change and the Political Economy of Development Corridors in Eastern Africa. *Journal of Eastern African Studies* 14 (2): 291–309.

Cissokho, S. 2022. Infrastructure, Development and Neoliberalism in Africa: Review of the Concept of Transport Corridor (1945–2019). In *Transport Corridors in Africa*, ed. P. Nugent and H. Lamarque. James Currey: Melton.

Clapham, C. 2018. The Ethiopian Developmental State. *Third World Quarterly* 39 (6): 1151–1165.

Cormack, Z., and A. Kurewa. 2018. The Changing Value of Land in Northern Kenya: The Case of Lake Turkana Wind Power. *Critical African Studies* 10: 89–107.

D'Arcy, M., and A. Cornell. 2016. Devolution and Corruption in Kenya: Everyone's Turn to Eat? *African Affairs* 115 (459): 246–273.

Deloitte. 2016. *Africa's Changing Infrastructure Landscape: Africa Construction Trends Report.* Diegem: Deloitte University.

Doornbos, M. 2011. Researching African Statehood Dynamics: Negotiability and its Limits. In *Negotiating Statehood: Dynamics of Power and Domination in Africa*, ed. T. Hagmann and D. Péclard. Wiley-Blackwell: Hoboken.

Economic Consulting Associates. 2018. Evaluation Summary—Ashegoda Wind Farm. https://www.afd.fr/en/ressources/evaluation-summary-ashegoda-wind-farm. Accessed 19 Oct 2021.

Elliott, H. 2016. Planning, Property and Plots at the Gateway to Kenya's "New Frontier." *Journal of Eastern African Studies* 10 (3): 511–529.

Emirbayer, M., and A. Mische. 1998. What is Agency? *American Journal of Sociology* 103 (4): 962–1023.

Engel, U., and P. Nugent. 2010. The Spatial Turn in African Studies. In *Respacing Africa*, ed. U. Engel and P. Nugent, 1–9. Brill: Leiden.

Enns, C., and B. Bersaglio. 2020. On the Coloniality of "New" Mega-Infrastructure Projects in East Africa. *Antipode* 52 (1): 101–123.

Ethiopia Electric Power. 2017. Adama I Wind Farm Project Capitalisation Report. Addis Ababa, Ethiopia.

Ethiopian Rural Energy Development and Promotion Centre. 2007. Solar and Wind Energy Utilization and Project Development Scenarios. Addis Ababa.

Federal Democratic Republic of Ethiopia. 2017. Ministry of Water Irrigation and Electricity: Federal Democratic Republic of Ethiopia Power Sector Review March 2017. Addis Ababa.

Furtado, X., and J. Smith. 2007. Ethiopia: Aid, Ownership, and Sovereignty (No. 2007/28). https://www.geg.ox.ac.uk/sites/geg.bsg.ox.ac.uk/files/GEGWP2007_28Ethiopia-aid%2Cownership%2Candsovereignty-Furtado%26Smith.pdf.

Gadzala, A.W., ed. 2015. *Africa and China: How Africans and their Governments are Shaping Relations with China*. Lanham: Rowman & Littlefield.

Gambino, E. 2020a. Job Insecurity, Labour Contestation and Everyday Resistance at the Chinese-Built Lamu Port Site in Kenya. Asia Dialogue. https://bit.ly/35gqswC. Accessed 3 Apr 2020a.

Gambino, E. 2020b. La participation chinoise dans le développement des infrastructures de transport au Kenya: une transformation des géométries du pouvoir? [Chinese participation in Kenyan transport infrastructure: reshaping power-geometries?]. *Critique Internationale* 89: 95–114.

Gambino, E. 2021. The Political Economy of Sino-African Infrastructural Engagement: The Internationalisation of Chinese State-owned Companies in Kenya. The University of Edinburgh, UK. PhD thesis.

Gambino, E. 2022. Corridors of Opportunity? African Infrastructure and the Market Expansion of Chinese Companies. In *Transport Corridors in Africa*, ed. H. Lamarque and P. Nugent. James Currey: Melton. [Chapter 12].

Government of Kenya. 2007. *Kenya Vision 2030: A Globally Competitive and Prosperous Kenya*. Nairobi: Government of Kenya.

Government of Kenya. 2011. *Vision 2030 Development Strategy for Northern Kenya and Other Arid Lands*. Nairobi: Government of Kenya.

Greiner, C. 2016. Land-Use Change, Territorial Restructuring, and Economies of Anticipation in Dryland Kenya. *Journal of Eastern African Studies* 10 (3): 530–547.

GTZ-TERNA. 2005. *Wind Energy Program TERNA-Ethiopia Site Selection Report*. Ethiopia: Addis Ababa.

Hagmann, T., and D. Péclard. 2010. Negotiating Statehood: Dynamics of Power and Domination in Africa. *Development and Change* 41 (4): 539–562.

Harvey, P. 2018. Infrastructures in and Out of Time: The Promise of Roads in Contemporary Peru. In *The Promise of Infrastructure*, ed. N. Anand, A. Gupta, and H. Appel, 80–101. London: Duke University Press.

Hildyard, N. 2016. *Licenced Larceny: Infrastructure, Financial Extraction and the Global South*. Manchester University Press.

Hillman, J.E. 2018. The Belt and Road's Barriers to Participation, Reconnecting Asia. Center for Strategic and International Studies. http://bit.ly/2GGoquo. Accessed 14 Mar 2020.

Hodzi, O. 2018. China and Africa: Economic Growth and a Non-transformative Political Elite. *Journal of Contemporary African Studies* 36 (2): 191–206.

Hydrochina Corporation. 2012. *Master Plan Report of Wind and Solar Energy in the Federal Democratic Republic of Ethiopia*. Hangzhou: Hydrochina Corporation.

Infrastructure Consortium for Africa. 2018. *Infrastructure Financing Trends in Africa—2018*. Abidjan: Infrastructure Consortium for Africa.

Jacob, T., and R.H. Pedersen. 2018. New Resource Nationalism? Continuity and Change in Tanzania's Extractive Industries. *Extractive Industries and Society* 5 (2): 287–292.

Jessop, B. 1990. *State Theory: Putting the Capitalist State in Its Place*. Cambridge: Polity Press.

Jessop, B. 2016. *The State: Past, Present, Future*. Cambridge: Polity Press.

Kanyinga, K. 2016. Devolution and the New Politics of Development in Kenya. *African Studies Review* 59 (3): 155–167.

Kenyatta, U. 2021. President Kenyatta's full Speech at the Commissioning of Lamu Port, 20th May, Lamu. https://bit.ly/2Rrv8xl. Accessed 20 May 2021.

Kinyondo, A. 2019. Is China Recolonizing Africa? Some Views from Tanzania. *World Affairs* 182 (2): 128–164.

Kochore, H.H. 2016. The Road to Kenya?: Visions, Expectations and Anxieties Around New Infrastructure Development in Northern Kenya. *Journal of Eastern African Studies* 10 (3): 494–510.

Lampert, B., and G. Mohan. 2015. Making Space for African Agency in China-Africa Engagements: Ghanaian and Nigerian Patrons Shaping Chinese Enterprise. In *Africa and China: How Africans and Their Governments are Shaping Relations with China*, ed. A.W. Gadzala, 109–126. Lanham: Rowman & Littlefield.

LAPSSET Corridor Development Authority. 2020. 'Lamu Port', LAPSSET Corridor Development Authority. https://bit.ly/3u1sVWE. Accessed 20 Mar 2021.

Lavers, T., B. Tereffe, and F. Gebresenbet. 2021. Powering Development: The Political Economy of Electricity Generation in the EPRDF's Ethiopia. FutureDAMS Working Paper 014. https://bit.ly/3nadNWw. Accessed 22 Sep 2021.

Lesutis, G. 2019. How to Understand a Development Corridor? The case of Lamu Port-South Sudan–Ethiopia-Transport Corridor in Kenya. *Area* 52 (3): 600–608.

Links, S. 2021. Ascertaining Agency Africa and the Belt and Road Initiative. In *Global Perspectives on China's Belt and Road Initiative*, ed. F. Schneider, 113–139. Amsterdam: Amsterdam University Press.

Magufuli, J.J.P. 2017. Foreword. In *Tanzania's Industrialization Journey, 2016–2056: From Agrarian to a Modern Industrialized State in Forty Years*, ed. A.A. Mufuruki, R. Mawji, M. Marwa, and G. Kasiga, viii–ix. Nairobi: Moran Publishers.

Makundi, H., H. Huyse, and P. Develtere. 2017. Negotiating the Technological Capacity in Chinese engagements: Is the Tanzanian Government in the Driving Seat? *South African Journal of International Affairs* 24 (3): 331–335.

Massa, I. 2011. Export Finance Activities by the Chinese Government. Brussels: Directorate-General for External Policies. Available at: https://www.europarl.europa.eu/RegData/etudes/note/join/2011/433862/EXPO-INTA_NT(2011)433862_EN.pdf. Accessed 30 May 2021.

Migdal, J. 1994. Introduction: Developing a State-in-Society Perspective. In *State Power and Social Forces: Domination and Transformation in the Third World*, ed. J.S. Migdal, A. Kohli, and V. Shue, 1–12. Cambridge: Cambridge University Press.

Migdal, J. 2001. *State in Society: Studying How States and Societies Transform and Constitute One Another*. Cambridge: Cambridge University Press.

MOFEC. 2010. The Federal Democratic Republic of Ethiopia: Growth and Transformation Plan (GTP) 2010/11–2014/15.

MOFEC. 2016. Federal Democratic Republic of Ethiopia: Growth and Transformation Plan II (GTP II).

Mohan, G., and B. Lampert. 2013. Negotiating China: Reinserting African Agency into China-Africa Relations. *African Affairs* 112 (446): 92–110.

Mohan, G., and M. Tan-Mullins. 2019. The Geopolitics of South-South Infrastructure Development: Chinese-Financed Energy Projects in the Global South. *Urban Studies* 56 (7): 1368–1385.

Mold, A. 2012. Will It All End in Tears? Infrastructure Spending and African Development in Historical Perspective. *Journal of International Development* 24 (2): 237–254.

Mosley, J., and E.E. Watson. 2016. Frontier Transformations: Development Visions, Spaces and Processes in Northern Kenya and Southern Ethiopia. *Journal of Eastern African Studies* 10: 452–475.

Müller-Mahn, D., K. Mkutu, and E. Kioko. 2021. Megaprojects—Mega Failures? The Politics of Aspiration and the Transformation of Rural Kenya. *The European Journal of Development Research* 33: 1069–1090.

Musa, J. 2019. Why Talks on Port Stalled—Video. The Citizen. https://www.thecitizen.co.tz/news/1840340-5124384-8pdm7b/index.html.

Nantulya, P. 2021. Reshaping African Agency in China-Africa Relations. *Africa Centre for Strategic Studies.* https://africacenter.org/spotlight/reshaping-african-agency-china-africa-relations/ . Accessed 21 Oct 10 2021.

Nema, N. 2017. Twaha Among Sand Dunes Land "Grabbers" Summoned by NLC. Baraka FM, 24 February. https://bit.ly/3fk7aMg. Accessed 04 May 2020.

Nugent, P. 2018. Africa's Re-enchantment with Big Infrastructure: White Elephants Dancing in Virtuous Circles? In *Extractive Industries and Changing State Dynamics in Africa*, ed. J. Schubert, U. Engel, and E. Macamo, 22–40. Abingdon: Routledge.

Nugent, P. 2019. *Boundaries, Communities and State-Making in West Africa: The Centrality of the Margins*, vol. 144. Cambridge: Cambridge University Press.

Odhiambo, M.O. 2013. The ASAL Policy of Kenya: Releasing the Full Potential of Arid and Semi-Arid Lands—An Analytical Review. *Nomadic Peoples* 17 (1): 158–165.

OECD. 2015. Working Party on Export Credits and Credit Guarantees: Chinese Export Credit Guarantees: Chinese eExport Credit Policies and Programmes. Unclassified-TAD/ECG(2015)3. https://bit.ly/2yYdrLU. Accessed 24 May 2020.

Olivier de Sardan, J.P. 2011. The Eight Modes of Local Governance in West Africa. *IDS Bulletin* 42 (2): 22–31.

Oya, C. 2019. Labour Regimes and Workplace Encounters Between China and Africa. In *China-Africa and an Economic Transformation*, ed. A. Oqubay and Y.J. Lin, 239–263. Oxford: Oxford University Press.

Paget, D. 2021. Tanzania: The Authoritarian Landslide. *Journal of Democracy* 32 (2): 61–76.

Péclard, D., A. Kernen, and G. Khan-Mohammad. 2020. États d'émergence. Le gouvernement de la croissance et du développement en Afrique [States of émergence. [The governance of growth and Development in Africa]. *Critique Internationale* 89: 9–27.

Phillips, J. 2019. Who is in Charge of Sino-African Resource Politics? Situating African Agency in Ghana. *African Affairs* 118 (470): 101–124.

Polus, A., and W. Tycholiz. 2019. David Versus Goliath: Tanzania's Efforts to Stand Up to Foreign Gas Corporations. *Africa Spectrum* 54 (1): 61–72.

SaveLamu. 2011. 'SaveLamu Holds Protest at NEA and KPA Offices', Save-Lamu. Available at: https://www.savelamu.org/protest-in-lamu/. Accessed 22 April 2020.

Schindler, S., and J.M. Kanai. 2021. Getting the Territory Right: Infrastructure-Led Development and the Re-emergence of Spatial Planning Strategies. *Regional Studies* 55: 40–51.

Schlimmer, S. 2018. Talking 'Land Grabs' is Talking Politics: Land as Politicized Rhetoric During Tanzania's 2015 Elections. *Journal of Eastern African Studies* 12 (1): 83–101.

Soulé-Kohndou, F. 2019. Bureaucratic Agency and Power Asymmetry in Benin-China Relations. In *New Directions in Africa-China Studies*, ed. C. Alden and D. Large, 189–204. Abingdon: Routledge.

Soulé-Kohndou, F. 2020. 'Africa+1' Summit Diplomacy and the 'New Scramble' Narrative: Recentering African Agency. *African Affairs* 119 (477): 633–646.

Subera, R. 2013. Federalism and Decentralisation. In *Routledge Handbook of African Politics*, ed. N. Cheeseman, D. Anderson, and A. Scheibler, 22–37. Abingdon: Routledge.

Sun, Y., Jayaram, K. and Kassiri, O. 2017. 'Dance of the Lions and Dragons', McKinsey Global Institute. https://mck.co/39tUQV6. Accessed 20 Mar 2020.

Swainson, N. 1980. *The Development of Corporate Capitalism in Kenya, 1918–77*. London: Heinemann Educational.

Taylor, I. 2020. Kenya's New Lunatic Express: The Standard Gauge Railway. *African Studies Quarterly* 19 (3–4): 29–52.

The Citizen. 2019. How the Dream for a Port in Bagamoyo Became Elusive. The Citizen. https://www.thecitizen.co.tz/news/1840340-5124384-8pdm7b/index.html.

The National Christian Council of Kenya. 1972. *Ready for Change: Development in Northern Kenya*. Nairobi: The National Christian Council of Kenya.

Tsubura, Machiko. 2018. 'Umoja Ni Ushindi (Unity is Victory)': Management of Factionalism in the Presidential Nomination of Tanzania's Dominant Party in 2015. *Journal of Eastern African Studies* 12 (1): 63–82.

Wang, Y., and U. Wissenbach. 2019. Clientelism at Work? A Case Study of Kenyan Standard Gauge Railway Project. *Economic History of Developing Regions* 34 (3): 280–299.

Wethal, U. 2019. Building Africa's Infrastructure: Reinstating History in Infrastructure Debates. *Forum for Development Studies* 43 (3): 473–499.

Wight, C. 1999. They Shoot Dead Horses Don't They? Locating Agency in the Agent-Structure Problematique. *European Journal of International Relations* 5 (1): 109–142.

Wight, C. 2006. *Agents, Structures and International Relations: Politics as Ontology*, 2nd ed. Cambridge: Cambridge University Press.

Wissenbach, U. 2019. Kenya's madaraka Express: An Example of the Decisive Chinese Impulse for African Mega-infrastructure Projects. In *Duality by Design: The Global Race to Build Africa's Infrastructure*, ed. N. Gil, A. Stafford, and I. Musonda, 315–352. Cambridge: Cambridge University Press.

Wolrd Bank 2018. GDP Growth (aanual %)—Ethiopia. https://data.worldbank.org/country/ethiopia?most_recent_year_desc=false. Accessed 31 July 2020.

Zajontz, T. 2021a. Debt, Distress, Dispossession: Towards a Critical Political Economy of Africa's Financial Dependency. *Review of African Political Economy.* https://doi.org/10.1080/03056244.2021.1950669.

Zajontz, T. 2021b. Infrastructure. In *Yearbook on the African Union,* ed. U. Engel. Brill: Leiden.

Zajontz, T. 2020b. The Chinese Infrastructural Fix in Africa: A Strategic-Relational Analysis of Zambia's 'Road Bonanza' and the Rehabilitation of TAZARA. University of St. Andrews. PhD dissertation.

Zajontz, T. 2020a. The Chinese Infrastructural Fix in Africa: A Critical Appraisal of the Sino-Zambian "Road Bonanza." *Oxford Development Studies.* https://doi.org/10.1080/13600818.2020.1861230.

Zajontz, T., and I. Taylor. 2021. Capitalism and Africa's (Infra)structural Dependency: A Story of Spatial Fixes and Accumulation by Dispossession. In *Africa and the Global System of Capital Accumulation,* ed. E.O. Oritsejafor and A.D. Cooper. New York: Routledge.

Zajontz, T. forthcoming. "Win–Win" Contested: Negotiating the Privatisation of Africa's Freedom Railway with the "Chinese of Today". *Journal of Modern African Studies* 60 (1).

Zawdie, G., and D.A. Langford. 2002. Influence of Construction-Based Infrastructure on the Development Process in Sub-Saharan Africa. *Building Research & Information* 30 (3): 160–170.

Zenawi, M. 2012. States and Markets: Neoliberal Limitations and the Case for a Developmental State. In *Good Growth and Governance in Africa: Rethinking Development Strategies,* ed. A. Norman, K. Botchwey, H. Stein, and J.E. Stiglitz. New York: Oxford University Press.

Ziso, E. 2018. *A Post State-Centric Analysis of China-Africa Relations: Internationalisation of Chinese Capital and State-Society Relations in Ethiopia.* London: Palgrave MacMillan.

CHAPTER 8

The AIIB and China's Normative Power in International Financial Governance Structure

Zhongzhou Peng and Sow Keat Tok

8.1 Introduction

The Asian Infrastructure Investment Bank (AIIB) was initiated by Chinese President Xi Jinping and Premier Li Keqiang during their respective visits to Southeast Asian countries in October 2013 (AIIB 2015c). The purpose of this bank is to provide support to Asian infrastructure

---

This chapter is a reproduction of the journal article: Peng, Z., Tok, S.K. "The AIIB and China's Normative Power in International Financial Governance Structure." *Chin. Polit. Sci. Rev.* 1, 736–753 (2016). https://doi.org/10.1007/s41111-016-0042-y

---

Z. Peng (✉)
School of Social and Political Science (SSPS), Melbourne University, Melbourne, VIC, Australia
e-mail: zpeng@student.unimelb.edu.au

© The Author(s), under exclusive license to Springer Nature Switzerland AG 2025
K. G.Cai et al. (eds.), *China and Global Economic Governance, Volume I: China's BRI & AIIB and Global Economic Governance*, Politics and Development of Contemporary China,
https://doi.org/10.1007/978-3-031-73212-6_8

construction. According to an oft-cited study by the Asian Development Bank (ADB) in 2009, between 2010 and 2020, the Asia region needs $8 trillion to develop its infrastructure, of which 68% would be for new capacity. As for how it is spent, 51% would be for electricity, 29% for roads, and 13% for telecommunications (Bhattacharyay 2010). Compared to the astronomical amount of need, the World Bank (WB) and the ADB only provide about 20 billion U.S. dollars each year in the Asian region (Renard 2015, p. 2). The AIIB, with an authorized capital of $100 billion, seeks to contribute to this specific area.

The influence of this bank was rather limited, since the US and Japan have rejected this initiative at the early stage of its formation (New York Times 2014). Considering the enormous influence the US and Japan have in the financial governance area, both globally and in Asian region, it was a general assumption that 'the AIIB would start out as a modest venture involving mainly Asian and Middle Eastern countries' (Wihtol 2015, p. 7).

However, on March 12, 2015, the announcement of the United Kingdom (UK) which announced its intention to join the AIIB has changed the situation dramatically (the United Kingdom 2015). Although the UK is not the first European country that made the decision (Luxembourg joined a few days ahead of the UK), its political and financial clout in international politics made its announcement a trigger of the scramble for the founding membership of the AIIB. In a span of days, a group of Western government, including France, Germany, and Australia, made the similar announcement to join the AIIB. As a result, when the signing ceremony of the Articles of Agreement (AOA) was held in Beijing on June 29, 2015, the AIIB had become a significant multilateral financial institution involving 57 Prospective Founding Members (PFMs). After the AOA had been signed by all 57 PFMs between June 29, 2015 and December 31, 2015, the AIIB opened for business on January 16, 2016 and Jin Liqun, former Ranking Vice President of the Asian Development Bank (ADB) was elected as the first president of the AIIB.

The establishment of the AIIB, especially the agreement with major European states who have been the close allies of the US, was regarded

---

S. K. Tok
Asia Institute, Melbourne University, Melbourne, VIC, Australia
e-mail: sowkeat.tok@unimelb.edu.au

as a diplomatic triumph for Beijing over Washington. Quite a few articles put their focus on how Jin Liqun, the leader of Chinese negotiating team, used the economic interest to gain support from the allies of the US (Financial Times 2015). Some others suggest that the AIIB will become a great challenge to the existing US-led financial institutions, especially the WB, the ADB, and even the IMF (The Economist 2015a, 2015b). This article, on the other hand, seeks to analyze the normative implications of the AIIB rather than its diplomatic influence. Through the lens of normative power concept, this article argues that the AIIB is both a successor of Chinese norms in the financial governance area and a broader platform of Chinese normative projection. However, while the AIIB may serve as a new vehicle for Chinese normative diffusion, the inclusion of developed Western economies, the interactions with other institutions, and the internal governance structure might also challenge and shape China's normative approach in global financial governance area.

8.2 The Conceptual Framework of Normative Power

The concept of normative power is formulated by Ian Manners through a series of articles (Manners 2002, 2006, 2013). Based on his research of the EU's foreign policy, Ian Manners argues that the EU has 'evolved' into a form of governance which 'transcends Westphalian norms' (Manners 2002, p. 240). Specifically, Manners argues that the EU embraces norms, such as human rights, democracy, and rule of law, and puts these norms at the center of its relation with its member states (Manners 2002, p. 241). In addition, the EU has been diffusing these norms to other countries and other regions through economic and political interactions. Moreover, the EU aims to change the regime of other countries during its normative diffusion. Building upon these characters of the EU's foreign policy, Manners (2002, p. 239) defines the EU as a normative power which has 'the ability to shape conceptions of "normal" in international relations.'

Since its formation, normative power literature has become one of the most influential branches among the discussions of the EU's external behavior. Throughout the debates on normative power concept, one of the core research agendas is the criteria, and an international actor needs to meet to qualify as a normative power. In Manners' aforementioned article (Manners 2002), the EU is a normative power because of its internal implementation of the norms, plus its policy to diffuse these norms to other countries and regions (Manners 2002, p. 238–245). However, for an international actor to gain normative power, self-representation alone is not enough. Even if there are modifications of policies among its partners, it is possible that these actions are motivated by political and economic interests rather than true belief in the norms and regimes. Indeed, as some scholars point out, the reactions of other countries can be 'half-compliance' or 'fake-compliance' if they do not accept the normative component of the EU's policy (Noutcheva 2009) As a result, it is as important that the alleged normative power can convince its partners to accept the normative principles and to transform their policies to converge to these common clauses.

In this regard, the external perceptions of the EU's partners are considered by some scholars as an essential factor during the evaluation of the EU's foreign policy (Lucarelli 2007). Based on this discussion, Kavalski (2013) takes a step forward and argues that external perception is another essential criterion of normative power qualification. He argues that since normative power emerges from the interaction with the others, the recognition of the counterparts is also crucial for an international actor to qualify as a normative power. As he states, 'normative power emerges in relation to the inter-subjective environment to which its agency is applied' (Kavalski 2013, p. 250; emphasis in original). Zupancˇicˇ and Hribernik (2013) agree with Kavalski's argument. They contend that 'normative power is more than a rather vague notion that someone is "doing good". This "good" should also be recognized and, consequently, accepted as "good" by the other' (Zupancˇicˇ and Hribernik 2013, p. 111). Lucarelli also argues that the role of the EU '[is] determined by both an actor's own conceptions about appropriate behavior and by the expectations of other actors' (Lucarelli 2007, p. 257). As a result, the feedback from relevant others is another determinant of the EU's political identity.

To sum up, existing literature sets three criteria for an international actor to meet to qualify as a normative power: internal norm construction, the diplomatic capacity of normative diffusion, and external perceptions of being a normative power. However, the current literature more or less presumes that the EU is the exclusive normative power in international relations. This assumption does not accord much attention to the fact that other international actors also have their series of norms to guide their foreign policy. In addition, some of these characters may as well be successful during their normative diffusion. This article resonates with the argument made by Larsen (2014) that normative power scholarship needs to take into account other potential normative actors in international relations. In the area of global financial governance, China is emerging as an influential normative actor, and it will be fruitful to examine the correlation between the establishment of the AIIB and the emerging normative power of China in international financial governance.

Because of its booming economy and large population, China has become an important actor in international relations and regional geopolitics. Since the introduction of reform and opening-up policy in the 1970s, China had experienced a ten % annual growth rate for nearly 20 years. Until now, China still has a 7% annual growth rate. As a result, China now has the world's second-largest nominal GDP which has exceeded 60 trillion RMB or 10 trillion USD in 2014 (National Bureau of Statistics 2015). The rise of its economic power has provided a broader platform for China to spread its norms of financial governance. In addition, the increasing clout in international economy has given China new appeals regarding international institutions and governance regimes. The AIIB, as a Chinese initiative, is an important vehicle to carry these Chinese norms. Meanwhile, through the programs of the AIIB, China is able to increase its normative influence in the Asian region and the globe. On the basis of the conceptual framework of normative power, the following parts of this article will analyze the linkage between the AIIB and China's normative power in international financial governance.

8.3 The AIIB and Chinese Normative Power in International Financial Governance

8.3.1 The AIIB Consists of Chinese Norms regarding International Financial Governance

The establishment of the AIIB is a milestone in China's financial policy. Together with the New Development Bank (NDB, also commonly known as the "BRICs Bank"), they are both new multilateral financial institutions in which China is the major shareholder. Compared to the NDB, whose capital is evenly held by Brazil, Russia, India, South Africa, and China (NDB 2014), the AIIB relies more on China's capital contribution. According to the AOA, China holds more than 30% of the AIIB's capital. This proportion is significantly larger than any other member of the bank. As a result, China will have the leading position in the policy-making of the AIIB, and thus, it can implement its norms of external assistance into the programs of the bank. Meanwhile, the entrance of other member states implies that they also endorse China's principles of foreign aid and investment. Therefore, the operation of the AIIB will enhance the Chinese normative influence in both the recipient countries and the AIIB's member states.

Foreign aid programs have been the major vehicle of China's normative diffusion. According to public information, the policies of AIIB will inherit China's traditional principles of external assistance. These principles include 'no strings attached,' 'mutual benefit,' and 'non-intervention.' As early as in the 1960s, when it commenced providing foreign aid to African countries, these key norms had been adopted by then Chinese Premier Zhou Enlai to guide China's foreign aid. In the first principle of the 'eight principles of foreign aid,' Zhou Enlai defined the basic rules of China's foreign aid as 'equity and mutual benefit' and that China 'never considers its assistance as a type of unilateral charity but rather as mutual aid.' The second principle states that China 'never asks for any privilege and never poses conditions' in its foreign aid program (Zhou 1964).

Although half a century has passed, since Zhou Enlai first presented these principles, up until now, Chinese official documents are still repeating his words. Since 2011, the Chinese government has published a series of white papers to review its foreign aid policy. All these annual reports start with the declaration that Chinese foreign aid is based on norms, including equality, mutual benefit, and no strings attached. For instance, the 2014 China's Foreign Aid White Paper makes this clear statement in its second paragraph:

> When providing foreign assistance, China adheres to the principles of not imposing any political conditions, not interfering in the internal affairs of the recipient countries and fully respecting their right to independently choosing their own paths and models of development. The basic principles China upholds in providing foreign assistance are mutual respect, equality, keeping promise, mutual benefits, and win–win. (State Council 2014)

The fact that Zhou's principles of 'mutual benefit,' 'no strings attached,' and 'non-interference' are all repeated in this report indicates that these normative approaches remain to be the guidelines of China's foreign aid and investment. China adheres to the belief that the political system is an internal business of each state. Thus, no country has the right to interfere or to decide the regime of another one. This position formulates China's interpretation of unconditionality in foreign aid programs. As China's special envoy for Africa, Liu Guijin, outlines, 'We don't attach political conditions. We have to realize the political and economic environments are not ideal. But we don't have to wait for everything to be satisfactory or human rights to be perfect' (Financial Times 2008).

This principle is also manifested in the policy framework of the AIIB. Chinese leaders and officials have expressed clearly that the AIIB will not impose political conditions on its investment (Reuter 2015). In addition, there is no mention of political requirements among the operating principles in the AOA. Article 13 of the AOA states that '[t]he Bank shall ensure that each of its operations complies with the Bank's operational and financial policies, including without limitation, policies addressing environmental and social impacts' (AIIB 2015a). Since the AOA has been agreed and signed by all 57 PFMs (AIIB 2015d), China has not only introduced its norm of unconditionality into the AIIB, but also successfully gained endorsement for this norm from all the member states of the bank.

In addition, the AIIB's preference for infrastructure construction is also in line with China's foreign aid and investment policy. Drawing on its own experience, especially the reform and opening-up policy, China holds the idea that for developing countries to increase its national power, the focus should be economic development. In addition, to accelerate economic development, infrastructure building is the foundation. Guided by this principle, a large proportion of China's foreign aid is devoted to infrastructure construction. According to the State Council, 44.8% of aid was used for economic infrastructure, while 27.6% was used for social and public infrastructure during 2010–2012 (State Council 2014). These infrastructure programs include the construction of hospitals, schools, water supply, public infrastructure, transport and communications, broadcasting and telecommunications, and power supply. China has also helped the construction of over 70 transport projects, including roads, bridges, airports, and ports. In Africa alone China has built 2233 km of railroads, 3391 km of highways (State Council 2014). It is clear that the programs of the AIIB will share this preference for infrastructure construction. As the first article of the AOA clearly announces, '[t]he purpose of the Bank shall be to foster sustainable economic development, create wealth and improve infrastructure connectivity in Asia by investing in infrastructure and other productive sectors' (AIIB 2015a).

The first series of projects of the AIIB goes to show that infrastructure building is the major target of this bank. The AIIB has approved four projects by June 2016: the national motorway project in Pakistan; the Dushanbe-Uzbekistan Border Road Improvement project in Tajikistan; the distribution system upgrade and expansion project in Bangladesh; and the national slum upgrading project in Indonesia (AIIB 2016b). These projects, with a total cost more than 2 billion USD, aim to increase the transportation ability, electric supply, and urban infrastructure in developing countries. The official documents of these projects reveal that not only the AIIB, but also the recipient countries recognize that infrastructure building is essential for them to achieve economic growth. For instance, Pakistan government describes that the national motorway project "plays an important role in the development of micro and macro economy" (AIIB 2016b). Similarly, Bangladesh government has identified electricity supply as "a major constraint on GDP growth, and overall economic development" (AIIB 2016b). These official statements are in line with Chinese norms of infrastructure construction. None of these projects contain political conditions whatsoever. These projects manifest the AIIB's commitment to foster infrastructure construction is not just rhetoric. It has already put effort to increase infrastructure building in the Asian region. In addition, through this process, China's norm of infrastructure construction and unconditionality will also be spread in this area.

However, although the AIIB may well be understood as a platform for China to enhance the influence of its norms regarding financial governance, the structure of this institution, as well as the interactions between China and other member states, will possibly pose a challenge to China's cultivation of its normative influence. To start with, it is undoubtedly a significant achievement of China to persuade a group of major European countries, including Britain, German, and France to join the AIIB. Their decisions to become PFMs indicate that they, unlike the US, do not oppose the norms and structure proposed by China. However, this does not mean that China has successfully persuaded these Western countries to accept its norms of financial governance holistically. When analyzing the motivations of Britain, German, and other European countries to join the AIIB, reports often note that they are attracted by political and economic interests. For instance, German and France are aiming at the contracts of construction projects they can get from the AIIB. Britain is seeking to have the European center of the AIIB in its country, so that it can expand its financial influence in the globe (The Diplomat 2015). There is hardly any proof that the join of these countries means that they have accepted Chinese way of foreign aid and investment. In contrast, some countries, including Britain and Australia, have been suggesting that they aim to improve the governance structure of the AIIB, so that it will be more integrated with international regime (the United Kingdom 2015; the Guardian 2015b). As a result, even though the AIIB has successfully gained support from European countries, it does not mean that Chinese norms have been diffused and accepted by these states. China's financial policy may face considerable internal questioning and challenge during the operation of the AIIB.

Moreover, the AIIB has targeted to establish broader cooperation among regional financial institutions in infrastructure construction area. Up until now, China has declared that the AIIB will enhance the relationships with the ADB, the African Development Bank, the Inter-American Development Bank, the West African Development Bank, and the Caribbean Development Bank to channel more capital into the fields of infrastructure, environmental protection, education, and health care in developing countries. However, if the AIIB seeks to establish cooperation with WB, ADB, and other institutions, it has to adopt the norms of environment protection, good governance, and social security in its policy framework. Indeed, the analysis shows that some changes have undergone in China's policy. For instance, China's recent Foreign Aid White Paper has included environmental protection as a part of China's goals and achievements in this field (State Council 2014). The AIIB has also listed environmental protection and urban development as its areas of engagement. It has also produced an Environmental and Social Framework to regulate its operation, which has recently been approved by the Board of Directors (AIIB 2016a). It is thus interesting to observe how far will the AIIB move beyond the traditional "economic centralism" in China's foreign aid policy and be more integrated into international aid structure.

To sum up, since Chinese norms of financial governance underpin the setup of the AIIB and its policy, the AIIB provides a more direct channel for China to present its norms of financial governance to its Western partners and to increase the influence of its normative power. However, during the internal bargaining and external interactions, China may review and reassess its norms of foreign aid and foreign investment through workings within the AIIB.

8.3.2 The AIIB is a Litmus Test of China's Position in the Reform of Global Financial Governance

Aside from the norms of foreign aid and foreign investment, the AIIB is also a manifestation of China's normative appeals regarding the financial governance structure. In recent years, China has been actively promoting the reform of governance structure in major multilateral financial institutions. In Chinese rhetoric, the aim is to establish a fair governance structure in multilateral organizations (Lu 2011, p. 89). The key point of this reform is the redistribution of voting rights. China has been suggesting that currently, the share of voting rights of the emerging countries in the WB and the IMF does not correspond to their actual economic status. For instance, before 2010, China had only 2.8 and 5.5% voting rights in the WB and the ADB, respectively, and is ranked only 6th in terms of voting rights in the International Monetary Fund (IMF). On the other hand, Japan and the US had a combined 23.6 and 26% in the WB and the ADB, respectively. They also have the two largest shares of voting rights in the IMF: the US has 17% and Japan has 6%. The unbalance distribution of voting rights is also substantial between developed countries and developing countries. Before 2008, the G7 countries had a combined 41.2% voting rights in the IMF, while Brazil, Russia, India, China, and South Africa (BRICS) together have only 14.2% (Chen and Tan 2013). China argues that the developing countries, especially emerging countries, such as the BRICS, have less proportion of voting rights than their economic weight in the world economy (Cui and Chang 2013, p. 25). In contrast, although the economic clout of developed countries is diminishing, they still have an enormous share of voting rights, so that they can control the policies of the organizations. As a result, the voting rights distribution should be reformed, so that it can fit the new structure of the global economy.

Aside from the unbalance distribution of voting rights, China has also been criticizing the US's unilateral veto power in the IMF. According to the IMF's governance structure, major decisions need 85% of votes to get passed. Since the US has a share of more than 16% of voting power, it actually has the ability to block any decision that is against its own interest. China argues that this unilateral veto power makes IMF a tool of the US to execute its policies and suggests that it is not "fair" to other countries (Lu 2011).

China has been actively promoting its understanding of a 'fair governance structure' in international financial institutions in recent years. The strategy of China is to establish a coalition of emerging economies and developing countries to push forward the reform in the IMF and the WB. The major partners of China in this issue are Russia, Brazil, and India. Together with South Africa, they are called the 'BRICS' group. In September 2009, China, Russia, Brazil, and India jointly announced that the IMF should transfer 7% of the voting rights from developed countries to developing countries (BRICS 2009). China also suggests that the management level of the IMF should have more representatives from developing countries (Cui and Chang 2013, p. 24).

The effort of China and other developing countries has resulted in limited reforms in existing institutions. In 2010, the WB presented a new distribution of voting rights. Under this new framework, the developed countries will transfer 3.13% of voting rights to developing countries. Meanwhile, China's voting rights have increased from 2.77 to 4.42%, which makes it the third biggest shareholder in the WB. On the other hand, the IMF also made a decision to reform its governance structure in 2009. The reform plan raises the weight of GDP which is beneficial to the emerging economies and developing countries. According to this decision, the voting rights of China, Brazil, and India will increase from 3, 1.7, 1.9 to 6, 2.3, and 2.6%, respectively (G20 2009).

Despite the progress mentioned above, there is room for Chinese appeals. Although the reform plans of the IMF have given China the largest increase of voting rights and provided the emerging economies more power in the governance structure, the US still controls the veto power in the IMF. Meanwhile, China has not been able to increase its share of voting rights in the ADB. Until March 2015, China's voting rights was only 5.47%. Even though China has been actively promoting its blueprint of financial governance order, it has yet been influential enough to shape existing institutions through internal mechanisms, since the US, as well as Japan, has a dominant position in the current regime structure.

In this light, the AIIB, as a Chinese initiative, serves as a vehicle of China to manifest its illustration of an ideal financial governance structure. The first character of the AIIB is that it has a lean management arrangement. A week after the AIIB was inaugurated, Jin Liqun stated at the World Economic Forum that the bank will be "lean, clean and green." In terms of the "lean" commitment, the AIIB will maintain a small number of employees in its early stage of operation. It will start an initial staffing level of 50, and increase its workforce only to between 100 and 150 in the first year (Wall Street Journal 2015). The AIIB will also abandon a resident board of directors, instead the board of directors shall "function on a non-resident basis" and "meet as often as the business of the Bank may require, periodically throughout the year" (AIIB 2015a: Article 27.1). Compared with the World Bank, which has over 12,000 staff and consultants, and the ADB, which has 3000 employees, the AIIB's workforce scale is significantly smaller. More importantly, operating without a resident board of directors should save the bank money and friction in decision-making. The resident board costs the World Bank some \$70 million annually. In addition, there have been complaints that "'[t]here was often a certain tension between the management and the board members whose resident staff wanted to find out about projects at an early stage" (Wall Street Journal 2015). These arrangements reflect that the AIIB represents a more efficient management structure in which China has repeatedly attempted to introduce to international institutions.

Meanwhile, the AIIB carries another essential Chinese norm regarding financial governance: a supposedly fairer distribution of voting rights. According to the final text of the AOA, the voting rights of AIIB are divided into two parts: Asian countries and regions have 70–75% of voting rights, and the countries and regions outside Asia have 25–30%. The voting rights of individual countries consist of three parts: its share of the capital, basic voting rights, and 600 votes of PFMs. In specific, the share of the capital is calculated according to the weighted average of GDP (60% market exchange rate and 40% purchasing power parity). The basic voting rights constitute 12% of the total voting rights and are divided evenly among all the members (AIIB 2015a). It is worthy to note that the basic voting rights and PFM votes have a 15% proportion in the total voting rights. In contrast, in the IMF, the basic voting rights count only 5.5% of the total voting rights. As a result of this complex formula, Asian developing countries, excluding China, have a combined 30% voting power in the bank. In comparison, European developed countries together have around 20% votes (AIIB 2015a). This distribution ensures that Asian developing countries can have considerably larger influence in the institution than what they have in the WB and the ADB. In addition, the Board of Directors incorporates 12 representatives from 12 different countries from Asia, Europe, South America, and Oceania

(AIIB 2015b). These settings in the AIIB's governance structure can be regarded as an improvement of fairness among members, since it increased the basic votes and the decision power of the smallest member quite significantly.

However, according to the calculation of capital shares, China has 26.06% of total voting rights in the AIIB. The AOA has stated that the Board of Directors needs 75% of total voting power of the members to 'take decisions on major operational and financial policies and on delegation of authority to the President under Bank policies' (AIIB 2015a: Article 26). This means that China will have the single unilateral veto power in the bank's major policymaking, just like what the US has in the IMF. Although Beijing suggests that the successive entrance of new members will dilute China's voting power in the institution and that China will not use its veto power (China Daily 2016), it still needs a large economy, such as Japan to reduce China's share of voting rights to less than 25%. The gap between China's normative appeal of governance structure and the actual setting of the AIIB indicates that the AIIB is not only a larger platform for China to diffuse its norms, but also a dilemma for China to face: it either abandons its veto power and undertakes the risk of losing control of the AIIB's decision-making process, or it obtains veto power which will undermine its normative approach in financial governance. After the AIIB commences its business this year, the decision-making process of the AIIB's investment programs will continue to examine the extent of which China will balance its normative principles and practical interests.

8.3.3 The AIIB Will Improve the External Perceptions of China's Normative Power?

The prior parts have discussed the AIIB's impact on the normative aspects of China's foreign financial policy. However, as the debate of normative power concept has revealed, having a normative approach is not enough for an international actor to become a normative power (Kavalski 2013). The perceptions, as well as the level of acceptance, are also essential factors which determine whether an actor has normative influence. Judging from this assumption, the analysis of the AIIB's influence should also encompass its effect on the views of other countries regarding China's normative power. In this area, China's image is controversial. On the one hand, there is proof that China's understanding of foreign aid, and good governance is acquiring more support in the African region. On the other hand, in recent years, China's foreign aid policy has been a major target of Western criticism for its disregard of social development and environmental protection. In this sense, the AIIB will underpin the shaping of the external perceptions of the normative power of China in financial governance area. Since the AIIB had become a multilateral institution with more than 50 members, it will significantly increase the interactions among China, Western developed countries, and emerging countries. Through the cooperation with developed countries, the operation of the AIIB will take into account the social and environmental policies. Thus, this institution will give China a chance to improve its image among Western countries and expand its normative influence among developing countries.

China's foreign aid and foreign investment policy, especially its operations in African region, have been a widely discussed topic in recent years. African countries, as the direct recipients of China's aid, usually have a positive feedback of China's financial policy, and they have been adopting the Chinese way of state governance. Since the end of the Cold War, Africa's perception of China has developed from an ally against colonialism to a reliable economic partner. Chinese aid, especially its infrastructure construction programs, has made African countries recognize that China's policy will bring actual benefit to them. In addition, African leaders repeatedly showed the public appreciation of China's norm of unconditionality. They are comfortable that there are no benchmarks and preconditions, no environmental impact assessment to hinder the negotiations (Brautigam 2011a). Moreover, China is also perceived as an alternative model of development to African countries. As a Nigeria diplomat states:

> China has become ... a good model for Nigeria in its quest for an authentic and stable development ideology ... China [is] a lesson to Nigeria on the enormous good that a focused and patriotic leadership can do to realize the dreams of prosperity and security for the citizens. (Manji and Marks 2007)

Aside from African political elites, African civil society also has a positive perception of China's existence. In a study of the African perceptions of China, Keuleers (2015, p. 812) finds out that 36% of respondents indicated that China "helps a lot" and an additional 30.5% said China "helps somewhat." As a result, two-thirds of respondents hold a positive or very positive view regarding China's role in the African region. In another survey which covered 250 students and university staff from nine African countries, the result shows that the majority of the respondents (74%) believe that China's way of development is a positive model for their country. Overall, half of the respondents think that China's policy is more beneficial to African than Western policy and only 20% of the respondents agree that China is practicing neo-colonialism to Africa (Sautman and Hairong 2009). In addition, more than half of them (60%) think that China's policy of non-interference is a good thing. Similarly, in BBC's annual poll of global perceptions, the most favorable views of China are found in Africa where no surveyed country has less than 65% of positive views (BBC 2015, p. 37).

In contrast to the overall positive image of China among African countries, Western developed states, including European countries and the US, regarded China as a negative normative power in Africa. The conventional Western aid programs not only provide financial assistance, but also impose social and political requirements to the recipient countries. For instance, the EU includes a human rights clause in its aid agreement with African, Caribbean, and Pacific countries. According to this clause, the EU has the right to withdraw or suspend its aid if there is human right violation in the recipient countries (Cotonou Agreement 2010: Article 8). In contrast, Chinese aid programs focus on infrastructure alone. This approach is considered to be 'far simpler and does not overstretch the weak capacity of many African governments faced with multiple meetings, quarterly reports, workshops, and so on' (Brautigam 2011b, p. 761). Another criticism targets the unconditionality and non-interference principles in Chinese aid programs, especially those targeting African countries (Brautigam 2011a). The focus is China's omission of social, environmental, and governance standards applied by the West. For instance, the president of the European Investment Bank accused the Chinese of 'unscrupulous' behavior (Condon 2012, p. 16). The non-governmental organization Human Rights Watch presents a popular critic that 'China's growing foreign aid program creates new options for dictators who were previously dependent on those who insisted on human rights progress' (Leonard 2008). To sum up, the West has been describing

China's approach in Africa as unethical and perceiving China as a negative normative power in this region.

Focusing solely on the external perceptions of China's partners of its foreign aid programs, China's norms appear widely accepted by the target countries of its financial policy. Indeed, African countries find China a more amicable collaboration partner and thus receptive to China's principles, given their common experience as victims of colonialism, and identify each other as peers in the developing South. China's norms, when compared to most Western paradigms, better meet the developmental needs of African countries. China's principles of equality and non-interference have, by and large, differentiated itself with the Western approach which is considered by some Asian and African countries as a new form of colonialism (Larsen 2014).

However, the fact that China is perceived as a negative normative power by Western observers sheds light on the relationship between Chinese norms and the international normative structure. It illustrates that although China's normative clout is expanding globally, it is still viewed by most of the Western observers as a country, whose democracy and human rights conditions are below the international standard (Zhang 2011, p. 241). As a result, China is still regarded as the 'other' in international normative structure. This analysis illustrates that there is a lack of interaction and integration between China's norms and the international normative structure. China has been playing its own game with its own rules. In addition, Western countries are becoming more and more frustrated, because they think that China is compromising their efforts of promoting their norms.

This skepticism is manifested in some initial responses toward the AIIB among developed countries. Since the AIIB's normative guidelines are distinct from existing policies of external assistance, there are concerns that the AIIB will lack transparency and accountability. This has been the major argument of the US and Japan to oppose the formulation of the AIIB. Japan's finance minister Taro Aso says that Japan will 'consider' joining the AIIB if 'it proves to be a credible institution complying with generally accepted governance and environmental standards.' Taro Aso further states that the AIIB has to 'ensure debt sustainability, taking into account its impact on environment and society' (Japan Times 2015). The White House National Security Council, in a statement to The Guardian (2015a), makes this declaration:

> Our position on the AIIB remains clear and consistent ... Based on many discussions, we have concerns about whether the AIIB will meet these high standards, particularly related to governance, and environmental and social safeguards ... The international community has a stake in seeing the AIIB complement the existing architecture, and to work effectively alongside the World Bank and Asian Development Bank.

Despite these concerns and doubts regarding the AIIB, the establishment of this bank has resulted in substantial changes in the perceptions of China's involvement in financial governance. To start with, compared to the WB and the IMF, the AIIB is a new institution which serves an immensely different goal: infrastructure construction. Compared to the enormous need of fund regarding infrastructure construction in the Asian region, what each institution can provide is far from sufficient. Since the WB and the ADB are both focusing on reducing poverty, the formation of the AIIB is rather a complement to the existing institutions than a direct challenge (People's Daily Online 2014). Indeed, the AIIB has formulated cooperation with the WB, the ADB, and the European Bank for Reconstruction and Development in its initial projects. It has also agreed to strengthen its cooperation with the European Investment Bank. Indeed, the AIIB, along with the Chinese norm of infrastructure construction, is welcomed by many existing institutions. The president of the WB, Jim Yong Kim, the head of the IMF Lagarde, and the president of the ADB Takehiko Nakao have expressed their support of the AIIB. The United Nations (2015, p. 73) has addressed the launch of the AIIB as "scaling up financing for sustainable development" for the concern of Global Economic Governance. These statements prove that there is sufficient space for the AIIB to cooperate with existing international governance structure rather than to challenge or replace it. Moreover, the AIIB (2016a) has introduced the Environmental and Social Framework. This framework, which has put into operation in February 2016, aims to provide 'a mechanism for addressing environmental and social risks and impacts in Project identification, preparation and implementation' to '[e]nsure the environmental and social soundness and sustainability of Projects' (Article 5). The framework also makes clear reference to the idea of sustainable development which includes economic, social, and environmental aspects (Article 8). The inclusion of the Environmental and Social Framework implies that China is willing to apply international standards to the AIIB's operation. As Jin Liqun underlines, the AIIB will adhere to the highest standard in the globe (Xinhua Net 2016). This stance will help to bridge the gap between China's norms and Western norms regarding external assistance, thus improving the external perceptions of China's normative power.

Moreover, the successful launch of the AIIB not only complements the current governance structure, but also enhanced China's normative diffusion in the sense that existing institutions have taken actions to integrate China into the governance structure. For instance, in March 2015, the ADB decided to raise the annual fund for infrastructure and other projects by nearly 40% to 18 billion US dollars. This is regarded as a response to the founding of the AIIB. It also signals that the launch of the AIIB has diffused the norm of infrastructure construction and changed the policy of other institutions. In the financial governance area, the AIIB has also caused a series of reactions. In December 2015, after more than half decade of stagnation, US Congress finally approved the reform plan of the IMF which was formulated in 2010 to increase the voting rights of China and other emerging countries. This was undoubtedly spurred on by the formation of the AIIB. For a while, China and other emerging economies are displeased with the slow process of IMF reform, which has given China considerable moral weight to gain the support of US allies in Asia and Europe (The Economist 2015b). The formation of the AIIB is partly a result of such an advantage. In the same month, the IMF agreed to add Chinese RMB to the Special Drawing Rights (SDRs). This is the first time in over 15 years that the IMF makes changes to the list of currencies comprising the SDRs. Supported by the US, the IMF believes that the inclusion of RMB will make the SDRs more diverse and representative of the international society (IMF 2015).

The analysis of the AIIB's management arrangements reveals that this bank is a manifestation of China's norms regarding governance structure in international institutions. Recent developments indicate that rather than perceiving the AIIB as a challenge of the WB and the IMF, it is more reasonable to regard it as a complement to the existing institutions. Through the cooperation with other institutions, the AIIB can foster China's integration into the international aid structure, so that it will no longer be treated as the 'other' in this area. Moreover, the other international institutions have made changes in their policies to accommodate China's appeals regarding the global financial governance structure. These developments shed light on the spill-over effect of the AIIB on the international financial governance structure. Therefore, through the operation of the AIIB, China's preference of infrastructure building will emerge a fundamental norm in external assistance policies in the Asian region.

8.4 Conclusion

This article studies the establishment of the AIIB and its connections with the normative power of China in international financial governance. It argues that the AIIB, as a new multilateral financial institution initiated by China, will inherit Chinese norms regarding external assistance. These norms are set by Zhou Enlai in the 1950s and 1960s and have continued to be the guidelines of Chinese foreign aid programs. In particular, China does not bind political clauses (except the 'One China' policy) with its aid. For most of the time, China has not expressed any preference toward the recipient country's domestic regime. Meanwhile, Chinese foreign aid and foreign investment projects concentrate on the infrastructure sector.

China argues that compared to other political rights, economic development is more important for people in developing countries. Drawing on Chinese experience, infrastructure building is the foundation for developing countries to obtain steady economic growth. Based on the analysis of the AIIB's policy and Chinese leaders' statements, the AIIB is expected to adopt these norms. More importantly, the endorsement of the AOA by 57 member states will significantly enhance the normative influence of China in external assistance area. However, the inclusion of Western developed countries casts a challenge to China's ability to maintain its current preference for these norms during the operation of the AIIB. To cooperate with other members, China will have to increase its attention on social security and environmental protection in the infrastructure programs.

In addition to the external assistance area, the formulation of the AIIB is also closely connected to China's normative appeals regarding the existing financial governance structure. The boost of China's economic power has stimulated it well to enhance its role in financial institutions. Together with other emerging economies, especially the BRICS group, China has been actively promoting the reform of governance structure in the IMF and the WB. The key points of China's claim are the redistribution of voting power and the abolishing of unilateral veto power. The AIIB is a manifestation of China's appeals regarding management arrangements. It has a leaner staff structure and a non-residential board of directors which enhances the efficiency of policymaking. It also has a different formula for voting rights distribution according to which the developing countries have the largest share. However, whether China will abandon its veto power during the operation of the AIIB still remains uncertain.

The third implication of the AIIB is its future impact on the external of China's normative power. While China's norms of sovereignty, unconditionality, and infrastructure building are being accepted by developing countries, the preference for sovereignty and non-interference also makes China the 'other' in international normative structure. Even worse, China's role in international financial governance is perceived as negative by some Western observers. In this regard, the AIIB is an opportunity for China to improve the external perceptions of its normative power. The cooperation between the AIIB and other existing institutions will imply that the AIIB is a necessary complement to the external assistance framework in the Asian region. The inclusion of social and environmental framework in the AIIB's policy is a sign that China is willing to converge to the existing normative structure. Moreover, the formulation of the AIIB has triggered a series of policy changes in other institutions. These recent developments advance China's involvement in international governance structure. They also considerably expand China's normative influence in the Asian region. Both these effects bridge the gap between China's norms and Western norms regarding foreign aid. As a result, the external perceptions of China's normative power will be improved.

The boost of its economic power in the recent decades has enriched the normative power of China in international financial governance area. However, the normative influence of China is still limited, as it has not integrated with the international normative structure. The current structure remains deeply embedded within a value system dominated by the West. Inevitably, China will have to work within the existing structure even if it seeks to expand its normative influence in the international system. The AIIB is a new institution that carries many Chinese norms. It gives a China a broader platform to diffuse its norms. Meanwhile, the formation of the AIIB will amplify not only the chances, but also the challenges China will face during its norm diffusion. China has to tread carefully so as to ensure that its normative power is enhanced through the operation of the AIIB. The operations of the AIIB will be a barometer for China's normative power for years to come.

Acknowledgements Philomena Murray deserves a special credit for pushing the authors to write this piece on order in the first place. The authors would like to thank Zhimin Chen, Zhongqi Pan, and two anonymous reviewers at this journal for their insightful comments. This research is funded by China's National Humanities and Social Sciences Research Project 'China and the International Rule Making' (14BGJ021).

REFERENCES

AIIB. 2015a. Articles of Agreement. http://www.aiib.org/uploadfile/2015/0814/20150814022158430.pdf. Accessed 10 Mar 2016.

AIIB. 2015b. Board of Directors. http://www.aiib.org/html/aboutus/governance/Board_of_Directors/?show=1. Accessed 10 Mar 2016.

AIIB. 2015c. History. http://www.aiib.org/html/aboutus/introduction/history/?show=0. Accessed 10 Mar 2016.

AIIB. 2015d. Membership Status. http://www.aiib.org/html/aboutus/introduction/Membership/?show=0. Accessed 10 Mar 2016.

AIIB. 2016a. Environmental and Social Framework. http://www.aiib.org/uploadfile/2016/0226/20160226043633542.pdf. Accessed 28 Apr 2016.

AIIB. 2016b. Projects. http://www.aiib.org/html/PROJECTS/. Accessed 02 June 2016.

BBC. 2015. Countries Rating Poll. http://downloads.bbc.co.uk/mediacentre/country-rating-poll.pdf. Accessed 02 June 2016.

Bhattacharyay, B. 2010. Estimating Demand for Infrastructure in Energy, Transport, Telecommunications, Water and Sanitation in Asia and the Pacific: 2010–2020. ADBI Working Paper 248. Tokyo: Asian Development Bank Institute. http://www.adbi.org/working-paper/2010/09/09/4062infrastructure.demand.asia.pacific/.

Brautigam, D. 2011a. *The Dragon's Gift: The Real Story of China in Africa.* Oxford: Oxford University Press.

Bra¨utigam, D. 2011b. Aid 'With Chinese Characteristics': Chinese Foreign Aid and Development Finance Meet the OECD-DAC Aid Regime. *Journal of International Development* 23 (5): 752–764.

BRICS. 2009. Meeting of BRIC Finance Ministers and Central Bank Governors Communique´, London, September 4, 2009. http://www.brics.utoronto.ca/docs/090904-finance.html. Accessed 15 May 2016.

China Daily. 2016. AIIB Chief Rules out China Veto Power. http://www.chinadaily.com.cn/business/2016–01/27/content_23265846.htm. Accessed 15 May 2016.

Chen, T., and Y. Tan. 2013. Predicaments of the IMF Quota and Voting Rights Reform and its Countermeasures. Studies of International Finance 2013–08, 3.

Condon, M. 2012. China in Africa: What the Policy of Nonintervention Adds to the Western Development Dilemma. *PRAXIS: The Fletcher Journal of Human Security* 27: 5–25.

Cotonou Agreement. 2000. Partnership Agreement between the Members of the African, Caribbean and Pacific Group of States of the one part, and the European Community and its member states, of the other part. Cotonou, Benin, 23.

Cui, J., and Chang, T. 2013. IMF Gaige Kunjing yu Zhongguo de Xianshi Xuanze [The Plight of IMF's Reform and the Feasible Selection of China]. Dangdai Jingji Kexue [Modern Economic Science] 35 (3).

Financial Times. 2008. China Defends Africa Aid Stance. http://www.ft.com/intl/cms/s/0/28a69bd4-479a11dd-93ca-000077b07658.html#axzz3qte3ef2w. Accessed 10 Mar 2016.

Financial Times. 2015. UK move to join China-led bank a surprise even to Beijing. http://www.ft.com/intl/cms/s/0/d33fed8a-d3a1–11e4-a9d3–00144feab7de.html#axzz3qte3ef2w. Accessed 10 Mar 2016.

G20. 2009. London Summit—Leaders' Statement, 2 April 2009. https://www.imf.org/external/np/sec/pr/2009/pdf/g20_040209.pdf. Accessed 10 May 2016.

IMF. 2015. Chinese Renminbi to Be Included in IMF's Special Drawing Right Basket. http://www.imf.org/external/pubs/ft/survey/so/2015/new120115a.htm. Accessed 10 Mar 2016.

Japan Times. 2015. Abe Administration Develops Rift over China's New Development Bank. http://www.japantimes.co.jp/news/2015/03/20/business/japan-could-join-china-backed-bank-aso/#.VuCtypx96hd. Accessed 10 Mar 2016.

Kavalski, E. 2013. The Struggle for Recognition of Normative Powers: Normative Power Europe and Normative Power China in Context. *Cooperation & Conflict* 48 (2): 247–267.

Keuleers, F. 2015. Explaining External Perceptions: The EU and China in African Public Opinion. *JCMS. Journal of Common Market Studies* 53 (4): 803–821.

Larsen, H. 2014. The EU as a Normative Power and the Research on External Perceptions: The Missing Link. *JCMS. Journal of Common Market Studies* 52 (4): 896–910.

Leonard, M. 2008. China's New Intelligentsia. Prospect Magazine 144: 2.

Lucarelli, S. 2007. The European Union in the eyes of others: Towards filling a gap in the literature. *European Foreign Affairs Review* 12 (3): 249–270.

Lu, Z. 2011. Hou Jinrong Weiji Shiqi Zhongguo Canyu Guoji Jinrong Tixi Gaige de Mubiao he Lujing——yi Zhongguo Canyu IMF Gaige Weili [Path and Objectives of China's Participation in the Reform of the International Financial System in Post-Financial Crisis Period—Taking Chinese Participation in IMF Reforms as A Case Study]. Dong Nanya Zongheng [Around Southeast Asia] 8: 87–91.

Manji, F., and Marks, S. 2007. *African perspectives on China in Africa*. Fahamu/Pambazuka.

Manners, I. 2002. Normative Power Europe: A Contradiction in Terms? *Journal of Common Market Studies* 40 (2): 235–258.

Manners, I. 2006. Normative Power Europe Reconsidered: Beyond the crossroads. *Journal of European Public Policy* 13 (2): 182–199.

Manners, I. 2013. Assessing the Decennial, Reassessing the Global: Understanding European Union Normative Power in Global Politics. *Cooperation & Conflict* 48 (2): 304–329.

National Bureau of Statistics of China. 2015. Gross Domestic Product. http://www.stats.gov.cn/tjsj/ndsj/2015/indexeh.htm. Accessed 10 Mar 2016.

NDB. 2014. Articles of Agreement. http://ndb.int/download/Agreement%20on%20the%20New%20Development%20Bank.pdf. Accessed 10 Mar 2016.

New York Times. 2014. U.S. Opposing China's Answer to World Bank. http://www.nytimes.com/2014/10/10/world/asia/chinas-plan-for-regional-development-bank-runs-into-us-opposition.html?ref=world&_r=1. Accessed 10 Mar 2016.

Noutcheva, G. 2009. Fake, Partial and Imposed Compliance: The Limits of the EU's Normative Power in the Western Balkans. *Journal of European Public Policy* 16 (7): 1065–1084.

People's Daily Online. 2014. The AIIB is a Complement Rather Than a Competitor. http://en.people.cn/n/2014/1028/c98649–8800974.html. Accessed 10 Mar 2016.

Renard, T. 2015. The Asian Infrastructure Investment Bank (AIIB): China's new Multilateralism and the Erosion of the West. http://www.egmontinstitute.be/wp-content/uploads/2015/04/SPB63-Renard.pdf. Accessed 20 May 2016.

Reuter. 2015. China's AIIB to Offer Loans with Fewer Strings Attached. http://www.reuters.com/article/usaiib-china-loans-idUSKCN0R14UB20150901. Accessed 10 Mar 2016.

Sautman, B., and Y. Hairong. 2009. African Perspectives on China-Africa links. *The China Quarterly* 199: 728–759.

State Council. 2014. China's Foreign Aid, April, Information Office of the State Council, People's Republic of China, Beijing.

The Diplomat. 2015. The AIIB Is Seen Very Differently in the US, Europe, and China. http://thediplomat.com/2015/05/the-aiib-is-seen-very-differently-in-the-us-europe-and-china/. Accessed 10 Mar 2016.

The Economist. 2015a. The Infrastructure Gap-Development Finance helps China win Friends and Influence American allies. http://www.economist.com/news/asia/21646740-development-financehelps-china-win-friends-and-influence-american-allies-infrastructure-gap. Accessed 10 Mar 2016.

The Economist. 2015b. Rich but Rash-To Challenge the World Bank and the IMF, China will have to imitate them. http://www.economist.com/news/finance-and-economics/21641259-challenge-worldbank-and-imf-china-will-have-imitate-them-rich. Accessed 10 Mar 2016.

The Guardian. 2015a. US anger at Britain Joining Chinese-led Investment Bank AIIB. http://www.theguardian.com/us-news/2015/mar/13/whitehouse-pointedly-asks-uk-to-use-its-voice-as-partof-chinese-led-bank. Accessed 10 Mar 2016.

The Guardian. 2015b. Australia on Brink of Joining China's Asian Infrastructure Investment Bank. https://www.theguardian.com/australia-news/2015/mar/20/australia-on-brink-of-joining-chinas-asianinfrastructure-investment-bank. Accessed 10 Mar 2016.

The United Kingdom. 2015. UK Announces Plans to Join Asian Infrastructure Investment Bank. https://www.gov.uk/government/news/uk-announces-plans-to-join-asian-infrastructure-investment-bank. Accessed 10 Mar 2016.

United Nations. 2015. World Economic Situation and Prospects 2015, New York. http://www.un.org/en/development/desa/policy/wesp/wesp_archive/2015wesp-ch3-en.pdf.

Wall Street Journal. 2015. How China Plans to Run AIIB: Leaner, With Veto. http://www.wsj.com/articles/how-china-plans-to-run-aiib-leaner-with-veto-1433764079. Accessed 10 Mar 2016.

Wihtol, R. 2015. Beijing's Challenge to the Global Financial Architecture. https://asianstudies.georgetown.edu/sites/asianstudies/files/GJAA%202.1%20Wihtol,%20Robert_0.pdf.

Xinhua Net. 2016. AIIB President Committed to "Highest Possible Standard". http://news.xinhuanet.com/english/2016–01/17/c_135017516.htm. Accessed 10 Mar 2016.

Zhang, X. 2011. A Rising China and the Normative Changes in International Society. *East Asia* 28 (3): 235–246.

Zhou, E. 1964. Speech in Accra, Ghana. 15 January 1964.

Zupancˇicˇ, R., and M. Hribernik. 2013. Normative Power Japan: The European Union's Ideational Successor or Another "Contradiction in Terms"? *Romanian Journal of Political Science* 13 (2): 106–136.

CHAPTER 9

The Asian Infrastructure Investment Bank and Status-Seeking: China's Foray into Global Economic Governance

Hai Yang

9.1 Introduction: China in Quest of Great Power Status and the AIIB

Attending its phenomenal economic growth in the past few decades, China has been seeking great power status (Larson 2015). Bolstered by its enhanced stature after the 2007/08 global financial crisis, Chinese

---

This article was previously published as: Yang, H. (2016). "The Asian Infrastructure Investment Bank and status-seeking: China's foray into global economic governance." *Chinese Political Science Review*, 1(4), 754–778. This version contains updates and minor revisions.

H. Yang (✉)
University of Macao, Macao, China
e-mail: haiyang@um.edu.mo

© The Author(s), under exclusive license to Springer Nature
Switzerland AG 2025
K. G.Cai et al. (eds.), *China and Global Economic Governance, Volume I: China's BRI & AIIB and Global Economic Governance*, Politics and Development of Contemporary China,
https://doi.org/10.1007/978-3-031-73212-6_9

foreign policy aiming to redefine the country's regional and international role has continued apace (Swaine 2010; Yan 2014). More lately, China has redoubled efforts in global economic governance by undertaking a series of high-profile institution-building actions, seen by many as a clear statement of intent from Beijing that it desires to challenge American supremacy (Shapiro 2015) and set new trading-investment rules in Asia (Kahn 2015). In the case of the AIIB, a recently established multilateral development bank (MDB), China played a decisive role over the course of two years that culminated in the launch of the institution in January 2016. Despite strong headwinds from the United States (US), China brought together fifty-six states, including a host of US allies in Europe and Asia–Pacific, as the AIIB's founding members.

Many studies have discussed the China-led MDB, looking at its institutional features, prospects, and challenges (Chin 2016; Humphrey 2015; Greenwood 2016), potential implications for the Bretton Woods institutions and international development (Kawai 2015; Liao 2015; Reisen 2015; Subacchi 2015), and most of all, the multiplicity of rationale motivating China to initiate the bank (Callaghan and Hubbard 2016; Dollar 2015; Ren 2016; Sohn 2015; Xing 2016). While extant literature tends to consider China's motivations from a rationalist perspective, this paper turns to the ideational motivations and contends at the core of the AIIB lies the enduring search of the Middle Kingdom for a greater status in its return to a major global power. On the one hand, the AIIB materialized in part because of persistent grievances of China and other developing countries about their under-representation and the glacial pace of reforms in the Bretton Woods system. On the other hand, by providing a real alternative, the AIIB injects a sense of urgency to revamp the anachronistic global economic governance architecture in favor of emerging economies. For nearly a decade preceding the AIIB, the US insisted that China stop freeriding the liberal international system and act as a responsible stakeholder (Nye 2013). Ironically, after China initiated the AIIB—a justifiable answer to the earlier criticism, US officials lobbied allies and partners to shun the project, on the grounds that the AIIB would pose a threat to its Bretton Woods counterparts and lead to a 'race to the bottom' (Pollack 2015). While many Western powers opted to join, the US and Japan remain on the sidelines.

Notwithstanding initial misgivings of Washington and Tokyo over the AIIB's (in)ability to embody and uphold governance and lending standards, they have overstated its potentially disruptive impacts. Given the financing gaps in Asian infrastructure (Elek 2014), Beijing has legitimate grounds for building a financial institution to complement the World Bank (WB) and the Asian Development Bank (ADB). The WB and ADB Presidents welcomed the new lender and signed co-financing agreements with it. Also, presupposing the AIIB's endgame is to fragment the incumbent architecture seems to run counter to the changing realities that attest to Beijing's will and ability to uphold international norms and practices. As for potential inter-organizational rivalry, among the seven projects approved by the AIIB thus far, four are co-financed with peer institutions (AIIB 2016).

The driving forces behind the creation of the AIIB are likely to be multifaceted. There are plausible arguments about Beijing's self-serving agenda to use the AIIB to export industrial overcapacity or channel foreign currency stockpile (Ren 2016) or multilateralize bilateral development finance (Stiglitz 2015). While manifold material incentives can be involved, this article contends that the overriding consideration for China to build the AIIB is ideational—searching for an international status befitting its role as a great power. This has to do with the fact that the funding capacity of the AIIB, and particularly, the financial contribution of China thereto pale into insignificance in comparison with the scale of Chinese industrial overcapacity, foreign currency reserve and overseas lending. Predicated on this premise, the question central to this research is: *how did China seek status in the AIIB case?*

The article proceeds as follows. It starts with a brief review of dominant theoretical perspectives on China's swift rise and its major implications. After reflecting on the major schools of thought in International Relations (IR) and drawing out their analytic limitations, the second part introduces the key tenets of Social Identity Theory, before contextualizing it in IR and complementing it with the theoretical construct of institutional innovation. The following sections move on to analyze, along the lines of the three status-seeking strategies with additional input from institutional innovation, to ascertain the dominant status-seeking strategy of China in the AIIB case. The conclusion summarizes the key findings and casts light on China's future policy choice in global economic governance.

9.2 China's Rise: Prevalent Theoretical Paradigms vs. Social Identity Theory

Much of the academic and policy debate has centered around whether the swift rise of China from the periphery to the center of global politics will be peaceful (Chen and Pan 2011; Christensen 2006; Friedberg 2005, 2011; Mearsheimer 2001, 2010; Yan 2014). Three main IR schools of thought offer rather contrasting answers. Neo-realists are preoccupied with the 'realties of power politics' and conceive of the global realm as a self-help system. A central argument flowing out of *realpolitik* strategic calculations is that as the relative weight of a new power continues to grow, it inexorably wants to rewrite the rules and establish for itself a new place that brings greater benefits (Organski and Kugler 1981, pp. 19–23). Dissatisfied with its under-privileged position in the post-1945 world order, China will in due course contest the supremacy of the US and disrupt the equilibrium of the order (Mearsheimer 2001). Such an interpretation is backed by China's military buildup, territorial claims, rejection of Western liberal values and institution-building outside of the established order.

In contrast to the realist view, liberal-institutionalists suggest that as a function of a rising state's integration into the global system, economic interdependence, and interaction with other states will shape its preferences in world affairs and push it to converge toward the current international order (Keohane 1998; Keohane and Nye 1987). Constructivists take issue with the realist and liberal-institutionalist explanations, and emphasize instead the role of ideational factors and their structuring effect on states (Finnemore 1996; Wendt 1999). They reckon, "States are socialized to want certain things by the international society in which they and the people in them live" (Finnemore 1996, p. 2). While some find little socializing effect (Kent 2013), others note modest but continual socialization of China to internalize certain global norms and practices (Johnston 2014).

In the stalemated debate about the rise of China, the prevalent theoretical lenses are helpful to varying degrees. Nonetheless, two analytic drawbacks stand out. First, discussions on whether China is a status quo or revisionist power seem to have missed the point, since China can and does revamp the current international order to better serve its expansive needs and interests. Second, the leading strands of IR literature cannot explain in an adequate fashion why China adamantly refuses to accept some international norms and increasingly challenges the global order (contrary to predictions of liberals and constructivists) but fights shy of drastically overhauling or reshaping the global system (at odds with the neo-realist hypotheses). In their search for theoretical parsimony, they tend to downplay or overlook the role of identity, or rather, Beijing's concern about its *relative status* in the world (Larson 2015, p. 325).

There has been research on the under-examined status concerns that so pervade the foreign policy of China and other rising states (Larson 2015; Larson and Shevchenko 2003, 2010, 2014). These seminal works invariably conclude that aspiring powers prefer to leverage their distinct strengths and win an enhanced status in a domain different from those where established powers dominate, rather than competing with or being assimilated into the elite club of established powers. While these studies have furnished ample evidence of the status concerns in the overarching foreign policy, their main conclusion is rarely borne out by examining closely and critically cases that constitute the rubric of grand status-seeking strategy. To gauge adequately the relevance of this scholarship, it is desirable to complement it with in-depth case studies and link, where appropriate, individual foreign policy to grand strategy.

For this purpose, this article looks at an illustrative case encapsulating China's great power aspiration—the AIIB, which brings into relief Beijing's resolve to seek a greater status in global economic governance. To probe how China sought status in the AIIB case, this study draws on conceptual insights from a vibrant theoretical tradition of social psychology: SIT. More substantively, it employs as a heuristic device the SIT's three standard identity management strategies as applied to IR. In the IR context, SIT posits an aspiring state may emulate or compete with established powers, or attempt to achieve national prestige on a new dimension (Larson 2015).

While in line with earlier SIT-inspired works on substantive grounds, this study diverges in two aspects. First, rather than starting with the presumption that rising powers follow the strategy of social creativity and fixating on finding confirming evidence as done previously, this article takes a different tack and investigates holistically all the three strategies before reaching a conclusion. Second, it deviates from the well-trodden research path by applying the SIT-informed perspective in IR in conjunction with insight on institutional innovation to extend its analytical rigor to this case study. In particular, it brings in institutional innovation, defined as "novel, useful, and legitimate change" (Raffaelli and Glynn

2015, p. 409), to study the manifestation of social creativity in the AIIB case. In so doing, this research contributes to: (a) theoretically, applying SIT at the micro level and combining it with institutional innovation in service of analyzing individual foreign policy; (b) empirically, adding reflections to the discussions about the AIIB and China's status-seeking behavior.

9.3   SOCIAL IDENTITY THEORY: MOBILITY, COMPETITION, AND CREATIVITY

Developed by social psychologists Henry Tajfel, John Turner, and their colleagues in Bristol in the 1970s, SIT has become one of the most prominent and conceptually mature theoretical approaches for studying intergroup relations. For Tajfel (1972, p. 272), social identity refers to "the individual's knowledge that he belongs to certain social groups together with some emotional and value significance to him of this group membership." Premised on a ubiquitous yearning for positive self-esteem, SIT suggests that individual members want their group to be superior and have greater value connotations in relation to comparison groups. While scholars diverge over the extent to which the need for positive self-esteem and social identity triggers intergroup discrimination, there is a broad consensus that individuals use their group membership to secure psychologically positive distinctiveness (Abrams and Hogg 1988). As a logical extension, how would individuals react when their group turns out inferior in intergroup comparison and is relegated to the lower rung of status hierarchy, and relatedly, what would they do to change their low status?

Tajfel and Turner (1979, pp. 43–44) laid out three distinctive reactions under contrasting conditions. When the structures and boundaries of intergroup relations are flexible and permeable, individuals will be motivated to disassociate themselves from the former group and move into a higher-status social group. To the contrary, when the structures and boundaries of intergroup relations are rigid, which renders it exceedingly difficult, if not impossible, for individuals to divest themselves of an undesirable group membership, they will prefer group strategies to secure positive distinctiveness for their group by: either directly competing with the reference group in its sphere of superiority (social competition); or creatively comparing their own group to the reference group on other dimensions, redefining negative attributes associated with the in-group as positive, and changing the reference group (social creativity). While social competition is concerned with the relative position of a group in a given area and is zero-sum (Turner 1975), social creativity is about identifying different dimensions to attain higher status and is not necessarily zero-sum.

Larson and Shevchenko (2003, 2010) first articulated SIT in the IR context and applied it to analyze the foreign policy of Russia (also Soviet Union) and China. Echoing the core SIT theoretical tenet in intergroup relations that individuals identify themselves with their group and act to others as group members instead of individuals, they suggest that SIT can be applied to interstate relations. In general, states as a classic social group in the international community are ranked according to a set of value-laden attributes including population, territory, economy, military, culture, among other constituent factors (Larson et al. 2014). When interstate comparison in a status hierarchy reflects adversely on the characteristics and accomplishments of a state—part and parcel of its identity, the state in question will seek to boost its relative status by following largely, albeit not exclusively, one of the three status-seeking strategies— social mobility, social competition, or social creativity. Of course, a state may integrate elements of the three strategies as they are ideal types and not mutually exclusive. Still, there should be a dominant one, because "the strategies have different goals and tactics, so that dominance of a particular management strategy alters the state's entire foreign policy" (Larson and Shevchenko 2010, p. 75).

As shown in Table 9.1, the framework of Larson and Shevchenko is fairly aligned with that of Tajfel and Turner. Just as ambitious individuals seeking a more positive identity, aspiring states search for a greater status. When the boundaries of the international society are flexible and permeable, a rising state adopts the social mobility strategy by mimicking the rules and norms of the established players to achieve upward mobility and eventually join the elite club. When opportunities for mobility are precluded and structures of the international society are seen as rigid and illegitimate, states wishing to change their position may resort to social competition or social creativity. The former denotes that rising powers go head-to-head with status quo powers with a view to replacing the dominant group in salient geostrategic and geopolitical domains. The latter relates to the efforts of emerging powers to seek status and prestige on an alternative ranking scale like promoting new norms and institutions in world politics (Larson 2015).

Table 9.1 Three identity management strategies (Tajfel and Turner 1979; Larson and Shevchenko 2003, 2010)

	Structural conditions	SIT in intergroup relations	SIT in international relations
Social Mobility	Flexible and permeable boundaries between different social groups	Dis-identify with the erstwhile group and move into a higher-status group through talent, diligence, luck or whatever other means	Adhere to established rules of the game, follow common practices and join international organizations in hopes of being admitted into the elite club
Social Competition	Rigid and impermeable boundaries between different social groups	Compete directly with higher-status groups in their area of superiority and seek to reverse the subjective position of the in-group and the out-group	Engage in geopolitical rivalry, compete for sphere of influence, promote rival norms, values and institutions in order to equal or replace the leading powers
Social Creativity		Compare the in-group with the out-group on new dimensions, reframe negative attributes, or change the reference group	Find a distinctive niche, promote alternative models, norms and institutions in global governance to boost status

Insofar as the overall foreign policy is concerned, SIT expects China to follow the social creativity strategy by engaging in favorable comparisons with leading powers in a different area. Accordingly, it will eschew a drastic overhaul of the multilateral architecture and be averse to the risk of overt competition with the West. Despite its rising ambitions, China's technological and military capabilities remain far inferior to those of the US. In view of the virtually unbridgeable discrepancy in political and value system (Pan 2012), China has neither the intention nor the capacity to imitate and join the West, whatever the grouping may be. In reality, China has emerged as the undisputed leader of developing countries in regional and multilateral fora, challenging the primacy of status quo powers. Also, it has made headway in initiating new norms and rules in foreign policy and global governance (Chan 2013) and promoting its distinct model of political economy and development (Breslin 2011). All these seem to validate the SIT's prediction.

Nevertheless, a lingering question is whether the prediction would be equally conclusive if the perspective were switched to individual foreign policy. Based on empirical observations, this study anticipates that the dominant strategy used by China in the AIIB case is indeed social creativity (*contra* social mobility and social competition). To better apply the identity management strategies and specifically, in service of analyzing the manifestation of social creativity in the creation of the AIIB, it is useful to leverage insight from institutional innovation.

9.4 INSTITUTIONAL INNOVATION: USEFUL, NOVEL, AND LEGITIMATE

This section views institutional innovation as an empirical manifestation of creativity. Institutions, both formal and informal, are an important subject of research in the social sciences. Notwithstanding its relative stability, institutions change over time and adjust to shifting circumstances. For many institutionalists (Hargrave and Van de Ven 2006; Raffaelli and Glynn 2015), institutional innovation includes both radical innovation (creating new institutions) and incremental innovation (modifying existing institutions). Often, it is met with contestation due to the inevitable tensions between institutional stability and change (Hargadon and Douglas 2001, p. 476).

Among others, Raffaelli and Glynn (2015, p. 409) provide a relatively operational conceptualization and define institutional innovation as "novel, useful, and legitimate change that disrupts, to varying degrees, the cognitive, normative, or regulative mainstays of an organizational field." Institutional innovation, they argue, is situated at the intersection of the three interrelated and mutually reinforcing aspects—novelty, usefulness, and legitimacy. Institutional innovation must be novel in that it represents a new idea or design with distinguishable features from the existing ones, and useful in terms of having the ability to solve problems, particularly in domains where current organizations fall short. More importantly, they emphasize the need for the institutional innovation to be legitimate, as "the creation, transformation, and diffusion of institutions require legitimacy, a condition whereby other alternatives are seen as less appropriate, desirable, or viable" (Dacin et al. 2002, p. 47). Accordingly, different strategies are required for an institutional innovation to demonstrate innovativeness, gain legitimacy, and be widely accepted. Raffaelli and Glynn (2015, pp. 414–415) put forth two strategies: bridging from the old and familiar institutions or institutionalized practices to the new and creative ones; highlighting new beliefs, issues, problems, and opportunities. The former stresses the need for continuity between the past and the present and conformity to prevailing practices, whereas the latter frames an innovation as a response to the emergence of new opportunities or critical changes.

9.5 China's Status-Seeking Strategy: Evidence from AIIB

In what follows, the analysis leverages insights from the status-seeking strategies (applied to IR) and institutional innovation, to explicate how China sought an enhanced international status in the AIIB case. In so doing, it serves to theoretically ascertain whether social creativity is preferred over social mobility or social competition, and empirically to showcase how China sought status in this particular case.

9.5.1 Social Mobility: Conformity in AIIB Institution-Building

Social mobility emphasizes the need to respect and emulate the established rules and norms in order to join the elite club. Pertaining to institutional innovation, acting in accordance with common standards is vital to the AIIB's legitimacy because it bridges from the past to the present and renders the new bank more recognizable, appropriate, and legitimately distinct in the eyes of the relevant audiences. Aside from the AIIB's orthodox three-level governance structure (Board of Governors, Board of Directors, Management), elements of continuity and compliance can be found in China's evolving positions on some key issues. Overall, China followed international practices and was in favor of multilateralism in the setup of the AIIB, especially in the wake of the decisions of several Western countries to 'break ranks' with the US and partake in the China-led initiative.

As regards membership, China initially planned to build a regional bank constituted only by Asian and Middle Eastern countries; and China would contribute up to fifty percent of the total capital, which would translate into veto power over any decisions (Sun 2015). Unlike the common practice of forming international organizations, usually preceded by rounds of consultations and negotiations between main stakeholders, China unilaterally put forward the AIIB initiative and set March 31, 2015 as deadline for applying as a prospective founding member (PFM). As late as March 6, 2015, Chinese Finance Minister Lou Jiwei (2015) intimated, "the relative consensus among the twenty-seven members is that we first open to countries from the region and disregard provisionally the applications of countries outside the region." On March 12, 2015, then Chancellor of the Exchequer George Osborne unveiled the decision of the United Kingdom (UK) to join the AIIB, citing mostly commercial reasons. Although the UK was openly reprimanded by the US, France, Germany, and Italy followed suit and applied in concert for the PFM status within days. The involvement of major European governments not only divided the US, Japan, and other Western countries, but also transformed the AIIB from an obscure initiative into a serious multilateral. In response, Chinese officials quickly adapted the messaging and jettisoned the regional focus. On March 17, 2015, when speaking of the decisions of leading European powers to join the AIIB, Chinese foreign ministry spokesperson Hong Lei stated, "The AIIB is a multilateral development institution that is open and inclusive... The wide participation of countries in and out of the region exemplifies the representativeness of the AIIB" (Chinese Ministry of Foreign Affairs 2015). Given the heavy weight of Japan and South Korea in Asia, Chinese foreign minister Wang Yi conducted consultations on the AIIB with his counterparts from Tokyo and Seoul during their trilateral meeting on March 21, 2015 (Ren 2016). South Korea followed European countries and Australia to participate, but Japan, alongside its close ally the US, decided to stay outside. Up until its launch in January 2016, the new lender counted fifty-seven members, including thirty-seven Asian and twenty non-Asian countries. As stipulated in the Articles of Agreement (AOA), the AIIB remains open to members of the WB and the ADB (AOA, p. 2).

Another noteworthy shift relates to the nature of the bank. Early on, the Chinese policy community envisioned the AIIB, with China contributing half of the capital stock, as either a foreign aid agency or a market-oriented commercial bank, both closely associated with China's agenda (Sun 2015). As articulated in an opinion-piece on the Chinese government website, the AIIB can be used to "restructure its foreign aid policy to achieve desired results... serve as a very strong, but positive, external pressure to overcome China's internal political obstacles to further economic, trade and investment liberalization, such as currency internationalization, capital control deregulation, business globalization and financial marketization" (Zhang 2015). This does not necessarily mean the earlier visions are irrational, considering the imperative for China to reform its problematic foreign aid policy and domestic economic woes. Rather, linking the multilateral AIIB to China's internal agenda could foreshadow and aggravate external concerns about China using the bank for its narrow economic-political objectives. In face of intense scrutiny from outside, accommodating participants and staunch holdouts alike, Beijing steered away from the two extremes. Now the primary function of the AIIB, at least on paper, is neither to channel Chinese foreign aid nor stimulate domestic economic restructuring, but to focus on Asian infrastructure with the aim of fostering broad-based economic and social development in Asia (AOA, pp. 1–2).

With respect to the multilateral procedures, eight Chief Negotiators Meetings (CNMs) were convened after the signing of the Memorandum of Understanding on Establishing the AIIB in October 2014. Comprised of all the PFMs, the CNMs allowed several rounds of negotiations on the AOA, adopted at the fifth CNM in Singapore, and on key issues as regards the AIIB's shareholding, governance, and future lending activities (AIIB 2015b). In parallel, a select group of seasoned international experts and MDB veterans were asked to draft the AOA and map out key policy frameworks (Jin 2015a). These channels of consultation and negotiation gave the developed PFMs, notably European countries with rich experience in running multilateral organizations, the opportunity to "use their collective bargaining power to negotiate, guide, and shape the bank's AOA from within and enmesh China in a network of international norms and standards" (Sun 2015). As such, the AOA bears strong similarity to the charters of the WB and the ADB (Wan 2016, pp. 80–82). According to the AOA, the AIIB is to all intents and purposes compatible with international practice. Further, the decision to choose US dollar as lending currency instead of Chinese RMB reveals that Beijing was receptive to the concerns of advanced economies over China using the bank as a tool to promote RMB internationalization.

As a fast-rising power, China wants to be acknowledged and respected. As an institutional innovation, the AIIB needs to be recognized and accepted. The realization of both would require a certain degree of adherence to the existing practices. To legitimate the nascent lender and win broad support, China adapted its stance on *inter alia* membership, primary function, shareholding, and by implication, veto power regarding the AIIB. Undeniably, China's efforts at mitigating concerns and honoring multilateral practices signal conformity and allow external inputs to shape itself and the institution. In the specific domain of development finance, the mere act of creating a multilateral lender means that China has taken a major step to endorsing a multilateral approach.

That said, China is not prepared to go all the way and reproduce Western formats unreservedly. Thus far, China has shown very little enthusiasm to join the traditional donor club: Development Assistance Committee (DAC) of the Organization for Economic Cooperation and Development (OECD), a key platform where developed countries coordinate their development aid policy. The China-DAC Study Group, established in 2009 with the intention of strengthening dialogue and promoting mutual understanding between Chinese officials and OECD member states officials working in the field of development, has proven a failed attempt by the OECD to bring China into the current framework of development cooperation (Ohno 2013). Besides, as its economic clout continues to grow, China seems intent on becoming a proactive rule-shaper or rule-maker in global governance rather than a passive rule-taker. Persistent divergences over certain international norms and rising ambitions in global rule-making potentially tilt the rising power to a strategy of competition.

9.5.2 Social Competition: Is AIIB a Competing Initiative?

Social competition is a strategy preferred by status-seeking states, especially when they deem the status hierarchy as rigid and illegitimate. The ultimate goal is to equal and even supersede the dominant states in their areas of superiority. Due to the widely perceived illegitimacy of institutions underpinning global economic governance, competition in such a context was and continues to be compelling.

Firstly, the AIIB is without doubt a warranted answer of China and the Global South to their limited influence and the slow pace of governance reforms in the global economic architecture. For years, major emerging powers, most prominently the BRICS countries have been pressing the West to redistribute voting shares in the WB and the International Monetary Fund (IMF) on the basis of changed realities in the global economy. In purchasing power parity terms, the aggregate economic weight of emerging and developing countries overtook that of their developed counterparts in 2013, growing further to make up fifty-seven percent of global GDP in 2014 (Kynge and Wheatley 2015). That said, developing countries and emerging economies remain heavily under-represented. Moderate reforms in the WB and the IMF were proposed in 2010 to give more power to large emerging economies. Yet, US Congressional foot-dragging stalled the IMF quota and governance reform till December 2015. Even in the wake of the reforms, the imbalance has not been substantively addressed.

As the Global South continues to rise and the economic center of gravity shifts away from the industrial North, the legitimacy of the Bretton Woods system and many other global governance arrangements has been seriously challenged (Keukeleire and Bruyninckx 2011). In fact, China has taken the lead by creating channels of its own to redress the imbalance in global economic governance, as demonstrated by an array of parallel structures initiated unilaterally by Beijing or jointly with other developing countries (Heilmann et al. 2014). The AIIB is a case in point. As an official involved in the talks to found the AIIB noted, "China feels it can't get anything done in the World Bank or the IMF so it wants to set up its own World Bank that it can control itself" (Anderlini 2014). Born out of frustrations at the lack of substantive governance reforms in Western-backed international financial institutions, the AIIB was imbued with a strong sense of competition.

Secondly, the AIIB is set to become a purveyor of the competing worldview of China to decouple development lending from policy prescriptions. There is no denying that development assistance is no longer a *domaine reservé* of developed countries sitting on the OECD-DAC. DAC official development assistance enjoyed near-exclusive dominance in the 1990s but a small group of non-DAC countries have become consequential aid providers since the 2000s (Kim and Lightfoot 2011). China, in particular, has transitioned from an aid recipient to a 'net donor' (Chin 2012) and is in the vanguard among non-DAC donors. Through the Ministry of Commerce, state policy and commercial banks and state-owned enterprises, Beijing doles out sizable development finance to other countries with no/few strings attached. Due to diverging approaches, external observers have expressed doubts about the expanding operation of rising donors such as China and their disruptive effect on the international development landscape. Some lambaste China for its mercantilist approach, which is considered detrimental to Africa's sustainable development and Western efforts to promote democracy and human rights (Tiffen 2014), others lament that the bargaining position of Western donors and the role of neoliberal economic model have been undercut as emerging donors offer more appealing alternatives to aid-receiving countries (Woods 2008). Even in the face of recurrent criticism, China remains outside of DAC aid architecture and refuses to subscribe to DAC practices (Bräutigam 2011). While the multilateral AIIB is not expected to merely do the bidding of its most powerful member, it is likely to reflect the position of China and other (developing) borrowing countries, thus bringing more pressure to bear on traditional donors.

Thirdly, the AIIB features large among a series of Beijing-backed schemes, stoking controversy over their wider implications. Among others, in the fall of 2013, China unveiled the development framework dubbed as the Belt and Road Initiative (BRI). The BRI consists of the 'Silk Road Economic Belt' stretching from China via Central Asia, Middle East to Europe, and the '21st-century Maritime Silk Road' linking China through Southeast and South Asia all the way to the Mediterranean and Africa. The signature foreign policy of President Xi is seen as a grand strategy to advance China's political-strategic interests in the neighborhood and beyond (Johnson 2016). In July 2014, China, along with other BRICS members, created the NDB with a capital stock of $100 billion and the Contingent Reserve Arrangement (CRA) with a currency pool of $100 billion.

As the most successful China-led multilateral initiatives to date, the AIIB is undoubtedly related to the primacy of Washington and Tokyo in the WB and the ADB and their reluctance to accord Beijing an international standing corresponding to its increased economic heft. Also, the bank alleges to offer a rival model of governance and deliver loans at a faster speed with fewer conditions attached (Koh 2015). Nevertheless, does it have the ability to replace the established actors in international development? Despite the potential competition that can ensue from the AIIB's growing operation, it is neither able nor intended to become a substitute for the WB and the ADB. The new lender boasts $100 billion in total authorized capital—equivalent to about half that of the WB and two-thirds that of the ADB (Table 9.2), but its level of loan disbursements is, at least initially, unlikely to reach a scale to rival the two dominant players. Chinese authorities repeatedly stated that the AIIB does not aim to upend the present architecture but to play a complementary role. When commenting on the AIIB's ambitions at Brookings Institution, then President-designate Jin Liqun in charge of shepherding the bank into existence dismissed the claim that the bank would undermine the WB and the ADB, characterizing the AIIB as a 'sibling' to the other two lenders

(Jin 2015b). Jin pushed back again on such a claim at the 2016 Boao Forum for Asia, using the analogy of opening a new restaurant alongside the existing ones (Fung 2016).

Beyond rhetoric, the AIIB has been co-financing projects with established actors. At the time of writing (August 2016), four out of the seven approved projects of the AIIB are co-financed with existing MDBs such as the WB, the ADB, the European Bank for Reconstruction and Development (EBRD), or development agencies of traditional donors (AIIB 2016). Besides, regional development banks are not at all unprecedented. In addition to the ADB and the EBRD, the African Development Bank (AfDB), the Andean Development Corporation (CAF), the European Investment Bank (EIB), the Inter-American Development Bank (IDB) are notable examples and play an important role in regional development financing.

Table 9.2 A brief comparison of WB, ADB, and AIIB (Kawai 2015, p. 9; official websites of the three banks)

	WB	*ADB*	*AIIB*
Formation	1944	1966	2015
President	American (Jim Yong Kim)	Japanese (Takehiko Nakao)	Chinese (Jin Liqun)
Headquarters	Washington D.C., US	Manila, Philippines	Beijing, China
Membership	188	67	57 (founding member)
Total authorized capital	$252.8 billion	$163.5 billion	$100 billion
Average annual lending	40–50 billion	13–18 billion	10–15 billion
Major decision-making	85% majority	75% majority	75% majority
Board of Directors	26-member, resident	12-member, resident	12-member, non-resident
Largest shareholders	US (17%), Japan (7.9%), China (5%)	Japan (15.7%), US (15.6%), China (6.5%)	China (26%), India (7.5%), Russia (5.9%)
Combined voting power of developing countries	Emerging and developing countries: 42.1%	Developing member countries: 46.8%	Asian member countries: 75%
Priority of financing	Poverty reduction worldwide	Poverty reduction in Asia	Asian infrastructure

9.5.3 Social Creativity: AIIB as a 'Creative' Institutional Innovation

Social creativity seeks to attain preeminence in an area different from that of established powers. It does so by carving out a niche or promulgating new institutions, norms, and practices. The AIIB is a prime case of China's status-seeking via social creativity, which unfolds along the triad of institutional innovation: usefulness, novelty, and legitimacy.

Firstly, the AIIB is useful in the sense that it focuses explicitly on tackling the unmet funding shortfall left by the WB and the ADB in Asian infrastructure. On many occasions, Chinese authorities highlighted the geographical and thematic priority of the AIIB. In the first-ever official announcement about the bank, President Xi (2013) stated the purpose of the AIIB is to "help fund the infrastructural development of ASEAN countries and other developing countries in the region." In his speech at the AIIB opening ceremony, Xi reiterated that the Asia-focused lender "has a due role to play to raise the level of infrastructure financing and of economic and social development in the region." Over the past several decades, Asia has grown into an economic powerhouse and key driver of global growth. Yet, intra-regional development has been uneven and many Asian developing countries are in need of quality infrastructure. To tackle the paucity of Asian infrastructure investment, the WB and the ADB have supplied respectively $15 billion and $13 billion per annum (Kawai 2015, p. 11). But as specified in an oft-cited working report by the ADB in 2010, Asia needs infrastructure financing of $776 billion annually during 2010–2020 (Bhattacharyay 2010). Also, due to the uncertainty of investment returns, the scale of capital requirement and time frame, traditional donors are reluctant to finance infrastructure (Chin 2012). As such, the AIIB fills an important gap.

Secondly, a notable new feature of the AIIB vis-à-vis existing MDBs is its alternative governance model that combines efficient lending with high standards. A much-criticized problem with established MDBs is the huge operational costs and inefficiency as a result of risk-averse and bureaucratic procedures. For instance, the WB's resident Board of Directors brings a hefty annual financial cost of $70 million and represents an extra layer of management that holds up project preparation (Dollar 2015). For a loan to be delivered, the WB requires no less than four in-country missions during the project preparation phase and four formal review phases prior to loan approval, resulting in an average loan delivery time of sixteen months (Humphrey and Michaelowa 2013). Another widely recognized issue with the WB is the undue influence of the US on the overall disbursement of loans. As demonstrated by fine-grained empirical studies (Fleck and Kilby 2006; Kilby 2009), WB lending often caters to US foreign policy interests and its program loans are more likely to be approved after countries adopting pro-US policies, thus casting doubt on the independence of the world's foremost MDB.

Having pledged to a modern modus operanti of 'clean, lean and green,' the AIIB has undertaken several steps in governance structures and lending practices to set itself apart from other MDBs. In particular, two pronounced differences are worth mentioning since they offer a glimpse into the governance innovations that are conducive to a combination of improved efficiency with adequate safeguards. To minimize costs and streamline operations, the Beijing-based lender will have an unpaid, non-resident Board of Directors convening at regular intervals and work toward a clear division of responsibility between the Board and the management team in a bid to prevent the former from micromanaging. Adding to this is a technocratic approach that tries to depoliticize development financing and disentangle it from policy conditions, reflecting the view of China and other borrowing countries. Major terms for loans are said to be grounded on economic considerations (project conditionality) to safeguard the lender's financial position and generate moderate returns on a solid pipeline of bona fide bankable projects (Koh 2015). This is a notable departure from the unwritten rules pushed and enforced by the WB and the IMF that set macroeconomic and institutional reforms as conditions for loans. In many ways, the AIIB can be seen as a welcome change that breaks away from the legacies of multilateral development finance.

Thirdly, the AIIB is legitimate as it provides leadership and ownership for the Global South in global economic governance, apart from being multilateral and useful in delivering a needed global public good. For the moment, there are about 20 MDBs across the world including inter alia the WB, the ADB, the AfDB, the EBRD, and the IDB. But most if not all MDBs with a respectable amount of assets were established and remain dominated by the West, giving a rather insufficient voice to developing countries. For this reason, the AIIB has a rightful place to fill. As China's official news agency Xinhua (2015) put it, "As the increasing importance of emerging markets changes the landscape of a global economic order that has long been dominated by advanced economies, they also want a new institution that best serves their own interests. The AIIB answers that call." In a way, the AIIB has become an influential multilateral institution led by the developing countries due to its allocation of voting power. The bank's charter (AOA, p. 4) stipulates that no less than seventy-five percent of total authorized capital and nine out of twelve members in the Board of Directors must come from regional members, thus giving the driving seat to Asian developing economies. In addition to strong regional representation, BRICS powerhouses China, India, and Russia, counting an aggregate voting share of nearly forty percent, are the most influential players.

Of equal importance is the privileged position China enjoys in decision-making on the basis of its voting shares. Despite forgoing veto power in daily decisions, the world's second-largest economy is still the largest shareholder and has a voting share of twenty-six percent. As stipulated in the AIIB charter, major decisions require a super majority of "an affirmative vote of two-thirds of the total number of Governors, representing not less than three-fourths of the total voting power of the member" (AOA, p. 17). As such, China enjoys veto power over critical issues as circumstances warrant. Having said that, a simple majority will suffice over matters including project approvals. Besides, according to Jin Liqun, China neither plans to exercise its de facto veto nor is keen to retain it (Fu 2016). This is sensible as a veto-casting China will tarnish the hard-won reputation of the AIIB, worsen the concern about China's hidden agenda, and ultimately undermine its own status-seeking.

9.6 Conclusion

This article situates the AIIB in the broad context of China's search for greater power status on the world stage. By employing the SIT to study the developments leading up to the advent of the AIIB and its early operations, it makes the case that social creativity is the strategy favored by China in this emblematic case of status-seeking. Of course, the jury is still out on whether the new institution will be complementary or competitive. Nonetheless, China sought consistently to reassure the West that the AIIB is a useful, novel and legitimate addition to global economic governance, and indeed, the new MDB is shaping up to be a multilateral of such features. Admittedly, elements of social mobility and social competition were present, but they have proven inadequate when measured against the yardstick of Beijing's intention to join the elite club or the AIIB's ability to overturn the dominant players. Hence, this case study substantiates the validity of the SIT-informed perspective on the preferred status-seeking strategy of rising states and extends its explanatory power to particular foreign policies.

Empirically, three findings drawn from this analysis can be indicative of the strategic thinking behind a growing number of China-proposed alternative structures. The first and most obvious is that the new bank demonstrates China's dual-track approach to global governance. To create a favorable environment wherein rising powers can enhance status, China has started building novel institutions in parallel with its active push to modify the system from within. Second, in the setup of the AIIB, China largely respected international norms and practices. It was responsive to concerns of the established powers and modified its stance on a string of key issues. Third and finally, from the Chinese perspective, the role of the multilateral bank, as other structures set up by Beijing, is not competitive but complementary. It serves as a helpful, legitimately distinct alternative rather than aiming to undercut existing institutions. Following this positive experience with the AIIB, China will likely continue with similar thinking in its status-seeking through institution-building.

References

Abrams, D., and Hogg, M.A. 1988. Comments on the Motivational Status of Self-esteem in Social Identity and Intergroup Discrimination. *European Journal of Social Psychology* 18 (4): 317–334.

Anderlini, J. 2014. China Expands Plans for World Bank Rival. *Financial Times*, June 24, http://www.ft.com/intl/cms/s/0/b1012282-fba4-11e3-aa19-001 44feab7de.html.

Asian Infrastructure Investment Bank (AIIB). 2015a. Articles of Agreement, http://www.aiib.org/uploadfile/2016/0202/20160202043950310.pdf.

Asian Infrastructure Investment Bank (AIIB). 2015b. Report on the Articles of Agreement, http://euweb.aiib.org/uploadfile/2016/0204/201602 04112514995.pdf.

Asian Infrastructure Investment Bank (AIIB). 2016. Projects. http://euweb.aiib. org/html/PROJECTS.

Bhattacharyay, B.N. 2010. Estimating Demand for Infrastructure in Energy, Transport, Telecommunications, Water and Sanitation in Asia and the Pacific: 2010–2020. ADBI Working Paper 248. Tokyo: Asian Development Bank Institute.

Bräutigam, D. 2011. Aid 'with Chinese Characteristics': Chinese Foreign aid and Development Finance Meet the OECD-DAC aid Regime. *Journal of International Development* 23 (5): 752–764.

Breslin, S. 2011. The 'China Model' and the Global Crisis: from Friedrich list to a Chinese Mode of Governance? *International Affairs* 87 (6): 1323–1343.

Callaghan, M., and Hubbard, P. 2016. The Asian Infrastructure Investment Bank: Multilateralism on the Silk Road. *China Economic Journal* 9 (2): 116–139.

Chan, G. 2013. China Faces the World: Making Rules for a New Order? *Journal of Global Policy and Governance* 2 (1): 105–119.

Chen, Z., and Pan, Z. 2011. China in Its Neighbourhood: A 'Middle Kingdom' not necessarily at the Centre of Power. *The International Spectator* 46 (4): 79–96.

Chin, G.T. 2012. China as a 'Net Donor': Tracking Dollars and Sense. *Cambridge Review of International Affairs* 25 (4): 579–603.

Chin, G.T. 2014. The BRICS-led Development Bank: Purpose and Politics beyond the G20. *Global Policy* 5 (3): 366–373.

Chin, G.T. 2016. Asian Infrastructure Investment Bank: Governance Innovation and Prospects. *Global Governance* 22 (1): 11–26.

Chinese Ministry of Foreign Affairs. 2015. Foreign Ministry Spokesperson Hong Lei's Press Conference on March 17, http://www.fmprc.gov.cn/mfa_eng/xwfw_665399/s2510_665401/t1246361.shtml.

Chinese State Council. 2015. Action Plan on the Belt and Road Initiative. http://english.gov.cn/archive/publications/2015/03/30/content_2814 75080249035.htm.

Christensen, T.J. 2006. Fostering Stability or Creating a Monster? The Rise of China and US Policy Toward East Asia. *International Security* 31 (1): 81–126.

Dacin, M.T., Goodstein, J., and Richard Scott, W. 2002. Institutional Theory and Institutional Change: Introduction to the Special Research Forum. *Academy of Management Journal* 45 (1): 45–56.

Dollar, D. 2015. China's Rise as a Regional and Global Power: the AIIB and the 'One Belt One Road.' Washington DC: Brookings, http://www.brookings.edu/research/papers/2015/07/china-regional-global-power-dollar.

Elek, A. 2014. The Potential Role of the Asian Infrastructure Investment Bank. *East Asia Forum*, February 11, http://www.obela.org/system/files/AsianBank_AElek_0.pdf.

Finnemore, M. 1996. *National Interests in International Society*. Ithaca: Cornell University Press.

Fleck, R.K., and Kilby, C. 2006. World Bank Independence: A Model and Statistical Analysis of US Influence. *Review of Development Economics* 10 (2): 224–240.

Friedberg, A.L. 2005. The Future of US-China Relations: Is Conflict Inevitable? *International Security* 30 (2): 7–45.

Friedberg, A.L. 2011. *A Contest for Supremacy: China, America, and the Struggle for Mastery in Asia*. New York: WW Norton and Company.

Fu, J. 2016. AIIB Chief Rules out China Veto Power. *China Daily*, January 27, http://europe.chinadaily.com.cn/business/2016-01/27/content_2327 3436.htm.

Fung, E. 2016. AIIB not looking for Trouble, President says. *Wall Street Journal*, March 25, http://www.wsj.com/articles/aiib-not-looking-for-trouble-presid ent-says-1458896738.

Greenwood, L. 2016. AIIB: Now Comes the Hard Part. February 18, Washington DC: Center for Strategic and International Studies, https://www.csis.org/analysis/aiib-now-comes-hard-part.

Hargadon, A.B., and Douglas, Y. 2001. When Innovations Meet Institutions: Edison and the Design of the Electric Light. *Administrative Science Quarterly* 46 (3): 476–501.

Hargrave, T.J., and Van de Ven, A.H. 2006. A Collective Action Model of Institutional Innovation. *Academy of Management Review* 31 (4): 864–888.

Heilmann, S., Rudolf, M., Huotari M., and Buckow, J. 2014. China's Shadow Foreign Policy: Parallel Structures Challenge the Established International Order. China Monitor 18. Berlin: Mercator Institute for China Studies.

Humphrey, C., and Michaelowa, K. 2013. Shopping for Development: Multilateral Lending, Shareholder Composition and Borrower Preferences. *World Development*, 44, 142–155.

Humphrey, C. 2015. Developmental Revolution or Bretton Woods Revisited? The Prospects of the BRICS New Development Bank and the Asian Infrastructure Investment Bank. Working Paper 418. London: Overseas Development Institute.

Jin, L. 2015a. AIIB to Benefit Asia and Beyond. *China Daily*, December 28, http://www.chinadaily.com.cn/opinion/2015-12/28/content_22836923.htm.

Jin, L. 2015b. Building Asia's new bank. Speech at Brookings Institution, October 21, https://www.brookings.edu/events/building-asias-new-bank-an-address-by-jin-liqun-president-designate-of-the-asian-infrastructure-invest ment-bank.

Johnson, C.K. 2016. President Xi Jinping's "Belt and Road" Initiative. Washington DC: Center for Strategic and International Studies, March 28, https://www.csis.org/analysis/president-xi-jinping's-belt-and-road-initiative.

Johnston, A.I. 2014. *Social States: China in International Institutions, 1980–2000*. Princeton: Princeton University Press.

Kahn, R. 2015. Interview: A Bank Too Far? New York: Council on Foreign Relations, March 17, http://www.cfr.org/global-governance/bank-too-far/p36290.

Kawai, M. 2015. Asian Infrastructure Investment Bank in the Evolving International Financial Order. In *Asian Infrastructure Investment Bank: China as Responsible Stakeholder?* ed. D. Bob, 5–26. Washington DC: Sasakawa Peace Foundation USA.

Kent, A. 2013. *China, the United Nations, and Human Rights: the Limits of Compliance*. Philadelphia: University of Pennsylvania Press.

Keohane, R.O. 1998. International Institutions: Can Interdependence Work? *Foreign Policy* 100, 82–194.

Keohane, R.O., and Nye, J.S. 1987. Power and Interdependence Revisited. *International Organization* 41 (4): 725–753.

Keukeleire, S., and Bruyninckx, H. 2011. The European Union, the BRICs, and the Emerging New World Order. In *International Relations and the European Union*, eds. C. Hill and M. Smith, 380–403. Oxford: Oxford University Press.

Kilby, C. 2009. The Political Economy of Conditionality: An Empirical Analysis of World Bank loan Disbursements. *Journal of Development Economics* 89 (1): 51–61.

Kim, S., and Lightfoot, S. 2011. Does 'DAC-ability' Really Matter? The Emergence of Non-DAC Donors: Introduction to Policy Arena. *Journal of International Development* 23 (5): 711–721.

Koh, G. 2015. Exclusive: China's AIIB to Offer Loans with Fewer Strings Attached. *Reuters*, September 1, http://www.reuters.com/article/us-aiib-china-loans-idUSKCN0R14UB20150901.

Kynge, J., and Wheatley, J. 2015. Emerging Markets: Redrawing the World Map. *Financial Times*, August 3, http://www.ft.com/intl/cms/s/2/4a915716-39dc-11e5-8613-07d16aad2152.html.

Larson, D.W., and Shevchenko, A. 2003. Shortcut to Greatness: the New Thinking and the Revolution in Soviet Foreign Policy. *International Organization* 57 (1): 77–109.

Larson, D.W., and Shevchenko, A. 2010. Status Seekers: Chinese and Russian Responses to US Primacy. *International Security* 34 (4): 63–95.

Larson, D.W., and Shevchenko, A. 2014. Managing Rising Powers: The Role of Status Concerns. In *Status in World Politics*, ed. T.V. Paul, D.W. Larson, and W. Wohlfort, 33–70. Cambridge: Cambridge University Press.

Larson, D.W., Paul, T.V., and Wohlfort, W. 2014. Status and World Order. In *Status in World Politics*, ed. T.V. Paul, D.W. Larson, and W. Wohlfort, 3–32. Cambridge: Cambridge University Press.

Larson, D.W. 2015. Will China be a New Type of Great Power? *Chinese Journal of International Politics* 8 (4): 323–348.

Liao, R. 2015. Out of the Bretton Woods: How the AIIB is Different. *Foreign Affairs*, July 27, https://www.foreignaffairs.com/articles/asia/2015-07-27/out-bretton-woods.

Lou, J. 2015. Yatouhang chuangshi chengyuanguo zige queren sanyue di jiezhi [AIIB founding membership status confirmation ends at the end of March]. *Xinhua*, March 6, http://news.xinhuanet.com/politics/2015lh/2015-03/06/c_1114552782.htm.

Mearsheimer, J.J. 2001. *The Tragedy of Great Power Politics*. New York: WW Norton & Company.

Mearsheimer, J.J. 2010. The Gathering Storm: China's Challenge to US power in Asia. *Chinese Journal of International Politics* 3 (4): 381–396.

Nye, J.S. 2013. Work with China, Don't Contain It. *New York Times*, January 26, http://www.nytimes.com/2013/01/26/opinion/work-with-china-dont-contain-it.html.

Ohno, I. 2013. China's Foreign Aid and International Aid Community: From the Perspectives of Traditional Donors and Africa. In *A Study of China's Foreign Aid: An Asian Perspective*, ed. Y. Shimomura and H. Ohashi, 193–216. Basingstoke: Palgrave.

Organski, A.F.K., and Kugler, J. 1981. *The War Ledger*. Chicago: University of Chicago Press.

Pan, Z. (ed). 2012. *Conceptual Gaps in China-EU Relations: Global Governance, Human Rights and Strategic Partnerships*. Basingstoke: Palgrave.

Pollack, J. 2015. Joining the Club: How will the United States Respond to AIIB's Expanding Membership? Washington DC: Brookings, March 17, http://www.brookings.edu/blogs/order-from-chaos/posts/2015/03/17-joining-the-club-aiib-pollack.

Raffaelli, R., and Glynn, M.A. 2015. Institutional Innovation: Novel, Useful, and Legitimate. In *The Oxford Handbook of Creativity, Innovation, and Entrepreneurship*, ed. C. Shalley, M.A. Hitt, and J. Zhou, 407–420. Oxford: Oxford University Press.

Reisen, H. 2015. Will the AIIB and the NDB help Reform Multilateral Development Banking? *Global Policy* 6 (3): 297–304.

Ren, X. 2016. China as an Institution-Builder: The Case of the AIIB. *The Pacific Review* 29 (3): 435–442.

Shapiro, J. 2015. The Chinese Foray into Global Governance. Washington DC: Brookings, April 1, http://www.brookings.edu/blogs/order-from-chaos/posts/2015/04/01-china-global-governance-shapiro.

Sohn, I. 2015. AIIB: A Plank in China's Hedging Strategy. Washington DC: Brookings, May 11, https://www.brookings.edu/opinions/aiib-a-plank-in-chinas-hedging-strategy.

Stiglitz, J.E. 2015. Asia's Multilateralism. *Project Syndicate*, April 13, https://www.project-syndicate.org/commentary/china-aiib-us-opposition-by-joseph-e--stiglitz-2015-04.

Subacchi, P. 2015. The AIIB is a Threat to Global Economic Governance. *Foreign Policy*, March 31, http://foreignpolicy.com/2015/03/31/the-aiib-is-a-threat-to-global-economic-governance-china.

Sun, Y. 2015. China and the Changing Asian Infrastructure Investment Bank. Washington DC: Center for Strategic and International Studies, http://csis.org/publication/pacnet-43-china-and-changing-asian-infrastructure-bank.

Swaine, M.D. 2010. Perceptions of an Assertive China. *China Leadership Monitor* 32 (2): 1–19.

Tajfel, H., and Turner, J.C. 1979. An Integrative Theory of Intergroup Conflict. In *The Social Psychology of Intergroup Relations*, ed. W.G. Austin and S. Worchel, 33–47. Monterey, CA: Brooks-Cole.

Tajfel, H. 1972. Social Categorisation. In *Introduction à la psychologie sociale*, ed. S. Moscovici, 272–302. Paris: Larousse.

Tiffen, A. 2014. The New-neocolonialism in Africa. *Global Policy*, August 19, http://www.globalpolicyjournal.com/blog/19/08/2014/new-neo-coloni alism-africa.

Turner, J.C. 1975. Social Comparison and Social Identity: Some Prospects for Intergroup Behaviour. *European Journal of Social Psychology* 5 (1): 1–34.

Wan, M. 2016. *The Asian Infrastructure Investment Bank: The Construction of Power and the Struggle for the East Asian International Order*. New York: Palgrave.

Wendt, A. 1999. *Social Theory Of International Politics*. Cambridge: Cambridge University Press.

Woods, N. 2008. Whose aid? Whose Influence? China, Emerging Donors and the Silent Revolution in Development Assistance. *International Affairs*, 84 (6): 1205–1221.

Xi, J. 2013. Deepen Reform and Opening Up and Work Together for a Better Asia Pacific. http://www.fmprc.gov.cn/mfa_eng/topics_665678/xjpfwynml xycx21apec_665682/t1088517.shtml.

Xi, J. 2016. Speech at the Inauguration Ceremony of the Asian Infrastructure Investment Bank in Beijing. https://www.fmprc.gov.cn/mfa_eng/wjdt_665385/zyjh_665391/P020160119533074024860.pdf.

Xing, Y. 2016. The Asian Infrastructure Investment Bank and China's role in Regional Economic Governance. *East Asian Policy* 8 (2): 25–36.

Xinhua. 2015. China Voice: The Call of Times. June 29, http://news.xinhua net.com/english/2015-06/29/c_134366132.htm.

Yan, X. 2014. From Keeping a Low Profile to Striving for Achievement. *Chinese Journal of International Politics* 7 (2): 153–184.

Zhang, L. 2015. The AIIB: Making Room for China in the Global Economy. *China.org.cn*, April 20, http://www.china.org.cn/opinion/2015-04/20/content_35365944_2.htm.

CHAPTER 10

Conclusion

Yitan Li

China has risen dramatically since the late 1970s when the Chinese government led by Deng Xiaoping introduced the "Reforms and Opening" policies. It has transformed itself from a backward agrarian economy to an economic powerhouse in the last five decades. On the one hand, the global economic structure created through the Bretton Woods system after the end of World War II provided the foundation upon which China's economy grew rapidly. The post-World War II global economic system was created by the West, primarily led by the US, and thereafter remained dominated by the US-led Western coalition. China benefited tremendously from the post-World War II economic system. As indicated by Kevin Cai in the introductory chapter, China, albeit gradually, embraced and integrated itself into the post-World War II Western-dominated global economic system. For example, China's full accession to

Y. Li (✉)
Department of Political Science, Seattle University, Seattle, WA, USA
e-mail: liy@seattleu.edu

© The Author(s), under exclusive license to Springer Nature Switzerland AG 2025
K. G.Cai et al. (eds.), *China and Global Economic Governance, Volume I: China's BRI & AIIB and Global Economic Governance*, Politics and Development of Contemporary China,
https://doi.org/10.1007/978-3-031-73212-6_10

the World Trade Organization (WTO) in 2001 was one of the most significant milestones of China's integration with the Western liberal economic order.

On the other hand, once China was fully integrated into the post-World War II global economic system, it made rapid economic transformation by leaps and bounds. Utilizing its abundant and inexpensive labor forces and combining the innovation from the Global North and resources from the South, it gradually became the "factory of the world," dominating the global supply chain of manufactured goods.

As China rose since the turn of the century, the West, led by the US, started to show signs of decline, particularly in the areas of the economy, institutional efficacy, and global leadership. For example, a series of events started to undermine the US's hegemonic position and that of the Western coalition. The attacks on September 11, 2001 dragged the US into a war on terrorism. The world's attention and US strategic focus shifted to the Middle East. In the decade that followed, the US-led Western coalition was bogged down in Afghanistan and Iraq. The cost of the post-9/11 wars in Iraq, Afghanistan, Pakistan, Syria, and elsewhere led to significant ripple effects on the US economy, including job loss and interest rate increases. In 2007 and 2008, a financial crisis originated in the US due to the subprime loan crisis took a significant toll on the US economy, leading to major job losses and bank collapses. Although the US economy eventually recovered, the Obama administration, while recognizing the strategic importance of containing the rise of China through the "Asian pivot" strategy, took a soft approach to deal with China. When Donald Trump became the president, the Trump administration led the US to a radical path, shifting US foreign policy from multilateralism to unilateralism. The Trump administration escalated tensions between the US and China through a series of trade wars and protectionist policies. Meanwhile, in Europe, the European Union (EU) went through a Euro crisis and Brexit, casting doubts on the institutional efficacy of the EU.

It is in this confluence of global power politics that China started a more systematic and aggressive way of seeking a leading role in global economic governance. This volume is an attempt to examine China's efforts in seeking a new structure of global economic governance through the lenses of China's BRI and AIIB. Several broad questions were examined in this volume to help understand China's needs and behaviors in search of its place in global economic governance. Why did China establish the BRI and AIIB? Have the BRI and AIIB been successful and what

10 CONCLUSION 243

are the challenges and opportunities? And how have the BRI and AIIB influenced China's leadership roles in global governance?

10.1 WHY DID CHINA ESTABLISH THE BRI AND AIIB?

There is wide consensus among the contributors that the creation of the BRI and AIIB is a reflection of the changing power landscape of the international system and how China sees itself in terms of its needs and desires in the new landscape. There are theoretical and practical reasons from both the domestic and international perspectives for China's changing behaviors.

From a theoretical perspective, Enyu Zhang and Patrick James' chapter uses systemism to visualize the BRI in the context of the power transition theory. China's rise has been a classic case of power transition, in which the gradual buildup in China's capabilities as a rising power has led to significant changes in power dynamics between the dominant state (the US) and the rising state (China). When China approaches power parity with the US, a vicious cycle in which the rising power will become increasingly dissatisfied with the status quo will begin. The rising power thus seeks to challenge and eventually replace the dominant power as the preponderant state. China's increasingly more aggressive and assertive behaviors in its foreign policy are directly correlated to China's rising power status.[1] When China is no longer satisfied with the status quo, challenging the US is the natural next step. The BRI and AIIB are two specific mechanisms in a much broader scheme to challenge the preponderant US dominance.

There are both domestic and international reasons why China needed to establish the BRI and AIIB. From a domestic perspective, as China's economic growth started to reach saturation, Beijing needed to develop new directions to keep its economy growing. The BRI in particular serves as a way to outsource China's growth outwardly. Zhang and James find evidence that the uneven growth in China's inland, in particular, has led China to promote the BRI to help refocus its growth priorities.[2] Mark Beeson and Corey Crawford's chapter points out that China's domestic

---

[1] Enyu Zhang and Patrick James, "All Roads Lead to Beijing: Systemism, Power Transition Theory and the Belt and Road Initiative." *Chinese Political Science Review*, Vol. 8, No. 1, 2023, pp. 18–44.

[2] Ibid.

overcapacity in the building sector makes outward investment and infrastructure a necessary outlet.[3] China is also using the BRI to build roads in Central Asia, for example, to transport oil and other resources from Iran back to China, and sees the BRI as a "win–win" solution for all BRI participants.[4] Moreover, there is a clear need for China to diversify energy supplies and secure key maritime supply routes.[5] China's outward strategies are not only limited to labor and resource-intensive areas. China also hopes to export its technological innovation to help find ways to avoid the "middle income" trap.[6]

From an international perspective, there are ample reasons for creating the BRI and AIIB. First, as Kevin Cai's chapter shows, although China has benefited greatly from the existing economic order, through institutions such as the International Monetary Fund, the World Bank, the WTO, and the Asian Development Bank, as time went on, the existing system could no longer serve China's needs. China resorted to a two-track approach to increase its influence that would match its growing status.[7] On the one hand, Beijing started to push more vigorously for reforms within the existing system, such as increasing China's share in the weighted voting system in the IMF and the proposal to create an IMF-controlled international reserve currency to replace the US dollar. However, China has not been satisfied with the scope and pace of reforms in the existing multilateral institutions.[8] Hai Yang's chapter points out that the slow reforms in the IMF and the World Bank, particularly the US's foot-dragging action to stall IMF reforms, have made Beijing increasingly more impatient.[9] Zhongzhou Peng and Sow Keat Tok's chapter makes a similar observation that China has had very limited success in working with emerging

[3] Mark Beeson and Corey Crawford, "Putting the BRI in Perspective: History, Hegemony and Geoeconomics." *Chinese Political Science Review*, Vol. 8, No. 1, 2023, pp. 45–62.

[4] Zhang and James, "All Roads Lead to Beijing."

[5] Beeson and Crawford, "Putting the BRI in Perspective."

[6] Zhang and James, "All Roads Lead to Beijing."

[7] Kevin G. Cai. "China's Initiatives: A Bypassing Strategy for the Reform of Global Economic Governance." *Chinese Political Science Review*, Vol. 8, No. 1, 2023, pp. 1–17.

[8] Ibid.

[9] Hai Yang, "The Asian Infrastructure Investment Bank and Status-Seeking: China's Foray into Global Economic Governance." *Chinese Political Science Review*, Vol. 1, No. 4, 2016, pp. 754–778.

and developing economies to push for IMF and World Bank reforms, especially through the BRICS channel.[10] As a result, Beijing launched a parallel process, on the other hand, by creating the BRI and AIIB as a "bypassing" strategy to circumvent the US's dominance in global governance.[11] Although the BRI is primarily a unilateral initiative, while the AIIB is a multilateral institution, Beijing enjoys clear decision-making dominance in both processes.

Second, China has always seen itself as a developing country and long called for solutions to the problem of underrepresentation of the Global South. Within the existing multilateral institutional structure, Beijing has used the BRICS group as a bridge between developing and developed countries and a venue where the Southern countries can speak with "one voice."[12]

Finally, from a social constructivist perspective, Hai Yang's chapter suggests that China is using social creativity to promulgate alternative norms, models, and institutions through the AIIB.[13] Although China has largely respected international norms, rules, and practices so far, a new set of norms created by Beijing would benefit China more greatly by providing legitimacy for China and the normative foundation for alternative governance. China is using the AIIB, for example, to demonstrate its ideal financial governance structure and norm, which features leanness, cleanness, greenness, and the fairer distribution of rights.[14]

10.2   Have the BRI and AIIB been Successful and What are the Challenges and Opportunities?

One natural question to ask is whether the BRI and AIIB have been successful. While there is no clear answer to this question, the contributors have presented two sets of views: a relatively skeptical view and a

---

[10] Zhongzhou Peng and Sow Keat Tok, "The AIIB and China's Normative Power in International Financial Governance Structure." *Chinese Political Science Review*, Vol. 1, No. 4, 2016, pp. 736–753.

[11] Cai, "China's Initiatives."

[12] Ibid.

[13] Yang, "The Asian Infrastructure Investment Bank and Status-Seeking."

[14] Peng and Tok, "The AIIB and China's Normative Power in International Financial Governance Structure."

relatively favorable view. While each set of views is not clear-cut, it does present both challenges and opportunities for Beijing.

10.2.1 The Skeptical

Mark Beeson and Corey Crawford's chapter compares China's BRI with the post-World War II US Marshal Plan. While the Chinese hegemony is a reality, as the first non-Western hegemony, the BRI does differ from the US-dominated hegemony post-World War II. The US hegemon was benign and based on institutions of principles, norms, and rules. It also had a key focus on ideological contestation. Beijing, on the other hand, wants to present a hierarchical structure as a distinct Asian approach and invokes the "Silk Road" as a way to return to China's past glory. Although the BRI is much larger than the Marshal Plan in terms of dollar amount, China's BRI lacks specific provisions, rights, and obligations. The recent COVID-19 pandemic exposed some of the deficiencies. As a result, the BRI lacks geopolitical imperatives and narratives and comprehensive global institutional architecture as compared to the US Marshall Plan.[15]

Kevin Cai's chapter shares a similarly skeptical view. China has been using the BRICS, BRI, and AIIB to create a new international economic system to exclude the US. These efforts have benefited Beijing regionally, but they have not transformed into China's enhanced status globally.[16]

Serafettin Yilmaz and Bo Li's chapter presents a more mixed view of the BRI. There is no question that the BRI is created as an alternative to the US-led global system, the BRI does not seem to be positioned to function as a systemic alternative to the existing global model, much less to replace the existing system by force, nor is it poised to decouple from the established international structures and norms. The BRI, as a reformed and upgraded form of globalization, carries two risks. First, the BRI has a "dampening effect" on the prospects of China's participation in regional institution buildup. Second, the BRI may be causing a "diluting effect" by creating areas of overlaps across global and regional integration processes under globalization and regionalization.[17]

---

[15] Beeson and Crawford, "Putting the BRI in Perspective."

[16] Cai, "China's Initiatives."

[17] Serafettin Yilmaz and Bo Li, "The BRI-Led Globalization and its Implications for East Asian Regionalization." *Chinese Political Science Review*, Vol. 5, No. 3, 2020, pp. 395–416.

10.2.2 The Favorable

Frangton Chiyemura, Elia Gambino, and Tim Zajontz's chapter presents a favorable view of the BRI from the perspective of recipient countries in Africa. They argue that the Bretton Woods institutions are too expensive and unsuited to African requirements. China's BRI on the other hand has been seen as a suitable partner. Beijing has marketed a "no strings attached" approach, although the Chinese model is often accompanied by a stringent set of requirements, particularly about the choice of contracting firms.[18] Nevertheless, local actors and agencies, such as African bureaucrats and government officials, have often engaged with Chinese contractors. Their findings suggest that the political, economic, and legal-bureaucratic contexts within African states do matter. If the local agencies can crucially condition infrastructure projects with Chinese involvement, the overall positive experience with the BRI outweighs the negative.[19]

The positive effects of China's BRI have spilled over into other areas of cooperation. Charles Chong-Han Wu's chapter examines the effects of the BRI on the disputed sovereignty with ASEAN countries in the South China Sea. Using territorial peace theory as a framework, Wu demonstrates the pacifying effects of the Maritime BRI on countries in Southeast Asia. Beijing has been using the Maritime BRI as a way to build a community of norms and demonstrate its strong commitment to enhancing mutual political trust in ASEAN.[20]

10.3 How have the BRI and AIIB Influenced China's Leadership Roles in Global Governance?

As several contributors have pointed out, China wants to become a rule shaper and maker rather than a taker in global governance.[21] If China wants to use the BRI and AIIB to improve its leadership standing

---

[18] Frangton Chiyemura, Elisa Gambino, and Tim Zajontz, "Infrastructure and the Politics of African State Agency: Shaping the Belt and Road Initiative in East Africa." *Chinese Political Science Review*, Vol. 8, No. 1, 2023, pp. 105–131.

[19] Ibid.

[20] Wu, Charles Chong-Han, "The Maritime Silk Road Initiative and its Implications for China's Regional Policy." *Chinese Political Science Review*, Vol. 8, No. 1, 2023, pp. 63–83.

[21] Yang, "The Asian Infrastructure Investment Bank and Status-Seeking."

in global governance, how has Beijing fared? The contributors have presented a balanced assessment, which suggests that initiatives and institutions, such as the BRI and AIIB, have enhanced Beijing's leadership in global governance.

Several chapters have provided mixed views about China's leadership role. For example, the effects of these initiatives and institutions on China's global leadership may have benefited Beijing regionally, but have not transformed into China's enhanced status globally.[22] Although Beijing has been promoting the BRI as its signature foreign policy; some view the BRI as a cohesive strategy, while others believe it is a fragmented policy.[23] This is partly due to the fact that China's BRI lacks geopolitical imperatives and narratives and a comprehensive global institutional architecture.[24] Moreover, although China has enjoyed clear decision-making dominance in the BRI and AIIB, its actions have been constrained by partnership countries, such as in the cases demonstrated by Chiyemura, Gambino, and Zajontz, where African actors, through different agencies, have shaped the terms and conditions of China-African investment projects. Similarly, by examining the BRI in the context of regionalism, Yilmaz and Li argue that China's participation in regionalism through the BRI in East Asia has been stronger economically but much weaker politically. As a result, the effects of the BRI on China's global leadership may be limited.[25]

Others see the BRI and AIIB as having a more positive influence on China's leadership in global governance. Wu demonstrates the pacifying effects provided by China's Maritime Silk Road Initiative to countries in Southeast Asia.[26] By examining the role of the AIIB, Peng and Tok argue that the AIIB will significantly enhance China's normative power in the international society because of the unconditionality nature of the sponsored projects and the focus on infrastructure construction projects. As the economic gravity is shifting from the North to the South, the AIIB

---

[22] Cai, "China's Initiatives."

[23] Zhang and James, "All Roads Lead to Beijing."

[24] Beeson and Crawford, "Putting the BRI in Perspective."

[25] Yilmaz and Li, "The BRI-Led Globalization and its Implications for East Asian Regionalization."

[26] Wu, "The Maritime Silk Road Initiative and its Implications for China's Regional Policy."

is undoubtedly a response to the slow reforms in the IMF and World Bank.[27] Yang argues that China has certainly enhanced its leadership role in global governance, especially among the underrepresented countries in the South.[28]

On balance, China has demonstrated its intentions to seek a stronger leadership role in global governance. Initiatives and institutions such as the BRI and AIIB have effectively served Beijing's purpose. However, there may be limits on China's leadership roles.

10.4 Summary and Future Direction of Research

Evidence presented by the contributors in this volume shows that China has embarked on a quest for greater global economic leadership. All things considered, China today enjoys a much higher level of leadership than before. For instance, the much-anticipated meeting between Chinese President Xi Jinping and US President Joseph Biden on the sidelines of the 2023 APEC Summit in San Francisco demonstrates that China is now considered a global economic leader on par with the US. In the post-pandemic era, China's global economic leadership has a direct impact on the livelihood of the global economy. Countries worldwide look to both China and the US for cues and solutions to the world's economic problems. However, the current global economic system still operates on the basic post-World War II economic structure dominated by the US and the West. As suggested by several chapters in this volume, China is using the BRI and AIIB to create an alternative system to compete with, if not replace, the Western-dominated global economic structure. As shown in Italy's recent decision to withdraw from the BRI, Rome's decision casts further doubt about China's leadership roles through institutions such as the BRI and AIIB.

Several questions deserve more attention in future research. First, responsibilities come with costs. As China continues seeking a greater level of global economic leadership, is Beijing willing and able to sustain the costs associated with the increased leadership? This is especially true as China's economy starts to slow down and its domestic economic needs

---

[27] Peng and Tok, "The AIIB and China's Normative Power in International Financial Governance Structure."

[28] Yang, "The Asian Infrastructure Investment Bank and Status-Seeking."

increasingly become a higher priority for Beijing. Second, can economic strength alone give Beijing a stronger status in global leadership, as China and much of the rest of the world remain on diverging paths of political governance? The economic model, through initiatives and institutions, such as the BRI and AIIB, may have presented an alternative based on a much more hierarchical and unilateral philosophy and practice than the existing Western liberal order. This leads us to the third question—how can Beijing ensure that its actions in seeking greater global economic leadership do not threaten other countries, particularly the US-led Western coalition? For example, is Beijing's dual-track strategy still effective? Should Beijing take a multilateral or unilateral approach as it seeks more leadership roles? And finally, how should the rest of the world cope with China's continued rise? In the frameworks of BRI and AIIB for example, some countries have chosen to be part of these initiatives and institutions so they can be part of the process of shaping the rules and norms from within, while others have decided to remain on the opposite team to compete with Beijing. This is indeed a critical juncture that would determine the future of international politics.

INDEX

A

ADB, 17, 22–26, 81, 192, 193, 199–202, 207, 208, 217, 225, 226, 229–232. *See also* Asian Development Bank

AfDB, 156, 232. *See also* African Development Bank

African Development Bank, 156, 199, 230. *See also* AfDB

African state actors, 157, 158, 160–162, 166, 181. *See also* African state agency/agencies
agency of local governance actors, 157, 158, 161, 179, 181
agency of political elites, 157, 161
bureaucratic agency, 157, 158, 161
different state actors, 161

African state agency/agencies, 157, 160, 161, 163, 175, 180, 181. *See also* African state actors
agency of local governance actors, 157, 161, 181
agency of political elites, 157, 161
bureaucratic agency, 157, 161
lack of African agency, 157

African Union, 155

Agenda 2063 (African Union), 155

Agricultural Development Bank of China, 58

AIIB, 2–4, 6–8, 10, 13, 15, 17, 18, 20–27, 58, 60, 61, 80, 81, 100, 116, 125, 130, 137, 139, 141, 191–193, 195–204, 206–210, 213, 216, 217, 219, 220, 223–234. *See also* Asian Infrastructure Investment Bank

American hegemonic leadership, 5. *See also* American hegemony

American hegemony, 73–75, 85. *See also* American hegemonic leadership; hegemony

AMF, 137. *See also* Asian Monetary Fund

Andean Development Corporation, 230

© The Editor(s) (if applicable) and The Author(s), under exclusive license to Springer Nature Switzerland AG 2025
K. G.Cai et al. (eds.), *China and Global Economic Governance, Volume I: China's BRI & AIIB and Global Economic Governance*, Politics and Development of Contemporary China,
https://doi.org/10.1007/978-3-031-73212-6

252 INDEX

AOA, 192, 195, 197, 202, 203, 209, 225, 226, 233. *See also* Articles; Articles of Agreement
APT, 138. *See also* ASEAN Plus Three
APEC Dialogue on Strengthening Connectivity Partnership, 81
Aquino, 112
Aquino administration, 112
Arbitral Tribunal, 104, 109, 116. *See also* arbitration ruling; SCS Arbitration
arbitration ruling, 110. *See also* SCS Arbitration
ARF, 138. *See also* ASEAN Regional Forum
Arroyo, 111
Arroyo administration, 112
Articles, 17. *See also* AOA; Articles of Agreement
Articles of Agreement (AIIB) (AOA), 17, 125, 192, 225. *See also* AOA; Articles
ASEAN, 94, 99, 104–111, 116, 124, 137, 138, 231, 247
ASEAN Defence Ministers' Meeting Plus (ADMM-Plus), 138
ASEAN Plus Three, 137, 138. *See also* APT
ASEAN Regional Forum, 110, 137. *See also* ARF
Asian Development Bank, 2, 11, 53, 192, 207, 217, 244. *See also* ADB
Asian Infrastructure Investment Bank, 2, 7, 10, 58, 80, 100, 125, 191, 215, 231, 245. *See also* AIIB Environmental and Social Framework, 199, 207
Asian Monetary Fund, 137. *See also* AMF
Association of Southeast Asian Nations, 93. *See also* ASEAN

authoritarian developmental state, 163, 170, 181
autocratic developmental state agency, 165, 166

B

B3W, 28, 62. *See also* Build Back Better World
Bagamoyo project, 165, 166, 169
balance of, 1, 11, 12, 40, 73, 97, 162, 169. *See also* balancing
economic power, 1, 12
fear, 73
power, 11, 40, 97
balancing, 97, 101, 112. *See also* balance of, power
bandwagoning, 97, 101, 112
Bangladesh–China–India–Myanmar Economic Corridor, 35, 82. *See also* BCIMEC
BCIMEC, 82. *See also* Bangladesh–China–India–Myanmar Economic Corridor
Belt and Road Initiative, 10, 33, 34, 36, 47, 58, 64, 70, 94, 124, 126, 130, 132, 155, 158, 159, 165, 167, 229, 242. *See also* One Belt One Road
Belt and Road Forum for International Cooperation (BRFIC), 139. *See also* BRI
Better Utilization of Investment Leading to Development, 62. *See also* BUILD Act, 2018
BFA, 141. *See also* Boao Forum for Asia
Biden, Joe, 62, 86, 249
Biden Administration, 62
bilateral currency-swap agreements, 58
bilateral renminbi clearing agreements, 58

Boao Forum for Asia, 15, 81, 139, 230. *See also* BFA
Bretton Woods institutions, 73, 156, 216, 247. *See also* Bretton Woods system; BWIs system, 216, 241
Bretton Woods system, 216, 228, 241. *See also* Bretton Woods institutions
BRI, 2–6, 8, 10, 13, 15–18, 20–28, 33–40, 46–48, 53–65, 69–71, 78–86, 94, 104, 108, 115, 117, 124–127, 130, 132–137, 139, 141–145, 159, 165, 167, 229, 242–250. *See also* Belt and Road Initiative
BRI forum, 39
BRI global forum, 58
BRICS, 4, 9–10, 13–15, 17–20, 22–24, 58, 81, 200–201, 209, 227, 229, 233, 245–246
BUILD Act, 2018, 62. *See also* Better Utilization of Investment Leading to Development
Build Back Better World, 28, 62. *See also* B3W
Build-Operate-Transfer, 167
BWIs, 76, 80, 85. *See also* Bretton Woods Institutions
bypassing strategy, 3–4, 10, 12–13, 18, 26, 245

C
Caribbean Development Bank, 199
CCP, 38, 56, 60, 76, 79, 84. *See also* Chinese Communist Party
Central Leading Small Group, 38
Leading Small Group, 38
CCWAEC, 82. *See also* China–Central Asia–Western Asia Economic Corridor
century of shame, 77

Chiang Mai Initiative Multilateralization, 138. *See also* CMIM
Chief Negotiators Meetings, 17, 226. *See also* CNMs
China–ASEAN Defence Ministers' Informal Meeting, 138
China-ASEAN dialogue, 104
China–ASEAN FTA, 138
China-centered global economic order, 23, 25
China-defined norms and rules, 23. *See also* Chinese norms, rules, and standards
China–Central Asia–Western Asia Economic Corridor/ China–Central Asia–West Asia Corridor, 35, 59, 82. *See also* CCWAEC
China Development Bank, 81
China–Indochina Peninsula Economic Corridor, 35, 82. *See also* CICPEC
China Investment Corporation, 81
China model, 56, 80, 81
China–Mongolia–Russia Economic Corridor, 35, 82. *See also* CMREC
China–Pakistan Economic Corridor, 24, 59, 82. *See also* CPEC
China's foreign policy, 77–78. *See also* Chinese foreign policy
China's great rejuvenation, 56
China's Marshall Plan, 16. *See also* new Marshall Plan
China's normative diffusion, 196, 208. *See also* Chinese normative diffusion
China's normative influence, 210. *See also* Chinese normative influence

China's normative power, 7, 191, 195, 203, 204, 208–210, 248. *See also* Chinese normative power
China as a negative normative power, 205, 206
external perceptions of China's normative power, 203, 208, 210
external perceptions of normative power of China, 204
normative power of China in international financial governance, 195, 209, 210
China's norms, 206, 208, 210. *See also* Chinese norm(s)
China's norm of unconditionality, 204
China's norms of sovereignty, unconditionality, and infrastructure building, 210
Chinese Communist Party, 13, 15, 38, 72, 142. *See also* CCP
Third Plenum of the 18th CCP Congress, 38
Chinese Dream, 56
Chinese foreign policy, 2, 35, 55, 56
Chinese hegemony, 70, 76, 246. *See also* hegemony with Chinese characteristics
Chinese Marshall Plan, 78. *See also* China's Marshall Plan
Chinese normative diffusion, 193. *See also* China's normative diffusion
Chinese normative influence, 210. *See also* China's normative influence
Chinese normative power, 195. *See also* China's normative power
Chinese norms, 7, 27, 193, 195, 199, 202, 206, 209, 210. *See also* China's norms
Chinese norm of infrastructure construction, 198, 207

Chinese norms, rules, and standards, 27. *See also* China-defined norms and rules
CICPEC, 82. *See also* China–Indochina Peninsula Economic Corridor
civil societies, 130, 135, 166, 180
climate change, 28, 86
CMIM, 138. *See also* Chiang Mai Initiative Multilateralization
CMREC, 82. *See also* China–Mongolia–Russia Economic Corridor
CNMs, 17, 226. *See also* Chief Negotiators Meetings
COC, 108, 109. *See also* Code of Conduct on the South China Sea
Code of Conduct on Responsible Fishery, 111
Code of Conduct on the South China Sea/Code of Conduct (South China Sea), 108, 109. *See also* COC
Cold War, 5, 46, 54, 70–74, 85, 86
Cold War 2, 85
end of the Cold War, 77, 124, 138, 204
new Cold War, 46
Community for Common Destiny, 56, 76. *See also* Community of Common Destiny
Community of a Shared Future for Mankind, 56
comparative hegemony, 5, 75, 87
Confucius Institutes, 38
constructivist, 76, 218–219, 245
Contingent Reserve Arrangement, 14, 229. *See also* CRA
core–periphery, 131
COVID/COVID-19/COVID-19 pandemic, 38, 54, 62, 84, 246

CPEC, 59, 82. *See also*
China–Pakistan Economic
Corridor
CRA, 14, 18. *See also* Contingent
Reserve Arrangement
Cuban Missile Crisis, 74
currency-swap agreements, 58

D
debt-trap diplomacy/debt trap
diplomacy, 61, 82
debt-traps, 84
Declaration on the Conduct of Parties
in the South China Sea, 108. *See
also* DOC
democratic peace theory, 98
Deng Xiaoping, 2, 55, 56, 79, 241
Digital Silk Road, 37, 60
DOC, 108. *See also* Declaration on
the Conduct of Parties in the
South China Sea
Duterte, 107, 110, 111, 113, 114.
See also Duterte, Rodrigo
Duterte, Rodrigo, 94, 116. *See also*
Duterte

E
EAS, 138. *See also* East Asia Summit
East Asian FTA, 137
East Asia Summit, 137. *See also* EAS
EBRD, 230, 232. *See also* European
Bank for Reconstruction and
Development
economic corridors, 35, 82
economic interdependence, 85, 116,
218
EEZ, 112. *See also* Exclusive
Economic Zone
eight principles of foreign aid (China),
196

emerging countries, 200, 204, 208.
See also emerging economies
emerging economies, 13, 19, 26, 53,
201, 208, 209, 216, 228. *See also*
emerging countries
European Bank for Reconstruction
and Development, 207, 230. *See
also* EBRD
European Investment Bank, 205, 207,
230
European Union (EU), 54, 106, 139,
193, 194, 205, 242
Exclusive Economic Zone, 107. *See
also* EEZ
Export–Import Bank of China (China
Exim Bank)/China
Export-Import Bank, 58, 81

F
financial crisis (2008), 75, 79, 215,
242
global, 79, 215
Fitch Ratings, 19
Five-Year Plan, 38, 111
Foreign Aid White Paper (China),
196, 199
foreign aid (China), 100, 197–200,
204–206, 209–210, 225–226
eight principles of, 196
white paper, 196
foreign policy, 10, 34
Chinese, 2, 35, 55–56
of China, 219
of Russia/Soviet Union, 221
FTA, 138
China–ASEAN, 104, 138
China–Japan–Korea, 138–139
East Asian, 138–139
trilateral, 138
functionalists, 129

256 INDEX

G

G-20/G20, 62, 75, 201. *See also*
Group of Twenty
G-7/G7, 28, 200. *See also* Group of
Seven
GATT, 73. *See also* General
Agreement on Tariffs and Trade
General Agreement on Tariffs and
Trade, 73. *See also* GATT
GFC, 80. *See also* global financial crisis
Global Development Initiative, 125
global economic governance, 1–4, 7,
8, 10, 12–14, 18–20, 23, 26–28,
207, 215–217, 219, 227, 228,
232, 233, 242
reform of global economic
governance, 4, 13
global economic order, 3, 4, 10, 18,
20, 23, 25–28, 61, 232. *See also*
international economic order
China-centered global economic
order, 23, 25
global economic system, 2, 3, 4, 10,
12, 26, 241, 242, 249. *See also*
international economic system
global financial crisis, 79, 215. *See also*
GFC
global financial governance, 193, 195,
200, 208. *See also* international
financial governance
reform of global financial
governance, 200
global financial system, 7. *See also*
multilateral financial system
global governance, 10, 13, 17, 26,
28, 112, 124, 135, 222, 227,
228, 234, 245, 247–249. *See also*
global economic governance
globalism, 127, 128. *See also*
globalization
globalization, 6, 56, 124–136,
141–145, 246. *See also* globalism

anti-globalization, 124
BRI-driven globalization, 6, 126,
127, 143, 145
BRI-driven new globalization, 135
BRI-led globalization, 144
BRI-led globalization for East Asian
regional development, 136
BRI-led new globalization, 125,
136, 145
China's brand of globalization, 139
China's globalization drive, 126
China's version of globalization,
126
Chinese vision of globalization, 136
classical globalization, 126, 132
comprehensive globalization, 134
fourth wave of globalization, 126
globalization with Chinese
characteristics, 125
marine-based globalization, 134
new globalization, 124, 130, 136
new type of globalization, 124,
130, 137
traditional globalization, 134, 136
global public goods, 232
Global Security Initiative, 125
global trade liberalism, 130. *See also*
global trade liberalization
global trade liberalization, 129. *See
also* global trade liberalism
going out strategy, 55, 79
Great Depression, 71, 72
Great Western Development Program,
54, 55
Group of Seven, 62. *See also* G7
Group of Twenty, 14. *See also* G20
Going Out Strategy, 55, 79
governance
global, 10, 13, 17–18, 26, 28, 112,
124, 135, 222, 227–228, 234,
245, 247–249

global economic, 1–4, 7–8, 10, 12–14, 18–20, 23, 26–28, 207, 215–217, 219, 227–228, 232–233, 242
international, 130, 207, 210
international financial, 6, 195, 208–210
reform of, 200, 209
structure, 2, 6–7, 11–12, 163, 193, 199–201, 203, 207–209, 224, 232, 245
Great Depression, 71–72
Great Western Development Program, 54–55

H

Hague rulings, 10. *See also* SCS Arbitration
hedging, 97, 98, 101, 112
hegemon, 71, 72. *See also* hegemonic power
Benign Hegemon, 72
hegemonic
influence, 5, 75, 85
leadership, 5, 86
power, 70, 74, 132
rise, 71
transition(s), 5, 71, 86
war, 56, 72
hegemonic power, 74, 132. *See also* hegemon
hegemonic transition, 5, 71, 86
hegemony, 5, 71, 75, 77, 170
American, 72–75, 85
Chinese, 70, 76, 246
comparative, 5, 75, 87
with Chinese characteristics, 77
hegemony with Chinese characteristics, 77. *See also* Chinese hegemony
hide and bide, 79. *See also* tao guang yang hui

high-politics/high politics, 94, 95, 105, 107
Huawei, 27, 37, 61
Hu Jintao, 15, 55
Human Rights Watch, 205

I

IDB, 230, 232. *See also* Inter-American Development Bank
ideology, 71
IMF, 2, 4, 11–14, 17, 19, 23, 25, 26, 59, 62, 74, 193, 200–203, 207–209, 228, 232. *See also* International Monetary Fund
infrastructure gap, 24, 53, 156, 159
infrastructure-led development, 160, 162, 170
Innovation and Competition Act (2021), 62
institutional innovation, 7, 217, 219, 220, 223, 224, 226, 231
institutions, 2, 11–13, 25, 70, 72, 73, 75, 97, 104, 124–126, 128, 130, 132, 133, 139, 160, 193, 199, 208, 210, 221–224, 227, 231, 244–246, 248–250
international, 11, 23, 56, 57, 59, 62, 74, 80, 195, 202, 208
(international) financial, 7, 22, 201, 228
multilateral, 4, 11–12, 23, 25, 34, 40, 138, 204, 225, 229, 233, 244–245
regional, 126–127, 136–137, 141, 143–144, 246
Inter-American Development Bank, 199, 230. *See also* IDB
international economic institutions, 11, 58. *See also* international institutions

258 INDEX

international economic order, 3, 10, 25, 26, 28. *See also* global economic order

international economic system, 1–4, 12, 246. *See also* global economic system
  liberal international economic system, 2

international financial governance, 6, 191, 195, 208–210. *See also* global financial governance

international financial institutions, 7, 22, 201, 228. *See also* multilateral financial institutions

international hierarchy, 43

international institutions, 11, 23, 56, 57, 59, 62, 74–75, 80, 195, 202, 208. *See also* multilateral institutions

International Monetary Fund, 2, 11, 54, 57, 58, 73, 200, 227, 244. *See also* IMF

international normative structure, 206, 210

international order, 44, 58, 75, 218
  liberal, 72

international organizations, 39, 80, 135, 222, 224. *See also* IOs

international relations, 7, 34, 55, 71, 76, 193–195, 217, 222. *See also* IR

international reserve currency, 13, 54, 244

international society, 7, 77, 208, 218, 221, 248

international system, 43, 44, 47, 59, 73, 124, 125, 210, 216, 243. *See also* multilateral system; world system
  less liberal and more autocratic international system, 125

IOs, 80. *See also* international organizations

IR, 7, 39, 47, 76, 77, 217–219, 221, 224. *See also* international relations
  IR theory, 40, 76, 77, 86

J
Jiang Zemin, 55
Joint Marine Seismic Undertaking (JMSU), 111

K
Keeping a low profile and biding our time, 56. *See also tao guang yang hui*
Khrushchev, Nikita, 73
Kissinger, Henry, 77

L
Lamu port project, 177–180
Lancang-Mekong Cooperation (LMC), 138–139
liberal-institutionalist, 218
liberal international order, 72
liberal international system, 216
Li Keqiang, 81, 104, 191
low politics, 94, 105

M
major country diplomacy, 39
Malacca Dilemma, 55, 59
Mao, 10, 78
Marcos, 111, 114. *See also* Marcos Jr., Ferdinand
Marcos Jr., Ferdinand, 111, 114. *See also* Marcos
Maritime Silk Road, 82, 111, 114
  Initiative (MSRI), 5, 248

21st Century, 15, 16, 35, 36, 53, 83, 229. *See also* MSR
Maritime Silk Road Initiative, 5, 93, 94. *See also* MSRI
Marshall Plan, 4, 5, 70, 74, 83, 85
  Chinese, 16, 78
  new, 78
Memorandum of Understanding, 16, 17, 106, 164, 226. *See also* MOU
middle-income trap, 63
Middle Kingdom, 216
militarized interstate disputes(MIDs), 95, 101, 103, 104, 109
Mischief Reef Incident, 106
Monroe Doctrine, 84
Moody's, 22
MOU, 82, 113, 135. *See also* Memorandum of Understanding
MSR, 82. *See also* Maritime Silk Road
MSRI, 6, 94, 95, 98–100, 104, 105, 108, 110, 112–117. *See also* Maritime Silk Road Initiative
multilateral economic system, 13, 14, 20. *See also* international economic system
multilateral financial institutions, 195, 200. *See also* international financial institutions
multilateral financial system, 14. *See also* global financial system
multilateralism, 40, 137, 224, 242
multilateral institutions, 4, 11, 12, 23, 25, 40, 138, 244. *See also* international institutions; multilateral organizations
multilateral organizations, 11, 200, 226. *See also* multilateral institutions
multilateral system, 4, 12, 13, 18, 22. *See also* international system
multinational corporations, 130

N
NAFTA, 139
national interests, 17, 19, 27, 76, 78, 101, 105, 112
nationalism, 129
nation-state(s)/nation state, 124, 129, 130
NDB, 14, 18–20, 24, 26, 195, 229. *See also* New Development Bank
NELBEC, 82. *See also* New Eurasian Land Bridge Economic Corridor
neo-realist, 218–219
New Development Bank, 14, 58, 81, 195. *See also* NDB
New Eurasian Land Bridge Economic Corridor, 82. *See also* NELBEC
new Marshall Plan, 78. *See also* China's Marshall Plan
Nixon, Richard, 77
non-traditional security, 139
Normative
  diffusion, 193–194, 196, 208
  influence, 195–196, 198, 203–204, 209–210
  power, 6–7, 193–195, 199, 203–206, 208–210, 248
  principles, 7, 194, 203
normative diffusion, 193, 194
normative power, 6, 7, 191, 193–195, 197, 199, 201, 203, 205, 207, 209–211, 213
norm(s)
  Chinese, 7, 27, 193, 195, 198–199, 202, 206–207, 209–210
  diffusion, 7, 193–194, 196, 208, 210
  new, 221, 222
  global, 218
  international, 81, 206, 210, 217, 219, 226, 227, 234, 245
  Westphalian, 193

260 INDEX

O

Obama, Barack, 55
  Obama administration, 55, 81, 242
OBOR, 78. *See also* Belt and Road
  Initiative; One Belt One Road
OECD, 227. *See also* Organization for
  Economic Cooperation and
  Development
One Belt One Road, 9, 35, 78, 141.
  See also Belt and Road Initiative
  One Belt One Road Forums, 39.
    See also OBOR
Organization for Economic
  Cooperation and Development,
  227. *See also* OECD

P

parallel order, 13
People's Liberation Army, 56. *See also*
  PLA
People's Republic of China, 2, 15, 33,
  69, 141, 142. *See also* PRC
people-to-people exchanges, 37
periphery diplomacy, 55
PFMs, 17, 192, 197, 198, 202, 226.
  See also Prospective Founding
  Members
Pivot to Asia, 141. *See also* rebalance
  to Asia
Pivot/rebalance to Asia (US), 55
PLA, 57, 65. *See also* People's
  Liberation Army
PLAN, 83. *See also* PLA Navy
PLA Navy, 83. *See also* PLAN
power(s)
  emerging, 221, 227
  revisionist, 218
  rising, 23, 44, 46, 62, 64, 219,
    221, 226, 227, 234, 243
  status quo, 3–4, 10, 12, 18, 57,
    221–222

power transition theory, 4, 5, 34,
  42–44, 46, 47, 57, 64, 243
PRC, 34, 35, 37, 39, 46, 47, 56, 57,
  59, 60, 70, 74, 75, 77, 78, 80,
  81, 85, 86. *See also* People's
  Republic of China
Prospective Founding Members, 17,
  192, 225. *See also* PFMs
protectionism, 129

R

RCEP, 116, 137, 138. *See also*
  Regional Comprehensive
  Economic Partnership
realist, 71, 77, 95, 218–219
realpolitik, 218
rebalance to Asia, 55. *See also* Pivot to
  Asia
regional bloc(s), 129
Regional Comprehensive Economic
  Partnership, 116, 137. *See also*
  RCEP
regional integration, 127, 143, 144
  regional integration in East Asia,
    126
regionalism, 6, 127, 128, 130, 137,
  138, 141, 142, 144, 248
  China's regionalism, 143
  deeper regionalism, 137
  East Asia regionalism, 144
  East Asian regionalism, 126, 137,
    138, 141, 143, 144
  new regionalism, 130
  open regionalism, 137
  political regionalism, 137, 138
  regionalism in East Asia, 138
regionalization, 6, 124–129,
  141–145, 246
  China's regionalization policy, 143
  debate on regionalization, 126
  East Asian regionalization, 6,
    124–128, 136, 142–145

regionalization in East Asia, 126, 127, 145

renminbi, 16, 54, 58, 61, 79. *See also* RMB

Republic of China, 47

rise of China, 39, 69, 87, 218, 242. *See also* rise of Chinese power

rise of Chinese power, 11. *See also* rise of China

RMB, 16, 21, 23, 25, 27, 195, 208, 226. *See also* renminbi

Russian invasion of Ukraine, 126

S

Scarborough Shoal Incident, 106, 108, 109, 113

SCO, 78, 80. *See also* Shanghai Cooperation Organization

SCS, 94, 97, 99, 101, 102, 104, 105, 107, 109–113, 136. *See also* South China Sea

SCS Arbitration, 109. *See also* Arbitral Tribunal; arbitration ruling

SDRs, 23, 25, 208. *See also* Special Drawing Rights

Second World War/World War II, 2, 5, 11, 47, 57, 59, 70–73, 241–242

security dilemma, 96

Shanghai Cooperation Organization, 57, 78. *See also* SCO

Silk Road
  Economic Belt (SREB), 15, 16, 35–36, 53, 83, 94, 229
  Fund (SRF), 58, 81, 130
  on Ice, 38

Silk Road Economic Belt, 15, 16, 35, 36, 53, 83, 94, 124, 229. *See also* SREB

Silk Road Fund, 58, 81, 130. *See also* SRF

Silk Road on Ice, 38

Sino-African cooperation, 6, 157, 158

SIR, 34, 40, 47. *See also* Systemist International Relations

SIT, 219–222, 233, 234. *See also* social identity theory

social
  competition, 7, 220–224, 227, 233
  creativity, 7, 219–224, 231, 233, 245
  mobility, 7, 221–224, 233

social identity theory (SIT), 7, 217, 218, 220

social identity theory, 7, 217, 218, 220. *See also* SIT

SOEs, 79. *See also* state-owned enterprises

soft power, 80, 116, 157

South China Sea, 35, 36, 57, 82, 84, 94, 106, 108, 111, 112, 114, 116, 247. *See also* SCS

Soviet model, 72

Space Information Corridor, 35, 36, 38

Special Drawing Rights, 23, 54, 208. *See also* SDRs

spillover effect, 105, 108

SREB, 94. *See also* Silk Road Economic Belt

SRF, 130, 137. *See also* Silk Road Fund

Stalin, Joseph, 73

Standard & Poor's (S&P), 19

state
  actor(s), 6, 124, 157–158, 160–162, 166, 177, 181
  agency/agencies, 157–158, 160–163, 165–166, 169, 175, 180–181, 247
  capitalism, 72
  developmental, 163–166, 169, 181

state capitalism, 72

262 INDEX

state-owned enterprises, 79. *See also* SOEs
status quo, 40, 44, 46, 47, 57–59, 62, 79, 102, 218, 221, 222, 243
status-quo power(s), 3, 10, 12, 18, 222
status-seeking strategies, 221, 224
  social competition, 221, 227, 233
  social creativity, 220, 221, 231, 233
  social creativity strategy, 222
  social mobility, 221, 224, 233
  social mobility strategy, 221
string of pearls strategy, 84
sustainable development, 58, 99, 111, 207, 228
SWIFT, 58
systemism, 4, 5, 34, 41, 42, 48, 63, 243
Systemist International Relations, 34, 41–42. *See also* SIR
Systemist IR, 47. *See also* Systemist International Relations

T
tao guang yang hui, 2. *See also* keeping a low profile and biding our time
TCS, 137. *See also* Trilateral Cooperation Secretariat
Tencent, 27
territorial, 19, 83, 93, 95, 102, 103, 115, 156, 218
  conflicts, 97–98, 156
  disputes, 19, 95, 99, 102, 105, 107, 117, 145
territorial peace theory, 96–98, 101, 115, 247
TFP, 63. *See also* total factor productivity
three evil forces, 78
Tianxia (all under heaven), 76

total factor productivity, 63. *See also* TFP
TPP, 55. *See also* Trans-Pacific Partnership
trade
  agreement(s), 137
  diversion, 129
  liberalism, 130
  liberalization, 129
  regime, 138
trade diversion, 129
trail of trouble, 24
Trans-Pacific Partnership, 55. *See also* TPP
Tributary system (China), 76
Trilateral Cooperation Secretariat, 137, 140. *See also* TCS
Truman, Harry S., 73
Trump, Donald, 77, 242
  second Trump administration, 86
  Trump administration, 55, 64, 242
Truong Tan Sang, 116
Twenty-First Century Maritime Silk Road, 15, 35, 36, 83, 229

U
UN, 23, 25, 57–59. *See also* United Nations
United Nations, 57, 207. *See also* UN
United Nations Charter, 73
UN peacekeepers, 57
US–China relations, 60
US-China rivalry, 126

V
Vision and Actions on Jointly Building Silk Road Economic Belt and 21st Century Maritime Silk Road, 16, 35, 124
voting, 2

INDEX   263

voting power, 2, 7, 11, 13, 17, 21–23, 25, 200, 202, 233
    China's voting power, 203
    redistribution of voting power, 209
voting rights, 200–203
    basic voting rights, 202
    China's voting rights, 201
    distribution of voting rights, 200, 201
    voting rights distribution, 210
    voting rights of AIIB, 202
    voting rights of China, 208
voting share, 227, 233
voting structure, 7
voting system, 13, 20, 24
voting weights, 26

W
Washington Consensus, 74, 85
WB, 193, 199–202, 207–209, 217, 225–232. *See also* World Bank
West African Development Bank, 199
Western norms, 208, 210
Westphalian norms, 193
Whitsun Reef Incident, 107
World Bank, 2–4, 11–14, 17, 19, 22–26, 54, 57, 59, 61, 63,

73–75, 78, 159, 202, 217, 228. *See also* WB
world economic order, 21. *See also* international economic order
world system, 126. *See also* international system
World Trade Organization, 11, 57, 75. *See also* WTO
World War II/Second World War, 2, 5, 11, 47, 57, 59, 70–73, 241–242
WTO, 76, 82. *See also* World Trade Organization

X
Xi, 15, 76–81, 86, 113, 114, 116, 231. *See also* Xi Jinping
Xi Jinping, 13, 15, 17, 18, 33, 35, 38, 39, 55, 56, 76, 78, 79, 86, 94, 107, 116, 191. *See also* Xi

Y
yen, 58

Z
zero-sum, 60, 64
Zhou Enlai, 196, 209
ZTE, 27